Understanding Environmental Policy After Covid-19

Ömer Uğur and Emre Cengiz (eds.)

Understanding Environmental Policy After Covid-19

PETER LANG

Bibliographic Information published by the Deutsche Nationalbibliothek

The Deutsche Nationalbibliothek lists this publication in the Deutsche Nationalbibliografie; detailed bibliographic data is available online at http://dnb.d-nb.de.

Library of Congress Cataloging-in-Publication Data

A CIP catalog record for this book has been applied for at the Library of Congress.

ISBN 978-3-631-86112-7 (Print)
E-ISBN 978-3-631-86797-6 (E-PDF)
E-ISBN 978-3-631-86798-3 (EPUB)
10.3726/b19099

Peter Lang – Berlin · Bern · Bruxelles · Istanbul · New York · Oxford · Warszawa · Wien

This publication has been peer reviewed.

www.peterlang.com

Contents

Authors Contributing to the Book

Elif Acuner: Asst. Prof., Recep Tayyip Erdogan University, Ardeşen Tourism Faculty, elif.acuner@erdogan.edu.tr, ORCID: 0000-0002-7769-8705

Sıla Turaç Baykara: Assist. Prof. Dr., Izmir Demokrasi University, Faculty of Economics and Administrative Sciences, Department of International Relations, silaturac.baykara@idu.edu.tr

Muhammed Yunus Bilgili: Asst. Prof. Dr., Karadeniz Technical University, Faculty of Economics and Administrative Sciences, Department of Public Administration, mybilgili@ktu.edu.tr, ORCID: https://orcid.org/0000-0002-6062-8858

Hatice Çelik: Asst. Prof. Dr., Social Sciences University of Ankara, Institute for Area Studies, Department of Asian Studies, hatice.celik@asbu.edu.tr, ORCID: 0000-0003-1409-8865

Emre Cengiz: Asst. Prof. Dr., Gümüşhane University, Faculty of Economics and Administrative Sciences, Department of Political Science and Public Administration, Gunushane/Turkey, emrecengiz_58@hotmail.com

Kadir Caner Doğan: Assoc. Prof. Dr., Gümüşhane University, Faculty of Economics and Administrative Sciences, Department of Political Science and Public Administration, Gunushane/Turkey, kadircanerdogan@gumushane.edu.tr

Nisa Erdem: Res. Asst., Karadeniz Technical University, Faculty of Economics and Administrative Sciences, Department of Public Administration, asenhu5@gmail.com

Pelin Pınar Giritlioğlu: Assoc. Prof. Dr., Istanbul University, Faculty of Political Sciences Department of Political Sciences and Public Administration Urbanization and Environmental Problems Branch, pinozden@istanbul.edu.tr

Kamber Güler: Dr., Post Doc Researcher, Swiss Forum for Migration and Population Studies, University of Neuchâtel, kamberguler@gmail.com

Suna Ersavaş Kavanoz: Asst. Prof. Dr., Karadeniz Technical University, Faculty of Economics and Administrative Sciences, Department of Public Administration, sunaersavas@hotmail.com

Merve Suna Özel Özcan: Asst. Prof. Dr., Kırıkkale University, Faculty of Economics and Administrative Sciences, Department of International Relations, mervesuna@yahoo.com

Candan Yılmaz Ugur: Asst. Prof. Dr., Gumushane University, Faculty of Economics and Administrative Sciences, Department of Public Finance, candanyilmaz@hotmail.com

Omer Ugur: Assoc. Prof. Dr., Gümüşhane University, Faculty of Economics and Administrative Sciences, Department of Political Science and Public Administration, Gunushane/Turkey, omerugur@gumushane.edu.tr

Gökhan Zengin: Asst. Prof. Dr., Trakya University, Economic and Administrative Sciences, Public Administration Department, g_zengin@yahoo.com

Omer Ugur and Emre Cengiz

Understanding Environmental Policy After Covid-19: An Introduction

Human beings have been interacting with the environment since the moment they appeared on the stage of history and they have continued their life by taking advantage of the blessings offered by the environment.

Looking at the process until the industrial revolution, the damage caused by humanity to the environment did not exceed the ability of the environment to renew itself, and even if there was pollution, the environment was able to absorb a large part of this pollution. When the environmental pollution in the early 1900s and the environmental pollution in the 1970s are compared, the pollution increased 2.7 times in the last 70 years (Turner, 2008: 407). With the industrial revolution, the pressure on the environment has started to increase. All components of nature have begun to face the process of being negatively affected by this situation. The increase in production has increased the pressure on natural resources, and the increase in population has accelerated the transformation of agricultural areas into residential areas. As a natural consequence of this situation, environmental problems have started to occur, which is well above the rate of renewal of the environment/nature.

Tab. 1 shows the real-time population of the world population from 1950 to 2020 and the probable projection population until 2100. The table reveals how high the world population growth rate is.

It would not be wrong to say that the necessary perception about the environment was not formed in the world until the 1970s. The economic policies followed during the process have also been of a nature to prevent the formation of this perception. As a matter of fact, when we look at the economic policies of classical and Keynesian economists, we see that the issues of increase in production, prevention of unemployment and development are intensively covered. As for the environment, there is a prevailing opinion that "damages to the environment are the result of development and this situation is bearable". Again, in the process until the 1970s, environmental problems were considered on a local scale and a policy of treating after pollution was adopted (Uğur and Doğan, 2015: 46). However, by the 1970s, we can see that there is a transformation of thought about the environment in the world. Ecological problems experienced also demonstrate that environmental problems do not affect a single state or a

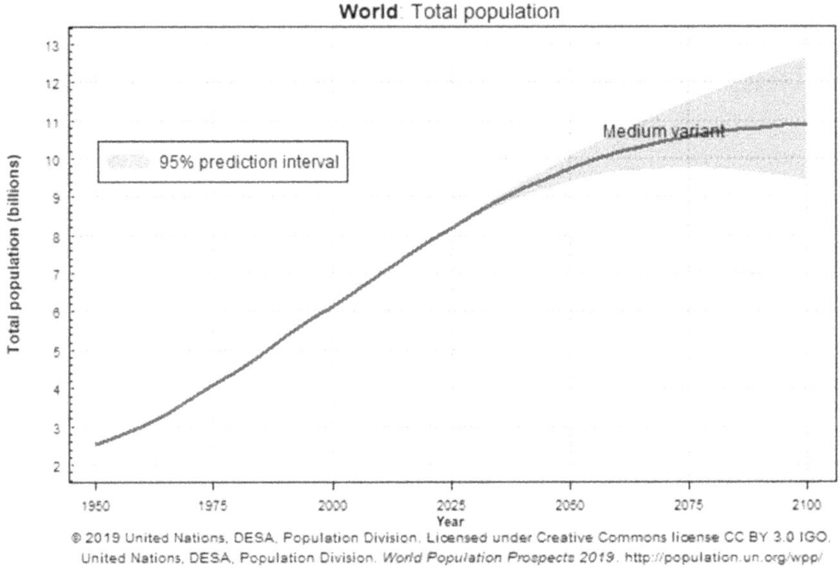

Tab. 1: World Population

single society anymore, on the contrary, each action that have cross-border effects independent from their origins and that is taken by a society or a state, gains a global dimension in the sense of affecting other societies and states seriously. As a result of this, the treatment policy for the emerging environmental pollution has also changed and took the form of prediction and prevention (Yildız and Yılmaz, 2015: 103). On the other hand, these years are also crucial in terms of addressing and attracting the attention of the world public to environmental problems. Cross-border effects of environmental problems, mutual interdependence between states and the necessity to fight against environmental problems collectively made reconciliation of mutual interdependence of states' independence and environment. The great shock after the report "Limits to Growth" published by the Club of Rome in 1972 is an indicator of this. The report, which was prepared in 5 sections, includes the following sections;

- The Nature of Exponential Growth
- The Limits to Exponential Growth
- Growth in the World System
- Technology and the Limits to Growth
- The State of Global Equilibrium

After the report was published, it brought with it discussions. For instance, in the part about natural resources; it is stated that if the use of non-renewable natural resources continues in the same way with the growth rate, it will be exhausted over the years. It can be said that this situation, which has a great impact in the world, has been beneficial to the development of environmental perception.

With the Stockholm Conference held by the UN in the same year, we can see that environmental problems have now been being discussed at the international level. As one of the important outputs of the Stockholm declaration; the protection and improvement of the human environment has been identified as an important issue affecting the welfare and economic development of all humanity and the protection of the human environment were declared as the common duty of all humanity and governments (UN, 1973: 3). In the light of these developments, which attract the attention and interest of all countries to the environmental issue, the point the world has reached is the emergence of the concept of "sustainable development". Sustainable development was used in the report "Our Common Future" -also known as the Brundtland Report- published by the World Commission on Environment and Development (WCED) in 1987 under the chairmanship of Norwegian Prime Minister Harlem Brundtland. In the 27th article of the Our Comon Future report, sustainable development is explained as follows

> "Humanity has the ability to make development sustainable to ensure that it meets the needs of the present without compromising the ability of future generations to meet their own needs. The concept of sustainable development does imply limits – not absolute limits but limitations imposed by the present state of technology and social organization on environmental resources and by the ability of the biosphere to absorb the effects of human activities. But technology and social organization can be both managed and improved to make way for a new era of economic growth." (UN, 1987:8).

Sustainable development is an important concept for the environment and people. Both production and population growth have increased the pressure on the environment and natural resources. This pressure on natural resources and the environment means the destruction of the world by human hands.

When we look at the world-wide comparison of biocapacity and ecological footprint (Fig. 1); a graphic above the biocapacity has emerged since the 1970s. This is another factor that shows us how important the concept of sustainable development is.

Despite the fact that after 1970's it started to be discussed among the states that there is a close relationship between environment and economy, and it is necessary to generate an absolute compliance between environment protection efforts

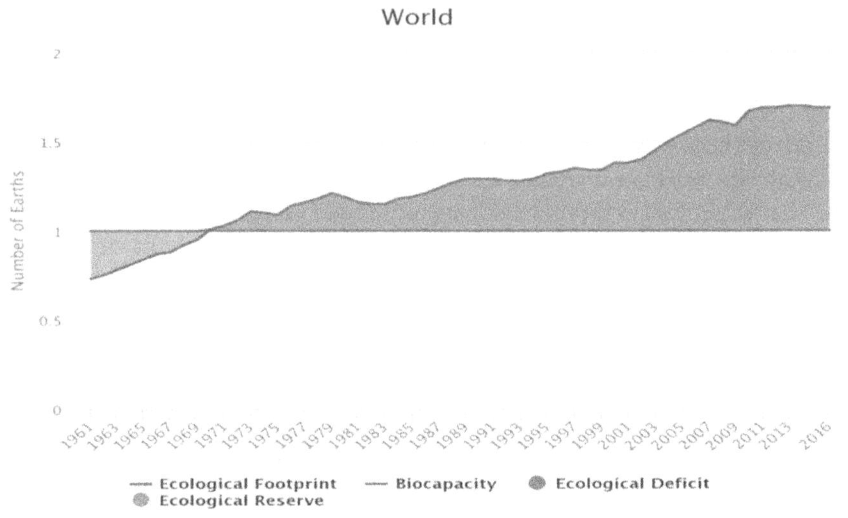

Fig. 1: Ecological Footprint and Biocapacity. Source: Ecological Footprint, https://theanthropocenedashboard.com/2019/08/02/ecological-footprint/

and development initiatives in order to eliminate the environmental threats arising in consequence of aforementioned relationship, they were not able to obtain significant results until 1990's. Certainly the reason of this situation is as also expressed by Giddens (2013) closely related with the fact that the hazards generated by environmental problems are substantial, urgent and prominent in daily life (Giddens, 2013: 12). However, in 1990's environmental problems, which emerged at global level, started to affect economic, political and social structures directly and generated the collapse indisputably, necessitates to take environmental issues into consideration more seriously. In this process, global climate change, which initiated the emergence of many environmental hazards as a direct consequence of basic production and consumption system and which affects all the relevant and irrelevant states and societies, generated the field that states wish to cooperate in the most during the establishment stage of international environment regime (Axelrod et al., 2005; Orhan et al., 2017; Susskind, 1994). This kind of desire was arisen because climate change both causes many global environmental problems and also because the increasing demand on natural resources that are gradually become more limited generate the risk of conflict between states (Swanson, 1999: 212; Yılmaz and Çiftçi, 2013: 3). And since complicated environmental problem is composed of problems that have no borders nor nations and that are connected with each other, states' addressing these problems within the framework of global cooperation creates a balance both in solution of problems that they are not able to solve by themselves and also between the conflicting economic and political interest of the states and therefore, initiated to find a fair solution. At this point, in spite of a fragmented and generally conflicting international system, which comprises of a large number of sovereign states, states constituted international cooperation and political coordination in the matter of solving problems of a global scale and that are affecting them or have a potential to affect them and therefore, enabled environmental issues to become a significant title in global politics (Vig., 2005: 4).

In this context, many conferences have been organized by the United Nations since 1972 to solve the environmental problems in the world (Tab. 2). Another important conference was held in Rio de Jenario in 1992. The Summit Agenda includes the following 4 main topics (For detailed information, see Report of the United Nations Conference on Environment and Development, Vol. 1, United Nations, New York, 1993).

- Rio Declaration,
- Climate Change Convention,
- Convention on Biological Diversity,
- Agenda 21

After ensuring that environmental issues become a significant title of global politics and that sustainable development is important for the future of the world in solving the problem; it was emphasized that countries should act in accordance with the basic principles adopted in line with the UN Conferences. It has been mentioned that development is substantial, but that it should be created by paying attention to the concept of sustainability while implementing development policies and that countries should fulfill their responsibilities. It has been stated as an action that especially developed countries' transfer of resources and technological aids to developing and least developed countries will offer important solutions to the environmental problems of the world. In addition, it was emphasized that global warming, climate change and the protection of biodiversity have emerged as the most essential problems of the world in the last 30 years and the necessity of finding solutions to them (Şahin and Yılmaz, 2017: 51).

Although providing the cooperation necessary for international climate regime, mobilized the states in the last period, due to a number of conflicts of interest dilemmas and complicated and problematical nature of the process itself, it does not come to fruition easily. Particularly the fact that negotiation of conflicting interests of so many states is virtually impossible and also the

Tab. 2: Sustainable Development and Climate Change Conferences (UN)

Sustainable Development	**Climate Change (Conference of the Parties COP)**
Stockholm 1972	COP 1 Berlin 1995
Rio 1992	COP 2 Geneva 1996
New York 1997	COP 3 Kyoto 1997
New York 2000	COP 4 Buenos Aires 1998
Johannesburg 2002	COP 5 Bonn 1999
New York 2005	COP 6 The Hague 2000
New York 2008	COP 7 Marrakech 2001
New York 2010	COP 8 New Delhi 2002
Rio 2012	COP 9 Milan 2003
New York 2013	COP 10 Buenos Aires 2004
New York 2015	COP 11 Montreal 2005
	COP 12 Nairobi 2006
	COP 13 Bali 2007
	COP 14 Poznan 2008
	COP 15 Copenhagen 2009
	COP 16 Cancun 2010
	COP 17 Durban 2011
	COP 18 Doha 2012
	COP 19 Warsaw 2013
	COP 20 Lima 2014
	COP 21 Paris 2015
	COP 22 Marrakech 2016
	COP 23 Bonn 2017
	COP 24 Katowice 2018
	COP 25 Madrid 2019
	COP 26 Glasgow 2021

Source: https://www.un.org/en/conferences/environment and https://unfccc.int/

insufficiency of scientific knowledge and technological infrastructure affects the process negatively. Nevertheless, states and other actors enable the continuation of the process by reaching an agreement on least common denominator against the fact of climate change. However, at this point, agreeing on least common denominator or acting accordingly will not be enough to overcome the rapidly increasing environmental problems. This, on the other hand, will bring economic, social and political problems in the global sense and lead to the emergence of greater problems. Indeed, the Covid-19 outbreak that we are experiencing today – which we can say is narrower when compared to environmental problems – has caused serious social, economic and political problems in the world and has brought about a great chaos in the world, albeit temporarily. Considering this situation, it can be said that increasing environmental problems and the economic, social and political problems it will cause will bring about more irreversible destruction in the world than the Covid-19 outbreak process. As a matter of fact, it is seen that the recent climate change and events related to global warming, beyond affecting all developed and least developed nations and societies, cause serious damages and losses.

In this context, the Covid-19 outbreak has more clearly revealed the increasing interdependence between states in the world and the need to jointly fight environmental problems. Because the Covid-19 outbreak has shown us a process in which each action in the globalizing world order directly affects all related and irrelevant nations and causes them great damage. These developments have once again revealed the necessity of preserving the ecological balance, which has become a more sensitive issue day by day, and brought up that cooperation between states and societies is an inevitable reality in this regard. In this context, we can say that it is imperative to experience a second perception change in terms of environmental awareness in the post-Covid-19 period. The first change in perception started with the developments in the 1970s and subsequent policy changes and the global discussion of environmental problems and the search for solutions. The process experienced since 2019 can be expressed as the second perception change and transformation process. Why do we say that? Because it would not be wrong to say that every state and every person knows what to do in terms of environmental problems, but sometimes has difficulties in applying what they need to do. However, after Covid-19, problems affecting the whole world emerged and both people and states had to do their part. This showed that not doing it in every sense is more costly than doing it. Therefore, the post-Covid-19 process will have an effect that will start the process of taking action and taking precautions as soon as possible beyond the global discussion of environmental problems and the search for a common point.

Certainly the reason of this situation is as also closely related with the fact that the hazards are substantial, urgent and prominent in daily life. The danger posed by the Covid-19 outbreak at the global level has directly affected the economic, political and social structures of the countries, causing an undeniable collapse, and inevitably creating a process that will necessitate a more serious consideration of environmental issues (Yilmaz Ugur, 2021: 292). It is seen that the global warming, flood disasters, forest fires and serious problems in agricultural products, which occur due to climate change, especially during the Covid-19 process, make states and the international community more willing to fight environmental problems than ever before. In fact, the willing attempts of the USA, which withdrew from the Kyoto Protocol on combating climate change in the early 2000s, using economic and political issues as an excuse, to combat Climate Change after the ecological crisis experienced ecological problemes especially in Texas during the pandemic period, confirms this situation. In fact, the extraordinary weather events in the world in recent years due to climate change and global warming have left all countries in economic, social and political difficulties and gave the impression that they may face worse. Therefore, it is inevitable that countries trying to overcome the shock of Covid-19 will gain a different dimension in their approach to the environment due to these two situations. In this respect, in the post-Covid-19 period, it will be possible to create an inclusive regime that has been struggling for a long time by bringing states and international organizations together and as well as including non-state actors in the process on a transboundary issue such as environmental problems that affects all areas of my life.

References

Axelrod, R. S., Downie, D. L., & Vig, N. J. (2005). The Global Environment: Institutions, Law and Policy. CQ Press, Washington

Giddens, A. (2013). İklim Değişikliği Siyaseti. Phoenix Yayınevi

Orhan, G., Kaya, Y., & Mazlum, C. S. (2017). Uluslararası Çevre Rejimleri: Oluşturulmaları, İşleyişi ve Özellikler. In Gökha Orhan, Semra Cerit and Yasemin Kaya (Ed.). Uluslararası Çevre Rejimleri. Dora Yayınevi, Bursa

Report of the United Nations Conference on the Human Environment. (1973). United Nations, New York

Report of the World Commission on Environment and Development Our Common Future. (1987). United Nations

Şahin, M., & Yilmaz, C. (2017). Financial Crises, Public Restriction and Environmental Issues. In M. Çelen, Ö. Zülfüoğlu and E. Robak (Ed.). The Political Economy of Public Finance. IJOPEC Publication, London

Susskind, L. E. (1994). Environmental Diplomacy: Negotiating More Effective Global Agreements: Negotiating More Effective Global Agreements. Oxford University Press, Oxford

Swanson, T. J. S. (1999). Global Environmental Problems and International Environmental Agreements: The Economics of International Institution Building. Edward Elgar, Cheltenham Cheltenham

Turner, M. G. (2008). A Comparison of the Limits to Growth with 30 Years of Reality, Global Environmental Change, 18, pp. 397–411

UĞUR, Ömer ve Kadir Caner Doğan. (2015). Avrupa Birliği'nin Sürdürülebilir Kalkınma Stratejisi: İklim Değişikliği Çerçevesinde Teoriden Pratiğe, Doğu Karadeniz Bölgesi Sürdürülebilir Turizm Kongresi Bildiriler Kitabı, 14–16 Mayıs, Gümüşhane

Vig, N. J. (2005). Introduction: Governing the International Environmnet. In R. S. Axelrod, D. Downie and N. J. Vig (Ed.). The Global Environment: Institutions, Law and Policy. CQ Press, Washington

Yildiz, B., & Yilmaz, C. (2015). Kirlilik Cennetlerinin Oluşumunda Çevre Vergilerinin Rolü, Gümüşhane Üniversitesi Sosyal Bilimler Elektronik Dergisi, 12, 102–120. (http://sbedergi.ghu.edu.tr/belgeler/sbe-cilt6-sayi12/MakalelerPDF/VI.pdf, 12.12.2015)

Yılmaz, N., & Çiftçi, A. (2013). "Arktika Bölgesi'nin Siyasal Önemi ve Siyasal ve Hukuksal Statüsünün Karşılaştırmalı Değerlendirmesi", Muğla Sıtkı Koçman Üniversitesi Sosyal Bilimler Enstitüsü Dergisi, Vol: 31, No: 2013 Güz, pp. 1–16.

Yilmaz Ugur, C. (2021). Struggling with Covid-19 Outbreak in the Framework of Global Public. In Goods, K. C. Dogan and Ö. Ugur (Ed.). Public Administration and Public Finance Research. Livre de Lyon Publication, Lyon

Muhammed Yunus Bilgili

Recommendations for the Post-Corona Era Within the Scope of Preventive and Reactive Environmental Policies

Introduction

People have been interacting constantly with their environment to meet their basic needs such as eating, drinking, sheltering, and maintaining body temperature. In the process of this interaction, humans have also caused environmental destruction by causing some changes to the natural environment while building their artificial environment. Industrialization, urbanization, and population growth in the 19th century increased the pressure on natural resources and created an accelerating effect on environmental degradation. By the 20th century, environmental issues began to be called catastrophes/crises and solutions were sought. These searches resulted in the beginning of creating environmental policies in which states set out their principles and goals for the environment. Despite the creation of environmental policies, the desired success in fighting the environmental issues has not been achieved, and the impact of these issues on human and environmental health has gradually increased. At the end of 2019, societies faced a global pandemic in addition to environmental issues such as climate change, desertification, deforestation, air, water, and soil pollution.

States have implemented many restrictions in order to reduce the speed of the COVID-19 pandemic, which started in China in December 2019, and spread rapidly all over the world, and to stop the pandemic. These restrictions have largely been measures to reduce human mobility. Therefore, the stagnation in economic activities in this process, led to a decrease in the use of oil and coal, resulting in a decrease in the amount of greenhouse gas emissions and an increase in air quality (Filonchyk and Peterson, 2020). Moreover, bans imposed on tourism under the COVID-19 measures have also had a positive effect on the protection of biodiversity (Elliott et al., 2020: 1192–1193). This positive situation the COVID-19 pandemic created on the environment can be a guide for regulations that will maximize environmental protection and reverse climate change (Gillespie et al., 2021: 1319). In this context, the measures within the scope of COVID-19 are seen to provide a kind of environmental restoration process. For the environmental improvement achieved in the COVID-19 restrictions not to be temporary, it can be said that environmental policies should be redesigned with a preventive approach to issues.

This study aims to introduce policy recommendations for the post-corona era within the framework of preventive and reactive environmental policies. First, environmental policy, environmental policy principles and environmental policy instruments were conceptually discussed within the framework of the study. Second, reactive and preventive environmental policies are examined in terms of definition, scope and content. Third and finally, the relationship between COVID-19 and the environment has been outlined, and proposals for reactive and preventive environmental policies have been presented for the post-corona era.

1. Environmental Policy

Urbanization, industrialization, population growth, intensive use of fossil fuels, and the concept of an economy based on continuous growth constitute the causes of environmental issues such as climate change, air pollution, deforestation, and reduction of biological diversity. With the gradual increasing impact of environmental issues on the lives of living things, states have begun to develop various policies to fight these issues. Environmental policy, in these circumstances, refers to the goals, objectives, principles and preferences determined to regulate the relation of society with the environment and the measures taken to protect and improve the environment (Keleş et al., 2012: 339–340; Pedersen, 2010: 26; Samancı, 2018: 208; Torunoğlu, 2006: 42).

Given that the administrative, financial, fiscal, economic, social and cultural structures of states are different from each other, there are also some differences in the environmental policies of states. Despite the differences, it should be noted that environmental policies unite around the objective of ensuring that society lives in a healthy environment and protect natural assets (Aydın and Çamur, 2017: 25; Torunoğlu, 2006: 42). In addition to this common objective, environmental policies also have objectives such as "ensuring societies live in a healthy environment", "protecting, developing and improving the environmental values of the society" and "providing social justice in allocating the burdens happening due to the implementation of environmental policy" (Keleş et al., 2012: 339–340; Samancı, 2018: 208). Achieving the objectives and targets set in environmental policies depends on the integration and consistent practice of these policies with other policy areas of the country such as economy, finance, culture, education and health. Therefore, there are important points to consider when creating environmental policies. These points (Keleş et al., 2012: 341–342):

- How the effects of environmental policies will be on ecosystems and their elements as well as on the population distribution should be determined.
- The long and short-term environmental and social costs of economic activities that may harm the environment should be calculated.
- The potential for economic activities to produce environmental consequences which are either difficult or impossible to recover should be taken into account.
- The precautionary principle should be applied for activities whose environmental impact is doubted.
- The short and long-term productivity of activities that will affect the environment should be distinguished, and how long-term environmental impacts will affect future generations and environmental elements should be taken into account.
- It should be evaluated whether the projects implemented within the framework of environmental policy will create a conflict of interest among the social segments and lead to environmental injustice.
- Consistency and coordination should be ensured between environmental policies and other policies such as industry, agriculture, urbanization, economy, health, and education.

When the above features are evaluated as a whole, it should be emphasized that a successful environmental policy should be designed with a holistic perspective including all physical, chemical, biological, cultural and social dimensions of the environment. It is possible to talk about the principles on which environmental policies created according to these features should be based.

1.1. Environmental Policy Principles

As mentioned earlier, environmental policies vary between countries. Despite these differences, the principles of sustainable development, prevention, polluter pays, precaution, cooperation and participation are often preferred principles in environmental policies.

The principle of sustainable development is based on the concept of sustainable development, defined in the 1987 report *Our Common Future*, as "not compromising the ability of future generations to meet their own needs while meeting today's needs" (United Nations, World Commission on Environment and Development, 1987: 54). Ensuring social development, protecting the environment and natural resources, increasing the quality of life, protecting biological and cultural diversity are the main elements of sustainable development (Eccleston and March, 2011: 59). Given that sustainable development takes economic, ecological and social factors into account, and it is an understanding that efforts are made to both protect the existence and improve the quality of these elements, therefore environmental policies to be created should be built based on this understanding (Samancı, 2018: 209).

The principle of prevention is based on the understanding that an activity that is likely to cause environmental pollution or damage can be prevented at the earliest possible stage and solved before the problem arises (Karaca, 2019: 39–40; Kaypak, 2013: 24). In other words, this principle is based on the understanding that prevention is better than cure (Read and O'Riordan, 2017: 5; Turgut Yılmaz, 2009: 111).

The polluter pays principle adopted by the Organization for Economic Cooperation and Development (OECD) in the early 1970s, polluters must cover the costs of protection, control, and removal measures determined by the public authority to maintain the environment in an acceptable condition (Beder, 2006: 2–3; Turgut Yılmaz, 2009: 121–123). This principle serves the purpose of internalizing the costs of environmental pollution, which is seen as a negative externality (Milon, 2019: 67).

The precautionary principle emphasizes that in the event of scientific uncertainty about the impact of a planned activity on the environment and human health, all necessary measures are taken (Akins et al., 2019). This principle aims to take measures by foreseeing the activities that will harm the environment and to prevent possible damages and protect the ecosystems in the long term (Samancı, 2018: 210). Therefore, the precautionary and prevention principles should be stated to be closely related to each other.

The principle of cooperation refers to the joint action of the central government, local governments, non-governmental organizations, private sector stakeholders, and individuals in the fight against environmental issues (Güneş, 2011: 269). This principle emphasizes also the importance of coordination and cooperation at the international level in the fight against environmental issues.

The principle of participation is based on the understanding that it is a democratic right for individuals or groups of individuals to have an influence and direct the environmental management process by participating in the decision-making and implementation processes related to environmental policy (Beder, 2006: 105; Reed, 2008: 2418; Yılmaz Turgut, 2009: 153).

Considering as a whole, environmental policy principles can be seen as indispensable priorities for a state to achieve the objectives and targets set within the framework of environmental policy. It is also important to choose appropriate instruments and methods as well as to determine the principles for achieving environmental objectives and targets.

1.2. Environmental Policy Instruments

Environmental policy instruments refer to the measures taken by states in order to prevent environmental issues such as air, water, soil and solid waste pollution, and depletion of natural resources (Liao, 2018: 1112; Mickwitz, 2003: 419). In other words, environmental policy instruments are methods that enable achieving environmental objectives and targets by connecting policy making and decision making with policy implementation (Huppes and Simonis, 2009: 239). These instruments can be classified under two categories: Administrative instruments and economic and fiscal instruments.

1.2.1. Administrative (Command and Control) Instruments of Environmental Policy

Administrative instruments are based on the understanding of determining the obligations individuals and companies must comply with in regards to environmental issues, with laws, regulations and other regulatory administrative acts in force in a particular country (Bilgili, 2012: 4). It is possible to mention many types of these instruments in practice, which are based on the state's compulsory mandate to make rules. The most common ones are orders and prohibitions (bans), standards, zoning, the obligation of notification, the obligation of classification, and environmental impact assessment.

Orders and prohibitions are restrictions imposed by law and/or regulatory administrative procedures, determining what individuals or companies carrying out activities that will have an impact on the environment should and should not do (Budak, 2000: 54). *Environmental standards* are the restrictions that are brought to make measurements in order to prevent pollutants that cause environmental pollution and not to exceed the environmental parameters determined based on these measurements (Ertürk, 2009: 207). *Zoning* is the determination of where economic activities (such as firms and households) in a certain area should be settled by the public authority (Campbell et al., 2014: 523). *The obligation of notification* is to notify the authorized administrative units by the persons who will carry out environmentally risky activities and to ensure supervision through this notification (Keleş et al., 2012: 398–399). *The obligation of classification* is a practice used in order to facilitate the inspection of the administrative authorities by showing the products and wastes in the dangerous goods class with special signs (Bilgili, 2012: 13–14; Budak, 2000: 55). *Environmental impact assessment* is a systematic process of determining the possible effects of economic activity on the environment and evaluating, reporting and auditing these effects (Jay et al., 2007: 287–288).

Having evaluated the examples presented on administrative instruments as a whole, these instruments seem to be based on the state's authority to issue orders and impose sanctions on those who do not comply. Furthermore, these instruments do not create flexibility and motivation for individuals to avoid activities that pose environmental risks. This flexibility and motivation are provided by the economic and fiscal instruments of environmental policy.

1.2.2. Economic and Fiscal (Market-Based) Instruments of Environmental Policy

Economic and fiscal instruments refer to the measures aiming to ensure that pollutants turn to environmental alternatives and internalize negative externalities through monetary motivation by increasing the cost of production and consumption activities that have an impact on the environment (Beder, 2006: 156). It is possible to classify the most preferred ones of this instrument, which has many types in practice, as environmental taxes, environmental fees (charges), subsidies, deposit-refund systems, and tradable permits.

Environmental tax is based on the understanding of internalizing the cost of negative externalities caused by environmentally harmful products by including them in the price of products and changing production/consumption patterns by creating financial pressure. Environmental taxes also serve the purpose of creating funds to be used for environmental purposes (Gabriela Cornelia and Carmen Lenuta, 2012a: 728–729). *Environmental fees* are based on the understanding that people who cause environmental pollution should bear the cost of this pollution. These fees can be charged for the prevention of pollution such as air, soil, water, and noise or for the services provided in these matters (Kaypak, 2013: 26). *Subsidies* are based on the principle of providing various monetary aids to companies in order for them to reduce the negative externality they create in the environment or to increase the positive externality they spread to the environment (Bilgili, 2012: 71). *Deposit refund systems* are the addition of a certain amount as a deposit to the prices of products with the potential to pollute the environment and the refund of the initial deposit to the user in case the product is returned by the user (Dace et al., 2013: 314). This practice guides producers to adopt more environmentally friendly production techniques, while encouraging consumers to return their waste to recycling systems (Zhou et al., 2020). *Tradable permits* are based on determining the maximum acceptable amount of pollution for a receiving environment (air, water, and soil) and dividing it by firms (Needham et al., 2019: 1430). If a firm produces less pollution than its quota, it can transfer its remaining tradable permits to the requesting firms. This instrument aims to increase environmental efficiency by dividing the marginal cost of pollution among pollutants (Lapan and Sikdar, 2019: 502).

The economic and fiscal instruments of environmental policy, as opposed to administrative instruments, offer flexibility to individuals and firms through economic motivation. Moreover, the income generated by the implementation of these instruments can help in the creation of environmental funds.

Environmental policies, created by considering the environmental policy principles and instruments discussed above, are divided into two as "preventive" and "reactive" environmental policies in terms of method.

2. Reactive and Preventive Environmental Policies

Reactive environmental policies emerged as a reaction to the problems in the early periods when the effects of environmental issues began to be observed (Gabriela Cornelia and Carmen Lenuta, 2012b: 719). This understanding also called a remediating policy, includes the measures applied to reduce or eliminate the effects after environmental issues occur. The aim of the reactive policy, which considers environmental pollution as an inevitable result of economic activities, is to improve the environment by reducing the damage (Bal, 2009: 189; Keleş et al., 2012: 352).

Within the framework of reactive policies, measures are taken to compensate for the damage done to the environment, to dispose of wastes resulting from activities of production and consumption, and to use environmental technologies (Becke, 2004: 6). This policy, for example, focuses on measures such as the release of gases into the air after filtration by requiring filters to be installed in the chimneys of incinerators instead of reducing the amount of solid waste generated in urban areas (Keleş et al., 2012: 353). From this point of view, it should be stated that reactive environmental policies usually tend towards the implementation of administrative environmental policy instruments.

It is possible to talk about some deficiencies of reactive policies. If problems are detected late and measures are delayed, ecosystems can suffer irreversible damage. Furthermore, it focuses only on a certain part of the environment-society relationship (such as air quality control). Therefore, it can be overlooked that an environmental issue may lead to another environmental issue (Simonis, 1984: 2–3). In this context, the reactive environmental policy approach should be emphasized to be a costly method in terms of economic, social and environmental aspects.

In the interaction process of people with the environment, it is often predictable which behaviors will harm the environment. In line with this, many environmental issues can be prevented by measures to be taken before they occur. But this is possible by developing a preventive understanding rather than a reactive understanding.

Preventive environmental policies reflect an understanding of taking the necessary measures, taking into account the possible future effects of human activities while the environment has not yet been harmed (Keleş et al., 2012: 353). In other words, preventive environmental policy is a long-term approach focusing on the development of economic, technological and social structures without causing disturbance to the ecological balance (Simonis, 1984: 6). For example, measures such as the production of engines that do not create noise or cause less noise pollution, the development of technologies for the reuse or recycling of waste, and the design of instruments requiring less energy are some of the preferred practices within the framework of this policy (Asolekar and Gobichandran, 2005: 3; Bal, 2009: 189). As can be seen from the examples presented, this policy focuses on the development of cleaner production technologies that benefit the protection and improvement of the environment and the implementation of structural changes in human-environment interaction (Staniškis and Katiliūtė, 2019). In this context, the preventive policy is an approach with the preference of reducing the impact of production activities on the environment and to use natural resources more effectively.

Given that environmental issues sometimes do not show their effect instantly, it is a necessity to prefer preventive methods. This policy is also less costly and more environmentally effective than reactive environmental policies (Simonis, 1984: 3).

The information presented above reveals that there are some important differences between reactive and preventive environmental policies. These differences were identified by Borda and Kiss (2011: 420) as presented in Tab. 1. As presented in Tab. 1, preventive environmental policy is a paradigm projecting radical changes in economic, technological, administrative, scientific, social and cultural structures to ensure environmental sustainability (Wynne, 1992: 127). Besides, an environmental issue can arise even if all measures have been taken. In such cases, the implementation of reactive policies becomes also a necessity. In this context, when it comes to environmentally risky activities, preventive measures should be applied if no damage has occurred yet, and if damage has occurred despite all measures, reactive methods should be applied.

Tab. 1: Comparison of Reactive and Preventive Environmental Policies

Characteristic	Reactive Environmental Policy	Preventative Environmental Policy
Environmental direction	Environmental ministry with department character	Environmental ministry with integrating and coordinating character
Resources of the regulation	Instruct, control, penalty, product fee	Environment friendly tax system, spontaneous, agreements, knowledge forming programs
Typical activity of the environmental bureaucracy	Control, penalty, avert of damage	Planning, collaboration in solving problems, advising
Technical solutions	End of pipe technologies	Clean production and consumption
Sponsor	Budget, separated funds	Business sphere, self governments, foundations
Period	Short term, apparent results	Long term, lasting results
Participants	Exclusive, green organizations	Spreading, civil organizations
Environmental sector	Well developed environmental industry and advisory network	Clean production advisors, information systems, educational programs

Reference: Borda and Kiss (2011: 420).

3. Environmental Policy Recommendations for the Post-Corona Era

States have started to take some measures to reduce the spread of the COVID-19 pandemic that emerged in China in late 2019. Restrictions such as banning public events, closure of schools, closure of country borders, prohibition of non-essential travel, and preferring the working from the home model were among these measures that have been intensively applied (Malliet et al., 2020: 868; Rousseau and Deschacht, 2020: 1149). Reduced transportation and production activities during the restrictions also triggered a decrease in the use of oil and coal resulting in a decrease in the amount of greenhouse gas emissions (Filonchyk and Peterson, 2020). This development has led to a decrease in air pollution and therefore an increase in air quality in China, India, Italy, France, Spain and many other countries (Şahin and Erensü, 2020: 6–7). Furthermore, tourism bans put in place during the pandemic have also provided a benefit in terms of protecting biodiversity by reducing the number of tourists (Elliott et al., 2020: 1192–1193). These positive effects that the COVID-19 pandemic created on the environment can be a guide for regulations that will maximize environmental protection and reverse climate change (Gillespie et al., 2021: 1319). The permanence of environmental improvements experienced during the pandemic can only be possible with the implementation of an effective environmental policy.

In the environmental policies that will be created to fight environmental issues in the post-corona era, first of all, issues should be correctly identified. Once issues are identified, the sources of these problems, their relationship with economic sectors and other policy areas should be determined. After these connections are established, the objectives and targets of the environmental policy should be set out in a measurable, auditable and realistic way. In addition, attention should be paid to ensure that the instruments and principles ensuring the achievement of the determined objectives and targets are consistent with each other.

Considering that the physical, chemical, biological and social effects of environmental issues on living and inanimate beings can vary in the short and long term, it should be stated that policies should be formed with a preventive perspective. In other words, while environmental issues have not yet occurred, choices for preventing the problem at its source should be prioritized at the forefront. At this point, precautionary and prevention principles should be considered as the basic principles of environmental policy and regulations should be made accordingly. Furthermore, accepting the concept of sustainable development, which projects the protection of the environment and natural resources, increasing the quality of life and protecting cultural diversity (Eccleston and March, 2011: 59), as the basic economic paradigm and principle is an element that can increase the effectiveness of the environmental policy. The ability to achieve structural transformations in environmental and human relations is directly related to the fact that citizens are adequately informed at this point. In this framework, the principles of participation and cooperation can ensure that citizens are informed about environmental issues.

To protect and improve the environment, preventive policies should be preferred in line with the perspective of the development of clean production technologies and the implementation of structural changes in the human-environment relationship (Staniškis and Juliūtė, 2019). In this context, it should be ensured that the environmental impact assessment method, which is directly related to the precautionary and prevention principles, should be extended to a wide range of practices. Moreover, economic and fiscal instruments should be put into practice, which will both bring the polluter pays principle into action and enable firms to turn to environmentally friendly technologies. At this point, it should be expressed that tradable permits, deposit-refund systems and environmental taxes will be functional instruments.

In the human-environmental relationship, even if all preventive measures have been taken related to environmentally risky activities, there is a possibility that some harm will occur. Therefore, in order to ensure efficiency in environmental policy, reactive practices should also be included. However, keeping in mind the disadvantages of reactive policies (e.g., irreversible damage to ecosystems if problems are detected late), it should be mentioned that this political choice should be taken into the account in the last instance. In summary, when it comes to environmental issues, prevention should be adopted as the fundamental paradigm of environmental policy, where prevention is cheaper and more effective than cure.

Finally, given that the restrictions put in place to prevent further spread of the COVID-19 pandemic have created some positive improvements on the environment, it should be noted that the self-renewal capacity of ecosystems (carrying capacity) has not been exceeded. In these circumstances, it should be stated that preventive environmental policies should be preferred in the post-corona era to increase the self-renewal capacity of ecosystems and ensure environmental sustainability.

Conclusion

The COVID-19 pandemic, affecting the whole world starting from China in late 2019, is basically a health problem but it has positively or negatively affected education, environment, management, and many other areas. Various restrictions put in place to stop the further spread of the outbreak have led to positive environmental improvements such as reduction of greenhouse gas emissions and protection of biodiversity. Therefore, COVID-19 appears to have led to an environmental restoration process. The fact that this restoration process is not temporary can be achieved by principles, instruments, methods and practices that will ensure effectiveness in environmental policies.

In the environmental policies which will be created to be implemented in the post-corona era, the sustainability of these systems should be taken as a basis by preferring practices that will not risk the self-renewal capacity of ecosystems. At this point, it is necessary to try to prevent the emergence of environmental issues by taking into account the possible consequences of activities that pose risks to the environment and ecosystems. This understanding of preventing environmental issue at their source requires the creation of environmental policies from a preventive point of view. It is possible to achieve some structural changes in human and environmental relations in favor of the environment with the design of preventive environmental policies with appropriate instruments, methods, and principles. In line with this information, it should be stated that the principles of precaution, prevention and sustainable development should be placed at the core of environmental policy. Furthermore, regulations should be created to enable the implementation of economic and fiscal instruments such as environmental taxes, deposit-refund systems and tradeable permits, which will lead producers to use environmentally friendly technologies.

Despite all the precautions taken, it is likely to occur some environmental damage in human and environmental interaction. In such cases, it is necessary to shift to reactive practices. Therefore, the priority should be preventive measures when creating environmental policies, and if an issue arises, reactive measures should be included. In other words, preventive and reactive approaches should be adopted together in the environmental policies which will be created for the post-corona era.

References

Akins, Ashli, Phil O'B., Lyver, Hugo F., Alrøe, and Henrik, Moller (2019). "The Universal Precautionary Principle: New Pillars and Pathways for Environmental, Sociocultural, and Economic Resilience", *Sustainability*, Volume: 11, Issue: 8, pp. 2357.

Asolekar, Shyam R. and Gobichandran, R. (2005). Preventive Environmental Management, *Foundation Books*, New Delhi.

Aydin, Ahmet Hamdi and Ömer, Çamur (2017). "Avrupa Birliği Çevre Politikaları ve Çevre Eylem Programları Üzerine Bir İnceleme", *Bingöl Üniversitesi Sosyal Bilimler Enstitüsü Dergisi*, Cilt: 7, Sayı: 13, ss. 21–44.

Bal, Durmuş Ali (2009). "Çevre ile İlgili Yeni Yaklaşımlar" (Ed. Mustafa Aydoğdu and Kudret Gezer), *Çevre Bilimi*, Anı Yayıncılık, Ankara.

Becke, Guido (2004). "Indirect Regulation-A Remedy to Cure the Defects of European Environmental Policy? The EMAS Regulation" (artec-paper, 116). Bremen: Universität Bremen, Forschungszentrum Nachhaltigkeit (artec). https://nbnresolving.org/urn:nbn:de:0168-ssoar-322644 (06.06.2021).

Beder, Sharon (2006). Environmental Principles and Policies: An Interdisciplinary Approach, *UNSW Press*, Sydney.

Bilgili, Muhammed Yunus (2012). "Çevre Politikası Araçları: Türkiye Örneği", Yayınlanmamış Yüksek Lisans Tezi, *Karadeniz Teknik Üniversitesi Sosyal Bilimler Enstitüsü*, Trabzon.

Borda, Jeno and Ferenc Kiss (2011). "The Environmental Policy of EU and the Sustainable Development", *Studia Universitatis "Vasile Goldis" Arad. Seria Stiintele Vietii (Life Sciences Series)*, Volume: 21, Issue: 2, pp. 417–420.

Budak, Sevim (2000). Avrupa Birliği ve Türk Çevre Politikası: Avrupa Topluluğu'nun Çevre Politikası ve Türkiye'nin Uyum Sorunu. *Büke Yayınları*, İstanbul.

Campbell, Heather E., Yushim Kim, and Adam Eckerd (2014). "Local Zoning and Environmental Justice: An Agent-Based Model Analysis", *Urban Affairs Review*, Volume: 50, Issue: 4, pp. 521–552.

Dace, Elina, Ieva Pakere, and Dagnija Blumberga (2013). "Evaluation of Economic Aspects of the Deposit Refund System for Packaging in Latvia", *Management of Environmental Quality*, Volume: 24, Issue: 3, pp. 311–329.

Eccleston, Charles H. and Frederic March (2011). Global Environmental Policy: Concepts, Principles, and Practice, *CRC Press*, Boca Raton.

Elliott, Robert J. R., Ingmar Schumacher, and Cees Withagen (2020). "Suggestions for a Covid-19 Post-Pandemic Research Agenda in Environmental Economics", *Environmental and Resource Economics*, Volume: 76, Issue: 4, pp. 1187–1213.

Ertürk, Hasan (2009). Çevre Bilimleri. 3. Baskı, *Ekin Yayınevi*, Bursa.

Filonchyk, Mikalai and Michael Peterson (2020). "Air Quality Changes in Shanghai, China, and the Surrounding Urban Agglomeration During the COVID-19 Lockdown", *Journal of Geovisualization and Spatial Analysis*, Volume: 4, Issue: 2, Article: 22.

Gabriela Cornelia, Piciu and Trică Carmen Lenuta (2012a). "Assessing the Impact and Effectiveness of Environmental Taxes", *Procedia Economics and Finance*, Volume: 3, pp. 728–733.

Gabriela Cornelia, Piciu and Trică Carmen Lenuta (2012b). "Trends in the Evolution of Environmental Taxes", *Procedia Economics and Finance*, Volume: 3, pp. 716–721.

Gillespie, Thomas R., Kate E. Jones, Andrew P. Dobson, Julie A. Clennon, and Mercedes Pascual (2021). "COVID-Clarity Demands Unification of Health and Environmental Policy", *Global Change Biology*, Volume: 27, Issue: 7, pp. 1319–1321.

Güneş, Ahmet M. (2011). "Yeni Anayasa Tartışmaları Bağlamında Çevre", *Gazi Üniversitesi Hukuk Fakültesi Dergisi*, Cilt: 15, Sayı: 3, ss. 259–283.

Huppes, Gjalt and Udo E. Simonis (2009). "Environmental Policy Instruments" (Ed. Jan J. Boersema and Lucas Reijnders), *Principles of Environmental Sciences, Springer*, Dordrecht; London, pp. 239–280.

Jay, Stephen, Carys Jones, Paul Slinn, and Christopher Wood (2007). "Environmental Impact Assessment: Retrospect and Prospect", *Environmental Impact Assessment Review*, Volume: 27, Issue: 4, pp. 287–300.

Karaca, Coşkun (2019). Çevre ve Kentleşme Politikası, *Ekin Yayınevi*, Bursa.

Kaypak, Şafak (2013). "Çevre Sorunlarının Çözümünde Küresel Çevre Politikalarının Önemi", *Muğla Sıtkı Koçman Üniversitesi Sosyal Bilimler Enstitüsü Dergisi*, Sayı: 31, ss. 17–34.

Keleş, Ruşen, Can Hamamcı, and Aykut Çoban (2012). Çevre Politikası, 7. Baskı, *İmge Kitabevi*, Ankara.

Lapan, Harvey E. and Shiva Sikdar (2019). "Is Trade in Permits Good for the Environment?", *Environmental and Resource Economics*, Volume: 72, Issue: 2, pp. 501–510.

Liao, Zhongju (2018). "Environmental Policy Instruments, Environmental Innovation and the Reputation of Enterprises", *Journal of Cleaner Production*, Volume: 171, pp. 1111–1117.

Malliet, Paul, Frédéric Reynès, Gissela Landa, Meriem Hamdi-Cherif, and Aurélien Saussay (2020). "Assessing Short-Term and Long-Term Economic and Environmental Effects of the COVID-19 Crisis in France", *Environmental and Resource Economics*, Volume: 76, Issue: 4, pp. 867–883.

Mickwitz, Per (2003). "A Framework for Evaluating Environmental Policy Instruments: Context and Key Concepts", *Evaluation*, Volume: 9, Issue: 4, pp. 415–436.

Milon, J. Walter (2019). "The Polluter Pays Principle and Everglades Restoration", *Journal of Environmental Studies and Sciences*, Volume: 9, Issue: 1, pp. 67–81.

Needham, Katherine, Frans P. Vries, Paul R. Armsworth, and Nick Hanley (2019). "Designing Markets for Biodiversity Offsets: Lessons from Tradable Pollution Permits", *Journal of Applied Ecology*, Volume: 56, Issue: 6, pp. 1429–1435.

Pedersen, Ole W. (2010). "Environmental Principles and Environmental Justice", *Environmental Law Review*, Volume: 12, Issue: 1, pp. 26–49.

Read, Rupert and Tim O'Riordan (2017). "The Precautionary Principle Under Fire", *Environment: Science and Policy for Sustainable Development*, Volume: 59, Issue: 5, pp. 4–15.

Reed, Mark S. (2008). "Stakeholder Participation for Environmental Management: A Literature Review", *Biological Conservation*, Volume: 141, Issue: 10, pp. 2417–2431.

Rousseau, Sandra and Nick Deschacht (2020). "Public Awareness of Nature and the Environment During the COVID-19 Crisis", *Environmental and Resource Economics*, Volume: 76, Issue: 4, pp. 1149–1159.

Şahin, Ümit and Sinan Erensü (2020). "COVID-19 Pandemisini ve İklim Krizini Birlikte Okumak", İPM–MERCATOR Politika Notu, Sabancı Üniversitesi İstanbul Politikalar Merkezi.

Samanci, Muhammed (2018). "Türkiye'de Çevre Politikalarının Mali Yönü" (Ed. Burak Hergüner and Erol Kalkan), *Türkiye'de Çevre Politikaları: Sürdürülebilir Kalkınma İçin Eksik Halkayı Tamamlamak*, Nobel Yayınevi, Ankara, pp. 203–228.

Simonis, Udo E. (1984). "Preventive Environmental Policy: Concept and Data Requirements", WZB Discussion Paper, No. IIUG dp 84–12, Wissenschaftszentrum Berlin (WZB), Berlin. http://hdl.handle.net/10419/82972 (06.06.2021).

Staniškis, Jurgis Kazimieras and Eglė Katiliūtė (2019). "Unsustainability Reduction in Enterprises by Incremental Innovations Implementation and Management", *Journal of Cleaner Production*, Volume: 236, Article: 117542.

Torunoğlu, Ethem (2006). Ötekilerin "Çevre"si, *Ütopya Yayınevi*, Ankara.

Turgut Yilmaz, Nükhet (2009). Çevre Politikası ve Hukuku, *İmaj Yayınevi*, Ankara.

United Nations, World Commission on Environment and Development (2013). "Report of the World Commission on Environment and Development: "Our Common Future"", https://digitallibrary.un.org/record/139811/files/A_42_427-EN.pdf (06.06.2021).

Wynne, Brian (1992). "Uncertainty and Environmental Learning: Reconceiving Science and Policy in the Preventive Paradigm", *Global Environmental Change*, Volume: 2, Issue: 2, pp. 111–127.

Zhou, Guangli, Yifan Gu, Yufeng Wu, Yu Gong, Xianzhong Mu, Honggui Han, and Tao Chang (2020). "A Systematic Review of the Deposit-Refund System for Beverage Packaging: Operating Mode, Key Parameter and Development Trend", *Journal of Cleaner Production*, Volume: 251, Article: 119660.

Nisa Erdem

Network Governance in Urban Environmental Management

Introduction

Network governance has been suggested as a new perception, which paves a way for a new paradigm in governance field. Network governance, which occurs as a third route against two main administration paradigms (traditional public administration and new public management), is in the position of an ancestor for the administration models titled variously as "new public governance", "public value approach", "new public service". On the other hand, network governance is also built upon a criticism of the initial paradigm concepts prior to itself. Within the scope of the prior administration paradigms, it has risen as a response to the gaps experienced regarding the resolutions for the issues. Besides, rather than suggesting that network governance is an excellent approach, it is considered a more beneficial method to elaborate on both the pros and cons of network governance, same as in any other governance approach.

The literature on network governance demonstrates that there are numerous and various conceptual works given in this field. Network governance is referred to and described through various terms and defined in different ways. Furthermore, based on the definitions, it seems to be possible to underline elements on network governance. Within this context, complexity, ambiguity, interaction, co-dependency, and mutual trust emerge as the fundamental principlas to encounter in the field of network governance. On the other hand, according to Juhola and Westerhoff (2011: 240), the increasing and widespread works given in the context of network governance eventuate in findings accessed based on the roles of network governance, its advantages, and restraints.

Correlatively in this study, the definition and the development of the term network governance are scrutinized, and its potential benefits for urban network governance and its critical aspects are reviewed. The theoretical aspect of the contributions of network governance to regional areas is scrutinized in this study. On the other hand, the field-researched case studies, which take place in practical terms for this potential, are given as references. Whilst the contributions and critical aspects of network governance being elaborated on, the results accessed are seen to be able to take place only under certain circumstances. Hence, this study attaches importance to the stress on the matters to pay attention on this basis. The analysis conducted within the scope of this study focuses on three special areas, which network governance contributes to during environmental management: the constitution of information and learning process, mobilizing resources, and enabling democracy and participation. In this study, the roles, contributions, and the restraints of network governance regarding the management of environmental issues, as in the scope of three areas.

1. Background: The Rise of the Network Governance

The occurrence of network governance is not "ipso facto". In as much as that public administration theories develop in a dialectic process. To perceive and understand network governance in its outlines, it is essential to review the prior public administration theories. To search for the roots of network governance means to set forth the reasons for it to emerge as well.

When Genç (2010: 147–148) express the outlines of traditional public administration and new public management paradigms, she also mentions that the concept of traditional public administration is based on bureaucracy, whereas new public management is based on market. Public interest, efficiency, the structure of duty and authority with precise boundaries, hierarchy, administrative responsibility, control, and results occupy an important place. Public administration by relevant traditional administrations was ensured in a long term. However, the changes and developments in economic policies have changed public policies. Under these circumstances, the role of the state and the traditional administration mechanism has changed, thus, decentralization recoups hierarchical administration, and interaction and participation recoups control. Therefore, the bureaucratic structure of traditional public administration and the way it is taken into service are not considered the sole and the best alternative. New public management occurred as a reflection of this change into public policies. New public management is based on a more flexible bureaucratic construct. In public service, citizens are considered as clients, and it is aimed to put the principles of activeness and efficiency in administration field into practice. Thus, private sector uses administrative methods parallel to these.

Along with this, mounting criticisms in recent years on the new public management model have put new public governance, new public service, digital era governance or public value to forefront. Negotiation of the role of the state in a new paradigm search has been agreed. The state proceeds to benefit from the market. This has parallels with new public management. In addition to this, new public management is firmly predicated upon the sense of free-market competition. Whereas, for instance, public value takes the complexity and ambiguity of institutions into consideration. Public value starts when it is agreed that the needs and the issues which citizens, societies and governments encounter have complex and heterogeneous constructs. Politics in traditional public administration is restrained to decision making and policy formulation. The role of politics in new public management, has narrowed down in support of market and private sector. However, public value model is conscious of the fact that public sector, unlike private sector, is composed of a political decision-making process; and, expands the political sphere of a public administrator, whose focus is on public value, by making a point of a collaboration in a different form (Köseoğlu ve Tuncer, 2014: 145, 156–157).

The mentioned paradigms are built upon a network governance in theory (Klijn and Koppenjan, 2012: 2). Accessing public value requires support of individuals, organizations and stakeholders and the formulation of a broader base consolidation. Hence, the idea of consolidating the skills which are prerequisites of effective poly dimensional thinking and mobilization is negotiated in the new complex model of polycentric network governance. Its focal point is to sustain the relations horizontally, vertically, and diagonally. This requires a different approach to public governance. This stems from that the issues citizens, communities and governments encounter are becoming complex and intersecting issues (Benington and Moore, 2011: 6, 15–16). The management of such issues aims to gather different resources around a common purpose and to acquire new perspectives regarding the nature of the issue. Therefore, network governance is both projected to elaborate on the complex public issues in public policy and it ensures network governance to be reviewed as an alternative model and criticism of prior approaches (Weber and Khademian, 2008: 334).

Hierarchy is based on powerful chains of commands and top-down approach. Market is based on a self-regulating administration. As for that, networks are based on the connections between actors. The fact that actors are interdependent indicates that they are unable to process decision making by themselves. Thus, one of the key features of network governance is collaboration. Actors search for common resolutions on common issues. Negotiation and consensus are inevitable in this sense. Network governance forms a broader interaction site between public-private partnerships and other stakeholder participations. This includes unofficial individual interactions as well. Actors hold various reasons and ideas to involve in the network. Moreover, the co-dependency amongst actors does not prevent the asymmetric power relations (Khan, 2013: 134). Since the unity of purpose amongst actors must not be confused with unity of interest. For instance, it is not possible to say that the collaboration between various actors who congregate within the frame of collaborations to be built against environmental issues would produce similar/parallel outputs for each actor. This reflects the diversity of both industry-specific differences among actors and the concerns about environmental issues. This diversity can be extended from protection of green spaces to construction of secure zones, from local development concerns to different dimensions.

2. The Defining Features of Network Governance

Network governance consists of many different conceptual theoretical works. Jones et al. (1997: 915) suggest that there have been different newly projected terms and definitions for network governance. Within the entrepreneurial network presented by Dubini and Aldrich (1991: 306) in this context; the distinguishments between individuals, organizations and networks are getting out of focus. Network governance focuses on the formulation of public policies in the fields of politics or administration (Üstüner, 2003: 49). Networks, in broader sense, are defined by their permanent change relations formed between individuals and groups (Weber and Khademian, 2008: 334). Torfing (2005: 307), describes network governance as: "(1) an imaginary framework, (2) that organizes itself within the boundaries set by forces, (3) which are normative, cognitive, external and which, (4) through negotiations, regulate the vertical articulations of interdependent although relatively autonomous actors in operational terms, and (5) that contributes to formulation of public objectives". It is possible to describe network governance in multiple ways and these descriptions enable the access to some fundamental and common concepts which are related with network governance.

Primarily, as Klijn and Koppenjan mentions (2012: 4–5), network governance is characterized by co-dependency, interactions and complexity. Network governance is related with co-dependency forasmuch as the political spheres in which network governance is conducted (such as environment, healthcare, education) are interrelated subjects. That is to say, network governance is a tool projected to overcome complex issues. In this sense, the actors involving in network governance are units that come from different and autonomous industries, however, that endeavor act in a co-dependent manner on a common matter. Network governance is related with interactions, since the actors not only try to act collaboratively, but also to generate new ideas through different perspectives. Interaction in network governance is an inevitable output. Network governance is related with complexity as well, as there is not a benchmark method to practise network governance. As aforementioned, network governance is considered an alternative way to bring a resolution on complex problems. Complex issues do not stem from a single cause. The causes are various and undetermined. Therefore, since it is not possible to eradicate a certain cause for a resolution for these problems, the resolutions are still subject to uncertainty.

On the other hand, mutual trust in network governance is essential. On the contrary of hierarchy-based and market-based approaches that form the logic of traditional public administration and new public governance, network governance is relies on mutual trust (Klijn and Koppenjan, 2012: 6–7). Networks can contribute to the enhancement of the trust and co-dependency between actors, although their interests may be different than one another (Juhola and Westerhoff, 2011: 240). To put on a clearer point, networks are not solely built on mutual trust, however, mutual trust plays a significant role in constructing networks and sustaining them. Thus, that actors have different interests do not prevent them from connecting to one another around a common objective. As Borzel (1998: 254) mentions the ways for using the term network vary to a significant extent on interdisciplinary basis. In addition, different disciplines share an understanding that is common and at a minimum with respect to network. Hence, networks form an interaction between various actors (that is, variety also signify a status of complexity and ambiguity) who aim to reach to common objectives related to any network governance matter. These relations more have the feature of co-dependency rather than a hierarchal order.

3. Environmental Management and Cities/Municipalities

For many years, natural resources of modern society have been increasingly used and consumed. Besides, the finite structure of these natural resources has frequently been neglected. Eventually, the world we inhabit is under serious and sharp environmental threats. The accelerated industrialization and urbanization, emerging overpopulations lead the natural resources become more finite. As a natural result of this, cities are under serious environmental risks.

It is worth mentioning two significant factors regarding environmental issues. Firstly, environment is a transboundary issue. Thus, environmental issues are far-off from being spaces in which national actors take place as sole actors. Environmental risks, impacts and results concern the entire planet as a whole. Therefore, it is known that all actors on sub-national, national and supra-national scales are being affected by environmental issues. Cities have a particular importance as they are concrete spaces in which these impacts are to be sensed at most. Citizens that inhabit cities are social entities that are directly concerned by environmental risks.

Secondly, environment has become one of the "complex issue" areas that have increasingly become questions of debate in today's academic literature. The nature and the extents of complex issues, that concern individuals as a whole and the society, are ambiguous. This ambiguity is estimated to have stemmed from the inadequate technical information regarding the structure of complex issues and alternatives of resolution. Consequently, it is not possible to have adequate information on the causes and impacts of these complex issues. The causative relations of the issues create areas which are diverse, co-dependent and hard to locate. Thus, it is not possible to formulate a method on a resolution for environmental issues. Resolution for environmental issues is subject to ambiguity. It is not possible to mention a certain resolution or a cluster of resolutions with respect to complex issues such as environment, healthcare or migration.

The fact that there is not a certain resolution method for environmental issues does not necessarily mean that the society is or would be left alone with these issues. Environmental issues are types of issues that require to be managed within the scope of different methods and types of understandings, same as in settlement of complex issues. Therefore, management of environmental issues could be considered an evaluation of procedural criticisms accessed within the sense of the occurrence of these issues, and a reformulation of new methods and strategies within the frame of the evaluations in question.

The state maintains its position of a significant actor in the process of environmental governance. Along with this, regulations of governance influence the role of national state in processes of decision making on environmental subjects. The connections between local and supra-national scales enable development of diagonal relations through by-passing national state (Jessop, 2005: 392–393). Hereby, local actors increasingly concern with supra-national/transnational networks.

Urban administrators are the actors who are responsible for defining the active acts of network administration and its practice. This is an essential acceptance to understand the key role of decentralization on environmental acts (Azevedo, 2016: 90, 93). Many municipalities/cities from all around the globe take an important role in the campaigns against environmental issues and are fundamental actors on the management of these issues. In addition to this, urban managements are both dependent to centralized government and act within a multi-level governance in which they are dependent to the other actors in society. Network governance, in this case, has occurred as an encouraging "new governance model" in which they could expand their capacities of legitimacy and practice, with respect to the field of environment (Khan, 2013: 133).

4. Network Governance in Urban Environmental Management

The concepts of public administration and new public management remain incapable in terms of providing efficient tools for the management of the issues encountered today regarding environment and other complex issues. One of the fundamental innovations which network governance approach introduced, within the frame of these issues, is that it has moved the participation framework, that can enhance collaboration and mutual dialog, to a broader sphere. This sphere, on the other hand, is surrounded with democratic tools in which citizens also could involve more. Hereby, a negotiation process, which enables the process of decision making on the management of the issues to be generated in a more efficient manner, is anticipated to be administrated.

In this sense, this study focuses on three remarkable themes as: "the constitution of information and learning process", "mobilization of resources" and "ensuring democracy and participation" which are assumed to contribute to the environmental management of network governance.

4.1. Building Learning Process

Environmental issues are complex and ambiguous issues to a great extent. Since there are numerous causes for environmental issues, there is not a standard method to settle these issues. There is a need for different perspectives on detecting the causes for environmental issues and their impact areas. One of the key factors which cities play in urban environmental management is to provide a common ground in which various actors congregate. Municipalities are administrative units of cities in this sense. Municipalities necessitate the participation of other stakeholders whilst searching for resolutions on environmental issues. Environment is a field that requires technical expertise, as well as being one of urban issues. Thus, environmental issues are far-off of being a field on which cities can settle a resolution by themselves. Collaboration enables municipalities to interact with various actors such as technical expert, academist, urban planner, in relation to environmental issues. The fact that diversity of actors from different industries occurs amounts the congregation of different perspectives regarding environmental issues. Hence, a space where information exchange on a common subject is possible is created.

Many transnational networks provide a complex organizational landscape for cities to access beyond their local boundaries (Acuto and Leffel, 2020: 1). In such constructs, the cause and effect relationships of environmental issues are examined, thus, rich seams of information in relation to social acceptance of particular norms are gathered. Therefore, social learning, debate and negotiation evolve into a process of an extensive negotiation. Above all, these transnational networks are composed of actors who typically represent many different interests. Learning is a way of producing and processing information. Networks enable production of information through interactions of other networks members. Negotiation processes in a network as well influence the processing of information. On the other hand, we can divide learning into two as: individual learning and collective (or institutional) learning. Whilst individual learning takes places on individual basis, collective learning is a reflection of individual learning on an institution (or a group) (Newing et al., 2010).

It is observed from academic studies and especially from field researches that network governance produces outputs in practical terms, with respect to the learning process within the field of environment. According to a research conducted by Khan (2013: 136), Vaxjö is a city which has the vision of being a residential site that is fossil fuel-free. In this sense, municipality staff in Vaxjö and people from different NGOs had the opportunity to congregate with different work groups. One of the advantages of network governance is the information which the stakeholders contribute to the process. On the other hand, there are also emphases on the necessity of these information being retrieved from higher management layers (national governments) as well (Bell and Park, 2006: 76). A field research conducted by Juhola and Westerhoff (2011: 243) shows that the distribution of climate-related information represents one of the key factors in creation of networks. Scholars, NGOs and other policy makers congregate at the end of a range of workshops and conferences so as to compile the information on the relevant subject.

4.2. Mobilization of Resources

Mobilization of resources refer to the situation of generating new resources or consumption of the current resources in more rational terms (Seltzer, 2014). Network governance admits the fact that the most efficient way to reach to common objectives is collaboration. Therefore, reaching to such objectives necessitate the mobilization of resources at the same time. Actors involving in network governance hold different interests and different material and moral resources. Different interests and resources lead to the situation of co-dependency among actors through common objectives. Actors interrelate with one another through common objectives for the sake of exchanging different resources (Borzel, 1998: 254, 258–259). In this sense, network governance forms a cluster of relations which organizes collective acts and sets distributed resources in motion (Kenis and Schneider, 1991: 36).

The resources which actors hold within network governance against environmental issues may differ. The resources need to be assessed as material and non-material feasibilities. For instance, the acts set in motion by NGOs, material feasibilities of private industries, effect sizes of local administrations, or services of information, experience and consultancy offered by institutions and organizations such as universities, research institutions or local administrative units; are among the resources which actors embody. These distributed resources can plan a capable strategic route for management of environmental issues by being gathered by urban managements, each of which hold a coordinator position.

Academic studies show that there are a wide range of actor participations in network governance. However, it is observed that private industry has a dominant role at times. This stems from the fact that environmental issues are not independent from economic issues. Network governance can be used to create a local market for environmental issues (Khan, 2013: 137–138). It is also observed in Vaxjö example that climate policies are influenced by commercial interests as well (Khan, 2013: 136). In a similar manner, Juhola and Westerhoff (2011: 243) manifest that the networks created among actors increase the success on the necessary financial appropriation. Urban managements and municipalities stress the importance of the networks to be created together with other local administrations to gather human and financial resources. Whilst part of the resources can be outsourced in this way, the rest may be procured from the institutional budget.

4.3. Participation and Democracy

In network governance, all the relevant individuals and groups of interest are assumed to be involved in the process and the system is considered to take the relevant demands into consideration. It is expected that there is to be a balance settled among different groups of interest, during the course of decision-making process. On the other hand, this reflects a negotiation process at the same time. Theoretically, it is possible that there is a relation between input and output emerging on itself, since mutual learning during the process is in question (De Rynck and Voets, 2006: 60–61). Network governance has the potential for enhancing flexibility and responsiveness in service providing, thus encourages negotiation. Emerging network governances are expected to be democratic and to expand participation as capable of embodying communities (Bogason and Musso, 2005: 3, 14).

For example, ROM project in Ghent canal zone was commenced as a temporary adjustment project for spatial planning and environmental issues. The canal zone has various areas of activity, which are intersecting, such as environment, economics and housing. The variety of areas of activity is related with interests, competencies and resources of multiple actors. This enables actors, who are willing to conduct an effective project, to be co-dependent and to negotiate with one another (De Rynck and Voets, 2006: 62, 65).

To increase the sensitivity of society on this matter, as well as various stakeholders, to sustain environmental management has an important place. Developing collaborations on environmental subjects aim for these collaborations remain sustainable. Therefore, collaborations are not only subject to various management processes, but also involve educating and informing society basis. The projects conducted on environmental field redound to consciousness-raising policies for society.

5. The Criticism for Network Governance in Environmental Management

Network governance offers various alternative methods during the process of environmental issues in cities. Part of these have been mentioned and supported along with field-researched case studies. Parallel studies in relation to this demonstrate that network governance concerns some risks at the same time. In other words, alternative resolutions that have been put forth within the frame of settlement of the issues, offer innovative approaches exercising through criticisms for traditional administrations, whereas, on the other hand, call for new risks on the fields which have not been experienced.

Problem areas that could be encountered during the process of learning:

- Process of learning is not unproblematic. It may not be possible for the information learnt on individual basis to be extracted to institutional sphere at all times. That is, learning process is both an individual and an institutional process. The trainings which individuals/staff, who are representatives of entities or institutions in governance process, receive could be presented as an example of individual learning process. Nonetheless, institutional learning process is constituted through reflecting the acquired information into institutional construct. However, it is not possible to say that the learning process in the latter redounds to success at all times.
- The individual/s who represent an organization in a governance network may be subject to a constant change and this can result in affecting learning process in negative terms (Newing et al., 2010).

- Policy learning processes in transnational networks are far from being easy tasks. One should not consider the networks solely information exchanges. Instead of this, policy learning in networks can be conceptualized as reframing and repetitive issues (Betsill and Burkeley, 2004: 490).
- Lastly, it is also a matter of fact that who are the actors in network structures in regard to environmental management due to the effects of actors to learning process (Newing et al., 2010).

Problem areas that could be encountered during the process of mobilization of resources:

- Environment and economics are not independent of each other. Network governance is practised with more difficulties in areas where economic interests are not in line with environmental interests. Economic concerns of private entrepreneurs may result in neglecting local factors and environmental sensitivities.
- In environmental management, it is expected from various stakeholders to have a common percept in collaboration process. Although, this may not be the case at all times. Collaboration, in case of being maintained by different perceptions of stakeholders, may create a difference in terms of an effective resource management (Robins et al., 2011: 1312).

Problem areas that could be encountered within the fields of participation and democracy:

- Whether network governance provides an actual participation is a problematic matter of concern. Participation ensures a negotiation among actors. In addition to that, it is possible for a new power balance to come to the surface within the context of network governance. It is known that network governance enhances the influence of urban notables to a great extent. In this case, there are times when citizen participation is less common (Khan, 2013: 137–138).
- Participation includes more than congregation of various actors. It also matters that actors participate in decision making processes to the same degree. Actors who engage in activities with regard to environmental subjects are expected to contribute to resolution processes as well, once having congregated. Whereas in Vaxjö example, it has been observed that the detailed research in regard to reaching the objective set is handed over to the strategic goals of the municipality (Khan, 2013: 136).
- The system can result in local notables on urban basis to be repressed out of the system, besides various individual and interest groups involving in the

process. This is the observed the most clear within private profit-oriented organisaitons. The expansion of profit-oriented organizations, instead of local administrations that perform various services, lead to the diminishing of "election" element. It especially leads to fulfilling services within a limited scope of activity instead of equilibrating local privileges on allocation of resources. Elections put preferences and priorities to forefront, wehereas assignations result in the repetition of prior models. In many cases, when fulfilling a task or service, the emphasis is on the individuals who have a business background and are assigned. However, it is unlikely of these individuals to be considered representatives of community/society as the same way in elected individuals.

Conclusion

It is considered likely that, against changing social needs in time, the understanding of serving the public will look for new ways to respond to this change. One of the key features of the areas of the most frequently encountered problems is that it comes to surface as a complex nature of issues and the ambiguity of resolution alternatives. The matters which are settled when issues are without difficulties, resolution alternatives are determined and they are taken as responsibility by the relevant entities or authorized persons; is emerging a much more grift systemic model today. In this life where everything is interrelated, there are also networks formed between problem areas, and, distributed techniques of management are facing difficulties to overcome these issues.

Within the scope of a paradigm search in public administration, disfunctional techniques proposed in public policies and network governance on conducting complex issues through innovative methods has become a frequently debated understanding. Network governance is described in various ways such as networks in literature, governance, governance networks, policy networks. The most fundamental feature of network governance is that these actors are co-dependent in terms of the objectives (that is, the term "objective" does not refer to the same concept with the term "interest") they are expected to reach and in terms of resources. This co-dependency is both a key factor in formation of a network and is a source of motivation which moves the network to the objective. Network governance suggests a collaboration and an interaction which is on a broader extent, contrary to the understandings which are hierarchy-based or market-based. Network governance enables the acquisition of learning outputs which actors could obtain through negotiation. The complex structure of problems play a key role in projecting network governance as a prerequisite/

necessity. Complexity brings about a state of ambiguity, and, it is attempted to settle this ambiguity by the affection of mutual trust.

Environmental issues are one of the most obvious complex issues. Neither the top-down management model of the understanding of traditional management, nor the corporatization strategies, which market-oriented approach is based on, are capable or competent in management of environmental issues. Urban managements/municipalities which are the entities in which environmental issues are to be sensed in the most concrete sense, prefer to expand their own capacities by utilizing mechanisms concordant to network governance understanding.

One of the most significant contributions that network governance makes to the efforts against environmental issues is it enables the occurrence of an interaction zone in which other actors conducting on environmental issues could participate as well. Thus, it becomes likely to maintain a multi-level learning process, including technical expertise, on environmental subjects. The sharing between cities also facilitates the exchange of beneficial examples, as well as information exchange, during the process of experience exchange and environmental management. Co-dependency between actors during the course of management of environmental issues to a particular purpose, allows the resources that actors own to be implemented, within this context. Municipalities, each of them hold a position of coordinator on this matter. Once for all, network governance enables a negotiation process in environmental subjects to occur between actors, hence, contributes the society to be involved in this process through various educational and informational mechanism.

In addition to this, not all the advantageous points which network governance provides urban environmental management with work without errors. To provide the relevant participation channels in network governance does not necessarily mean that these channels work in success at all times. In this sense, it becomes likely to encounter such cases where individual learning fails to be projected into the relevant institutional frame, learning process lacks sustainability, economic profits surpass environmental sensitivity, resources are not used efficiently, an unequal power balance emerges during negotiation process, the expected level of participation in decision making process fails to be accessed. Therefore, network governance practices are possible to be implemented as long as the convenient conditions are fulfilled.

References

Acuto, M., and Leffel, B. (2020). "Understanding the Global Ecosystem of City Networks", *Urban Studies*, Vol: 58, No: 9 pp. 1–17.

Azevedo, T. C. Portella, A. A., and Sanchez, F. I. M. G. (2016). "Munıcıpal Envıronmental Management: A Proposal of Instruments for Dıagnosıs of Publıc Envıronmental Polıcıes in the Metropolıtan Area of Salvador (MAS)", *Holos*, Vol: 32, No: 2, pp. 84–100.

Bell, S., and Park, A. (2006). "The Problematic Metagovernance of Networks: Water Reform in New South Wales", *Journal of Public Policy*, Vol: 26, No: 1, pp. 63–83.

Benington, J., and Moore, M. H. (2011). "Public Value in Complex and Changing Times", *Public Value*, Vol: 1, pp.. 1–30.

Betsill, M. M., and Burkeley, H. (2004). "Transnational Networks and Global Environmental Governance: The Cities for Climate Protection Program", *International Studies Quarterly*, Vol: 48, pp. 471–493.

Bogason, P., and Musso, J. A. (2005). "The Democratic Prospects of Network Governance", *American Review of Public Administration*, Vol: 36, No: 1, pp. 3–18.

Borzel, T. A. (1998). "Organizing Babylon – On the Different Conceptions of Policy Networks", *Public Administration*, Vol: 76, No: 2, pp. 253–273.

De Rynck, F., and Voets, J. (2006). "Democracy in Area-Based Policy Networks the Case of Ghent", *American Review of Public Administration*, Vol: 36, No: 1, pp. 58–78.

Dubini, P., and Aldrich, H. (1991). "Personal and Extended Networks are Central to the Entrepreneurial Process", *Journal of Business Venturing*, Vol: 6, No: 5, pp. 305–313.

Genç, F. N. (2010). "Yeni Kamu Hizmeti Yaklaşımı", *Türk İdare Dergisi*, Sayı: 466, ss. 145–159.

Jessop, B. (2005). Hegemonya, Post-Fordizm ve Küreselleşme Ekseninde Kapitalist Devlet, (Der: Betül Yarar ve Alev Özkazanç), İletişim Yayınları, İstanbul.

Jones, C., Hesterly, W. S., and Borgati, S. P. (1997). "A General Theory of Network Governance: Exchange Conditions and Social Mechanisms", *Academy of Management Journal*, Vol: 22, No: 9, pp. 11–45.

Juhola, S., and Westerhoff, L. (2011). "Challenges of Adaptation to Climate Change Across Multiple Scales: A Case Study of Network Governance in Two European Countries", *Environmental Science & Policy*, Vol: 14, pp. 239–247.

Kenis, P. N., and Schneider, V. (1991). Policy Networks and Policy Analysis: Scrutinizing a New Analytical toolbox'. In Marin and R. Mayntz (eds.), Policy Networks and Policy Analysis, Campus-Verlag, Frankfurt

Khan, J. (2013). "What Role for Network Governance in Urban Low Carbon Transitions?", *Journal of Cleaner Production*, Vol: 50, pp. 133–139.

Klijn, Erik-Hans and Koppenjan, Joop (2012). "Governance Network Theory: Past, Present and Future", *Policy and Politics*, Vol: 40, No: 4, pp. 187–206.

Köseoğlu, Ö. and ve Tuncer, A. (2014). "Kamu Yönetiminde Yeni Bir Yaklaşım Olarak Kamu Değeri: Kavramsal ve Kuramsal Açıdan Bir Tartışma", *Yönetim Bilimleri Dergisi*, Cilt: 12, Sayı: 24, ss. 145–170.

Newig, J., Günther, D., and Pahl-Wostl, C. (2010). "Synapses in the Network: Learning in Governance Networks in the Context of Environmental Management", *Ecology and Society*, Vol: 15, No: 4: 24. [online]: http://www.ecologyandsociety.org/vol15/iss4/art24/.

Robins, A., Bates, L., and Pattison, P. (2011). "Network Governance and Environmental Management: Conflict and Cooperation", *Public Administration*, Vol: 89, No: 4, pp. 1293–1313.

Seltzer, J. B. (2014). What is Resource Mobilization and Why is it so Important?, https://healthcommcapacity.org/resource-mobilization-important/#:~:text=Resource%20mobilization%20refers%20to%20all,as%20'New%20Business%20Development' (21.04.2021).

Torfing, J. (2005). "Governance Network Theory: Towards a Second Generation", *European Political Science*, Vol: 4, pp. 305–315.

Üstüner, Y. (2003). "Siyasa Oluşturma Sürecinde Ağ Yönetişimi Kuramı", *Amme İdaresi Dergisi*, Cilt: 36, Sayı: 3, ss. 49–65.

Weber, E. P. and Khademian, A. M. (2008). "Wicked Problems, Knowledge Challenges, and Collaborative Capacity Builders in Network Settings", *Public Administration Review*, 68 (82), pp. 334–349.

Suna Ersavaş Kavanoz

Environmental Governance: From International Environmental Regimes to Multi-stakeholder/Multi-level Collaborations

Introduction

With the 1980s, neo-liberal policies that limited the state's intervention and governance practices brought a multi-stakeholder management process. New collaborations to recoup the centralised role of the state occurred along with these years. The global localization understanding of the time brought a percept which entrusts the urban and sub-local managements by taking parts in international collaborations. Approaching environmental issues of the same period in terms of sustainability, focusing on the transboundary points of the issues, scale problem, common property concept; developed the percept of environmental governance in managing the issues, along with externalities, in question. It is possible that the most remarkable point here is that the stakeholders whom may be considered the source of environmental issues are synchronically the stakeholders of solution seeking. The citizen movements on the involvement accompanying the same period, and also, that the social movements on environmental subjects highlighted the requisite for approaching the environmental issues in terms of more democratic and political resolution processes; rallied the growth of the field of environmental governance. Social movements in numerous countries on environmental subjects compelled more participative decision making processes, by creating pressure that could entail changes in policies followed.

This study is to touch upon the percept of multi-stakeholder/multi-level collaborations, the influence, efficacity and amount of which has been increasing recently. The study aims to elaborate on the positive contribution to generating solutions, of the diversity of the stakeholders that take parts fundamentally in governance as embracing numerous approaches to environmental governance and which are included in the international environmental regimes that are the early practices of environmental governance.

1. About the Term: "Environmental Governance"

Governance is "*the set of values, policies and institutions concerned with the economic, political and social matters in a society, occurring via the interaction amongst private sector, state and civil society*" (Sipahi, 2010: 334). Governance concept elicits a response to the question of how organizations, rules, systems and decisions are made in heterogenous and considerably distinct societies; and tackles substantially with the issue of economic and political coordination in social life. Governance depicts the structure of sociopolitical instutions, their geographical scales, key stakeholders, organizations and the probability of changes in relations amongst these components. Governance discourse potently correlates with the changes in social and economical terms. Hence, it is no surprise that the term environmental governance comes to the fore as an enunciative term at a time in which state authority and legitimacy, to wit, issues of environment and resources are questioned more intensely (Bridge and Perreault, 2009: 476– 477).

According to Adger vd. (2003), environmental governance adresses to "the settlement of environmental conflicts by means of the constitution, reaffirmation or amending of institutional regulations that may alleviate or restrain the use of environmental resources". The emphasis in this definition is on the institutional regulations. Paavola (2007), in his study suggesting that environmental governance can be considered constitution, reaffirmation and amending of institutions to settle the conflicts on environmental resources in the most ideal manner; asserts that the new institutionalist approach illuminates the circumstance where the studies comprising of, in an interdisciplinary manner, political sciences, sociology and anthropology may attain the governance of voluntarily collective actions and the use of environmental resources; and that it determines the design principles that characterize the successful solutions for governance (Paavola, 2007: 94). Notwithstanding, if we are to define environmental governance as "the interaction amongst formal and informal institutions and stakeholders within society, which has an influence on identifying and marking out the environmental issues" (Sipahi, 2010: 334, as cited in Schreurs, 1999) we would notice the emphasis is on the stakeholders. In a broader definition: "environmental governance" to signify the broad range of political, economic, and social structures and processes that shape and constrain actors' behavior towards the environment. Environmental governance thus refers to the multiple channels through which human impacts on the natural environment are ordered and regulated. It depicts the soft infrastructure of acceptable behavioral norms, expectations and social perceptions relating to environment in the processes embodying the involvement of a wide range of stakeholders, along with its senses of establishing rules, establishment of institutions, pursuing and implementing (Levy and Newell, 2002: 2–3).

The consensus on that a production process, ongoing in a nonoptimal manner based on market mechanism, had underlied the early term environmental issues; opposition to economic growth and environmental protection developed such understanding that social costs to involve in the process by state intervention. This approach embarks on the recognition of administrative arrangements of the national state, thus, as the main stakeholder, of the national state. Sustainable development, attempered the conflict between environmental protection and economic growth, and placed environmental friendly economies on an advantaged position. Adoption of the same approach called for stakeholders diversity enabling economic stakeholders, civil society and public participation, as well as national state, in environmental issues. Therefore, the understanding of environmental governance emerged. Transboundary points of environmental issues has made a global environmental governance, in which international institutions also participate in governance process and international networks mount up, remarkable today (Sipahi, 2010; Uzel, 2006: 112–114). Global environmental governance understanding arose after sustainability arguments in 1990s. Global environmental governance has a framework which expresses the necessity that the constitution of international regimes, which pass beyond national state level, involving in the solution efforts for environmental issues, by taking notice of the global scale of environmental issues. Besides, NGOs, within the scope of democracy and social justice principles, are stakeholders of multi-national companies, local administrations; and of global governance in national states.

Moving out of micro scale, environmental issues have moved in to macro scale and have reached global catastrophes that threaten the future of the world (Kaypak, 2013: 20). In this context, environmental governance has come into the focus as a collective and alternative solution, anticipated with the object of fulfilling the significant gaps of traditional, local and national authorities which are incompetent in elaborating on transborder issues (Sipahi, 2010: 341). Global environmental governance is regarded as a fundamentally political process embodying the struggles concerning whom to possess the authority and legitimacy of proposing rules to guide to the practices of states, multi-national companies, social acts, individuals; and whom to benefit from or lose certain rules and their practices (Speth, 2002).

Focusing on geographical scales of governance, leads to the consideration of that scale as a political and destabilized spatial manifestation, by nature of the socio-environmental relations. Therebeside, environmental governance focuses on ways to put the emphasis on consistency and immeasurability problems, and, consistent adaptation forms of different individuals despite numerous political, economic and social tensions that may arise around the issues relating to environment and resources. Putting decision making and, in broad terms, political process to forefront, environmental governance bridges over regarding politics as a process of dreaming, questioning and creating collective environmental futures, in a creative manner (Bridge and Perreault, 2009: 485).

We can define environmental governance as development of participative, collaborative and multi-stakeholder infrastructures in decision making processes of multi-scales, in upscaling environmental policies, intersecting one another. When we say environmental governance, we refer to the efforts of different stakeholders to create solutions and to develop strategies collaboratively, as the key feature. The scales are not sharply indistinctive from one another. An ambiguity about scales, as well, is in question. An investment which an international business has made on local scale may result in an environmental issue for the investment, or, the decisions made by the influence of international political sphere may result in the same consequences. Many local administrations have been making alterations on cities in order for drawing the investments to their own region, hence, these alterations may lead to environmental issues at times. In this case, how accurate is suggesting that the scale is local? The assessments, not only on the space that environmental issues affect but also on the stakeholders causing such issues, would therefore bring more justice in sharing responsibilites for solutions.

2. From International Environmental Regimes to Multi-stakeholder/Multi-level Collaborations

Davidson and Frickel (2004) state that studies on environmental governance gather around six dominant terms as: pluralism, agency capture, ecological Marxism, social constructionism, ecological modernization, and global environmentalism. Different approaches to environmental issues have lead to the development of understandings relating to environmental governance, through different terms.

The approaches to environmental issues through multilateral collaborations, in which decision making and practicing policies are considered shared active responsibilities of both state and non-state actors, can be evaluated within the scope of post-hegemonic governance which shows moving away from state centric understanding (Karkkainen, 2004: 75). Interdependence conduces to environmental conflicts and force to settle these conflicts by the establishment, amendment or recognition of institutions (Paavola, 2007: 95). Institutions settle the conflicts through establishing authorizations on environmental resources, reaffirming or redefining them, redress certain balance between conflicting interests (Adger vd., 2003). Conceptualizing environmental issues as conflicts over environmental resources stress that selection of governance institutions is a matter of social justice rather than efficiency. Arguments over maintaining distinction between markets and politics, acknowledge that the founder institutions of both fields generate different power structures that help expanding power in society. This acknowledgment influences the plans and decisions, including the involvement and distribution of power, and the results of distribution (Paavola, 2007: 96–97).

The abundance of different approaches and criticisms to environmental governance field unveiled different governance models. Especially the incompetence in generating solutions, of the established governance models led to new pursuits. In this context Speth (2002: 1) mentions three different turnouts: Firstly, the need for new institutions on international basis and norm determination procedures. The second follows as subsidence of enterprises, from non-governmental organisations (NGOs), local administrations and other stakeholders, as bottom-up. Third is the necessity that the causes underlying environmental degradation (such as poverty, population increase, underdevelopment, inadequate technology) being conducted on in a more direct way.

Bulkeley (2005: 881) divides global environmental governance into three in terms of its fields and scales: first is the understanding in which nation state, which is based on the hierarchical model of environmental governance scale correlatively with regime theory and some structuralist descriptions, is considered primary field of political authority. Second follows as the understanding of state preferential field which is a collaborator in transnational network theories, regime theory and structuralist approaches, notwithstanding, deteriorates the hierarchical scale approach by the presence of horizontal networks. And, the third is the approach in which the authority that deteriorates, in relation with global civil society, the term "hierarchy of environmental governance" is positioned in networks that are nonstate fields, however, the focus is turned to nonstate stakeholders without scrutinizing closely the nature of state field.

Upon all of these divisions and evalutions within the scope of field and scale, it is possible to say that the environmental policies has undergone a horizontal alteration with the approach addressing to the role of international rules, norms and regimes and the criticisms over this approach; and a change towards an understanding remarking the significance of multi-stakeholder networks.

2.1. International Environmental Regime

Environmental issues were reviewed as issues which nation states will not be able to settle on their own, in terms of its transboundary character. Besides that, co-dependency, particularly ecological complex co-dependency, gap of practice and legitimacy issue, called for a transnational environmental governance. Due to the growth of environmental issues and, hence, the co-dependency, intensification of economical proceedings passing beyond national borders, the challenges faced during the course of practice of international conventions; transition from environmental management to environmental governance was supported through the thesis of practices of sustainable development, ensuring international systems a legitimacy and that they will come to the fore (Hayırsever Topçu, 2007: 97–104). Externalities is another cause to require governance. Global collective act can generate limited resolutions due to the fact that it is generally difficult to grasp the influences of "externalities". This fundamentally stems from both time-wise and spatial distribution of environmental issues. On the event of climate change, for instance, decrease and compliance costs may not only be transferred through spaces (to other nations) -but also through time- to future generations (Easty and Ivanova, 2002:10).

The term "regime" includes a connotation which the literature of international relations utilize more and is an international institution. Some environmental issues (i.e.: local air pollution and waste disposal) is within a restrained geographical scope or can be elaborated on a local scale. Furthermore, a set of issues from persistant organic pollutants to the extinction of fishing industry and climate change, calls for an efficient response in various spans of authority and, at times, a coordinated act on global level. Grasping the limits of settling transboundary environmental issues on their own, governments all around the world have started being stakeholders of an international environmental regime (Easty and Ivanova, 2002: 8). Inefficiency of the search within current bureaucratic structures for solutions for environmental issues have brought international and global level searches for solutions into question. Especially the transboundary point of environmental issues and diversity of stakeholders in the roots of issues call for multi-stakeholder in solution efforts. On the other hand, global ecological dependency bring collaborations forward in positive terms.

Spatial scales for environmental governance have bilateral influence. First, decomposition of the roots and solutions of environmental issues within their own scales uncover call forth the concerns on unequal distribution of benefits of costs and environmental issues. For instance, a problem such as global climate change may have stemmed from chief producers of greenhouse in the world at the first stage, however, the dramatic effects of these would mostly affect the low emission nations in the global south. The spatial distribution of environmental issues such as acid deposition, ozone depletion and transboundary water pollution passes beyond national borders and leads to difficulties in solution design and appliance. The major strategies to elaborate on these topics are determined as international environmental regimes (Lemos and Agraval, 2006: 308–309). Through international negotiations and processes of regime constitution; traditional studies on international environmental policy regarded global governance as a function provided principally by states system. The function of these types of regimes are depicted as fulfilling the gaps between state fields or expansion of the collective regionalism of states to atmosphere and oceans. Regimes both consolidate the interstate systems by reinforcing nation states, and, at the same time, diminish regional hegemony terms by enabling the "global community" (hegemonic states or collectives sometimes) regulate the processes occurring at spaces where the spaces are recognized as hegemonic state field (Bulkeley, 2005: 878).

Regime theory is based on the thesis that to manage global commons, there is the need for global institutions. Conventional environmental governance is criticized for focusing on ways to motivate the states to act in a protective and improving manner for global commons by reducing to, within international relations perspective, international environmental law and the institutions regulating the law. Regime analyses are criticized on the grounds that they are static, state centric and neglecting the majority of broader political and economic forces. We may collect the criticisms in terms of democracy of environmental regimes under three categories: first, the countries attending negotiation processes may not be democratic; second, limited participation from nonstate stakeholders (mostly participation of large NGOs), unequal distribution of power, information and resources between participating countries, the probability of strong countries imposing their own preferences, and for last, many international environmental conventions lacking an effective enforcement in terms of binding provisions (Lemos and Agraval, 2006: 300–301). It is another obstacle, but not the political and economic structures of developing countries, in achieving the set objectives that international systems are unable to regard developing countries as equal stakeholders in resolution processes. Compliance to governance principles are closely related with power balances on national and international level. It is considered unlikely for the countries where institutional structures are not supported with principles of law, to comply with governance principles (Bal vd. 2015: 186, 190).

Neo-marxists criticize international environmental regime in economic-political terms. Companies lobby for states to comply with conventions in the course of multilateral negotiations of environmental conventions. Moreover, to make institutional regulations fulfill the functions of environmental governance, they interact with one another, states or other nonstate stakeholders (Falkner, 2003: 72–73). International environmental regimes are also criticized over that capital owners using structural force over state governors since they can shape the contexts of resolutions that governments take; and multinational companies being incompetent in generating solutions due to the fact that they are capable of apply pressure on governments in the course of resolution taking (Newell, 2008: 508–515). Environmental governance is criticized over ensuring the legitimacy of certain accumulation regimes within the context of the relationship between private sector, state, civil society and capitalism. Neo-liberal environmental governance is regarded as set of regulations that includes nature and natural resources in the preference of market-based actors and practices (Bridge and Perreault, 2009: 482–492; Falkner, 2003: 83; Newell, 2008).

Governance, as international regime, is being used to depict the intergovernmental collaborative organizations, and, is again criticised as it considers the state as the central stakeholder. In regime theory, it is needed that enriched and complex political (and which can also function as forum for these negotiations) negotiation process between various stakeholders, companies above all, industry associations, NGOs, state institutions and international institutions gets attention by interstate relations are addressed to. Regime theory has also tended to portray regimes as rational, technical solutions to environmental problems that successfully overcome problems of collective action among states (Levy and Newell, 2005: 5–6). Authority and legitimacy, in nation states and regimes, are "social institutions composed of principles, norms, rules, and resolution procedures and programs, that manage the stakeholders interactions within particular subject areas and that are come on a consensus" (Bulkeley, 2005: 878, as cited in Young, 1997). Different models have occurred by approaching environmental issues through multilateral environmental conventions.

Responses to environmental deterioration, in one hand, have led to the occurrence of new governance forms in some cases, on the other hand, have become opportunities for companies and NGOs to carry forward their benefits or normative agenda, through especially institutional renovations. Every type of organization and institution have been collecting information, but are incompetent to coordinate the data (Speth, 2002: 11). Nonetheless, when objectives set are failed to practice, the institutions fall into disrepute, hence, the effectiveness of these institutions, who are incompetent of appliance, is harmed in terms of the supporters of these institutions (Andresen, 2007: 320). International environmental laws and agencies, have led to gaps in span of authority, information and practice, within current global environmental governance (Easty and Ivanova, 2002: 3).

Having enabled new global regimes, organizations, institutions, international collaborations to emerge and to develop; globalization of environmental issues have taken a competent position to contribute to searches for solution. Globalization, has also helped the international environmental groups to cross beyond the limitations of pressure negotiations with governments on subjects of environmental issues, by expanding the roles of these groups on social movements. We may consider the establishment of environmental international networks an effective effort as well, for solutions to environmental issues, thanks to information exchange and technological innovations. Since ozone depletion, climate change, carbon emissions are issues such as to exceed borders of a single country; international collaborations and institutional conventions are essential to struggle these issues (Lemos and Agraval, 2006: 300– 301). Efforts to develop the regime theory into new directions and to base on the grounds of criticisms of mainstream approaches brought forward a pluralist global governance approach, in which nonstate stakeholders play a more active role, and that develops opinions on "complex multilateralism" probably or revitalization (Newell, 2008: 508–515).

2.2. Environmental Governance Within the Scope of Multi-stakeholder and Multi-level Partnerships

According to Sanwal (2004: 1621), areas of environment require entirely new approaches grounding on decentralized multi-stakeholder networks, rather than institutional hierarchies based on international collaborations. Sustainable development are no longer issues related with governments. Mutual supportiveness is competent for supporting sustainable development. This concept describes the relations between international regimes and nonstate stakeholders. Sustainable development necessitate scientific and technological advices through the partial information of various industries and levels that are needed for political and technological alterations.

Multi-level governance is defined as "political structures and processes crosssing the boundaries of areas of administrative jurisdiction, which aims to overcome co-dependency in processes of social development and political resolution which exist within regional units" (Newig and Fritsch, 2009: 199, as cited in Benz, 2006). Multi-stakeholder governance is also a polyhedral governance model with its global, national and local extents. A system of three main shareholders, in which neither out of this model is dominant, is anticipated. Polyhedral and multi-stakeholder governance model is described as "network governance" or "governance as a network of relation" as well. Besides the abundance of stakeholders as public, private or hybrid of both, another component of network governance is the abundance of extents. The factors undermining the efficiency of traditional environmental institutions are international competition, growing liberalization on circulation of goods, more complex relations of producer and consumer that pass beyond further than national borders, the social extent of formulating considerably dynamic and rapidly changing environmental policies, the increasing awareness on incremental growth of new information on the causes and consequences of environmental deterioration and ambiguity of this information. In the earliest phase of formulating environmental policies, these "globalization" factors stressed that negotiations, collaborations, and mutual interaction between parties (state-civil society-market) needed to be a must, rather than an exception. Governance would be ensured by compliance and coordination between stakeholders. Plus, channeling and influencing such complex, differentiated and dynamic system would be ensured through network relations. This conceptualization relating to governance is based on the ground of resistance to the centralization of power in the neo-liberal form of globalization, within environmental governance arguments (Hayırsever Topçu, 2007: 138–165).

As a part of adaptive governance, governance of global environmental resources require multi-level solutions on institutional diversity, in which local, national and international levels proceed synchronically (Adger vd. 2003: 1101; Paavola 2007: 94, as cited in Ostrom 2005, 2009). A more inclusive global environmental governance paradigm pledges an expanded collaboration, not only for innovative governance strategies, but also for institutional benefits, social movements and NGOs, that may have been excluded from initial policy making processes. As an alternative for obviating arguments on democratism and to international regimes; networks that are multi-level, non-hiearchical, enriched in terms of information, and with flexible institutions and stakeholders step forth (Bulkeley, 2005; Lemos and Agraval, 2006: 300–301).

The focus within global governance has turned onto multi-level and multi-stakeholder activities, which embody an approach that is more participative, more informal and integrated than those of intergovernmental acts. These type of global networks primarily occurred on international level in which the incompetence of centralised government gives place to innovative structures resulting from the constant need of new policy resolutions. They are multisectoral partnerships linking different sectors and levels of governance and bringing together governments, international organizations, corporations, and civil society (Streck, 2002: 3). The effectiveness of less formalized and flexible networks could then point toward a more viable solution to protect the global commons (Bulkeley, 2005; Streck, 2002: 3). Networks help for the formation of pools for knowledge accumulation and exchange of information and experience. Global public policy networks could come to the fore in spaces that lack of information andd tools to elaborate on the complex policy subjects of national policy makers, or, when there is the need of building a response that is based on a large consensus of stakeholders. Nevertheless, networks may arise around subjects in which various stakeholders are expected to adopt a coordinated approach on turning international consensus into action (Streck, 2002: 5).

Sociopolitically, interscale environmental issues influence decision making processes, that are institutionalized on local, sub-national, national and transnational levels, and become influenced by them. A common formula to elaborate on the multi-level character of environmental issues, designs governance mechanisms on social and institutional constellation levels. Multi-level governance aims to resist to disintegration that is resolution characteristics organized by sector-based decision making, or, in reality, regional, social and political units. Restructuralization of interscale governance strategies helps to concede searching and social learning as well, through rendering possible the levels of less informal decision making, more transparency and higher representability in general (Lemos and Agraval, 2006: 308–309).

Some environmental issues having demonstrated effects on local and some having demonstrated on global scale, formed an opinion that environmental issues can be settled through adapting governance institutions scale onto environmental issues scale. Thus, it was inferred that environmental governance is capable of taking place in a multi-level manner (Adger vd., 2003: 1101; Newig and Fritsch, 2009: 198, as cited in Young, 2002). State centric analyses are being receded in order for evaluating the abundance of stakeholders and institutions that have an influence on ways of elaborating global environmental issues on different scales. From this perspective, global environmental governance is not an area of interstate negotiations and regimes on its own (Bulkeley, 2005: 880).

Newig and Fritsch, in their studies (2009) which manifests how and to what extent the existence of multi-levels in governance affects the providing and enhancing high quality environmental policy outputs skills of participant decision making, on 47 case studies of decision making in North America and Europe; demonstrate that face-to-face interaction affect ecological decision making standarts in positive terms, and a polycentric governance system that includes numerous agencies and governance level procures higher quality environmental outputs.

Networks, through the skills of immediately responding to urgent issues, provides the opportunity to fulfill the operational gap which currently characterizes the international environmental policy. Networks, at the same time, via their multisector and non-hierarchical structures, pledge to fulfill the participance gap which is generally the main cause beneath the international political gridlocks. The powerful environmental governance structures, that are based on the grounds of a set of networks that are coordinated and originated by international organizations, can fulfill the current participative, operational and institutional gaps in global governance, hence, can provide with a more successful path to conduct on environmental threats against our planet (Streck, 2002: 7–17). International networks have paved the way much for environmental governance through their flexibility, coupling resources, collaboration, sharing the best practices, and multi-stakeholder structure (Bulkeley, 2005: 881). Networks, taking advantage of current institutions, the power of both governments and civil society; provides with more rapid, fast, problem-specific process, comprehensiveness based on merit, access to recent technology knowledge, and synchronical proximity to local regions on both local and global scale (Easty ve Ivanova, 2002: 18).

It is possible to say that a network governance model, in which global environmental governance has been managed through international networks, which governments, local administrations, NGOs, private sector, relevant professionals in recent years participate in, has been on the increase. Especially global institutions excluding local stakeholders in terms of environment, and including top-down resolution process, has led to the increasing focus on environmental issues with more stakeholder networks. When we consider this in relation with wicked problem; different perspectives on environmental issues, arguments on defining the problem and its existence necessitate many stakeholders involve in policy making process collaboratively. International collaborations hold many alternatives thanks to the specialties of sharing information and resource, transfer of the best practices. Moreover, the interdisciplinary character of environmental subjects necessitate experts of various disciplines involve in collaborations. NGOs founded particulary with respect to environment have remarkably increased in number. Besides NGOs participating in both national and international collaborations on environmental issues, they try to exercise power over political field in terms of subjects related to environment to influence the resolution process. It is obvious that areas of civil society cannot be excluded from policy making processes when we consider of the potential of these areas turning into social movements, at the present time. The advancements on interaction technologies and social media nowadays, are capable of direct the attention of not only the areas of civil society, but also the public opinion, to environmental issues in individual terms. Furthermore, with the increasing professionalism of NGOs and their participation as stakeholder, the probability that the values they collaboratively represent and their strong defence may become grinded down, make us think non-organized and informal movements could achieve success on environmental issues.

Contemporary collaborations between governments and communities should also contain understandings of how individuals would respond to the interventions of environmental governance. Individuals and households, instead of communities and collectives, are the holders of certain rights and responsibilities. Environmental policy makers aim to influence the acts of individuals (Agrawal and Lemos, 2007: 41). Basic to the concept of environmental democracy is "the fight of the public to participate in- even collectively determin- decisions about technology". "The goal should be to render obsolete the "expert" status of government and industry's scientists in order "to make every citizen conversant at all levels of the environmental debate""" (Fisher, 1993:176, as cited in Thornton, 1991:15). It has been seen that community and local voices involving in environmental governance gain the advantage of time-wise and spatial knowledge that would help to settle the complex environmental issues and, at the same time, enable to benefit from environmental assets more equitably. It could help to overcome democratic deficit and legitimacy deficit stemming from higher level of participation of different stakeholders in environmental resolutions and practices, and state authorities being correlated with market-oriented tools. Contemporary shared governance strategies focus on how individuals subject would respond to governance efforts, rather than their historical counterparts. By means of such conjecture of individual responses, decentralizationist environmental governance aims to ascertain the eager collaborations of those subject to governance goals (Lemos and Agraval, 2006: 311).

Communities have unpeered, time-wise and spatial knowledge, which distant state institutions do not have in general, that could help settling the complex environmental issues. On the other hand, formal participation of community members in governance, may enable the benefits of environmental resources to be distributed in more equal terms. When NGos work with institutional commons, each common can obtain benefits that would move environmental goals forward. The acts of institutional commons would gain more social legitimacy. Furthermore, NGOs will be able to obtain financial resources to support their protection efforts. Lastly, participation of governmental institutions can contribute more authorization and consistency to the decentralizationist acts of community and market actors. The fact that no stakeholder has the essential skills to conduct on multiple sides, scales and co-dependencies of environmental issues on their own, necessitates the collaborations. Spatial knowledge of communities, jurisdiction and action capacity of states, and, fundamental human incentives set in motion through market changes; underpin the potentials of stakeholders of environmental governance (Agrawal and Lemos, 2007: 39–40).

Bulkeley (2005), suggests that the approaches, that reduce the resolution processes of spatial and scaled configurations of environmental governance from international to national, then to local scale; conceal various ways, in which such issues are discussed via composite management regulations that work through network terms, and are formulated, built, organized, and work interscales. And, within this context, she analyzes transnational municipial networks. Main chracteristics of new environmental governances can be construed as participative dialog, negotiation, transferred decision making and flexibility (Gunningham, 2009: 146). This approach can be interpret as involving nonstate stakeholders in decision making, rule making, regulation and further processes. New collaborative environmental governance enables local level to take more responsibility, through taking local conditions into consideration in a better way. Redesignation of "governance" mechanisms that also include cities -by means of, new forms of especially state-private collaboration and networks- is also closely related with how local is built in globalization (Jessop, 1995: 400). Swyngedouw, in his study where he suggests that the shift that has been experienced ever since post-1970s should be considered within the point of reorganization of geographical scale of economic and political life; uses the term "glocalization" to correspond to this shift. The concept *glocalization*, points to the transnational evolution of nation state on one hand, and the top-down evolution into local, urban and regional scales on the other hand. Also, it refers to increasing localization, regionalization and transnationalization starting synchronically between economic activities and company networks. The presence of institutions that will render service to new economic relations, along with the shift from management to governance, accompany this process as well. This concept also corresponds to global localization strategies of the fundamental structure of industrial, service and financial capital (Swyngedouw, 2004: 25–37).

Conclusion

Along with 1980s, questioning state sovereignty and the shift in state's span of intervention, has brought about the importance of supra-national and sub-national scales in decision making processes. Thus, the governance concept occurred in 1990s, led to the understanding of collaborative management in which private sector and civil society are included within the frame of collaborative understanding. Together with the transborder character of environmental issues of the time, environmental issues emerged from the multinational companies, passing beyond the spatial limits, investing in different cities, the rise of globalization and decentralization, questions against the environmental management of collective ownership; all these contradictions drove governance practices of decision making on environment, policy and strategy making forward.

In early terms, collaborations on environment were executed through international regimes open to the influence of multinational companies in which governments were at center. However, this model's approach that is inclined to disregard the unequalities between countries led to the criticisms within the context of developed countries being active on decision making process, being open to the influence of multinational companies, not managing to involve NGOs in the process. The necessity that governance of environmental issues execute on different levels and with a multi-stakeholder network approach showed itself through the inadequacies of international environmental regimes.

Every level containing multiple stakeholders is such as to pave the way for strategies for finding solution. Some environmental matters may need prompt action, by their characteristics. Even in such cases, prior preparation or that the points of view of different stakeholders are gathered and a solution is formulated is important. Hence, governance models that enable a multi-stakeholder and an intersecting multi-level bottom-up movement -that rises from more innovative base- can provide environmental issues with more realistic fight strategies.

Environmental issues, as a result of the uncertainties stemming from differentials of different actors on the causes of problem, the fact that an attempt for solution for an environmental issue has the potential of causing another problem, that it may not only be settled solely with technical approaches, and co-dependant relations particularly in economics and politics; remain one of the issues which have difficult solutions. Therefore, when it comes to environmental issues, it is essential to formulate practices to obtain skills of settling and managing a problem that is exceeding all these limits. Nation states, along with maintaining its significance in terms of being competent to execute the decisions made in rule making and international networks or regimes; environmental issues necessitate that different perspectives, values and information are included in understanding the problem and in contribution to solution strategies. Networks in which various stakeholders from countries particularly with different development rates are involved, are important in terms of the potential of converting distinctions in efforts for solution into knowledge.

References

Adger, W.N., Brown, K., Fairbrass, J., Jordan, A., Paavola, J., Rosendo, S., & Seyfang, G. (2003). "Governance for Sustainability: Towards a 'Thick' Analysis of Environmental Decision-Making", *Environment and Planning A*, 35, pp. 1095–1110.

Agrawal, Arun & Maria, Carmen Lemos (2007). "A Greener Revolution in the Making?: Environmental Governance in the 21st Century", *Environment: Science and Policy for Sustainable Development*, 49(5), pp. 36–45.

Andresen, Steinar (2007). "The Effectiveness of UN Environmental Institutions", *International Environment Agreements*, 7, pp. 317–336.

Bal, Harun, Neşe, Algan ve, & Pınar, Özdemir (2015). "Environmental Governance and Importance of Instituonal Framework from the New Institutionalist Perspective", *Journal of Doğuş Üniversity*, 16(2), pp. 179–191.

Benz, Arthur (2006). "Governance in Mehrebenensystemen", in Schuppert, G. F. (ed.), *Governance-Forschung. Vergewisserung über Stand und Entwicklungslinien. 2. Aufl age*. Baden-Baden: Nomos, pp. 95–120.

Bridge, G. & Perreault, T. (2009). "Environmental Governance", in. Castree, N., Demeritt, D., Liverman, D., and Rhoads, B. (eds.), A Companion to Environmental Geography. Oxford: Wiley-Blackwell, pp. 475–497.

Bulkeley, Harriet (2005). "Reconfiguring Environmental Governance: Towards a Politics of Scales and Networks", *Political Geography*, 24, pp. 875–902.

Davidson, Debta J. and Scott, Frickel (2004). "Understanding Environmental Governance", *Organization & Environment*, 17(4), pp. 471–492.

Easty, Daniel C. and Maria H. Ivanova (2002). "Revitalizing Global Environmental Governance: A Function-Driven Approach", in. Daniel C. Esty and Maria H. Ivanova (eds.), Global Environmental Governance: Options & Opportunities. New Haven, CT: Yale School of Forestry & Environmental Studies. Publications Series, pp. 181–204.

Falkner, Robert (2003). "Private Environmental Governance and İnternational Relations: Exploring the Links", *Global Environmental Politics*, 3(2), pp. 72–87.

Fischer, Frank (1993). "Citizen Participation and the Democratization of Policy Expertise from Theorotical Inquiry to Practical Case", *Policy Sciences*, 26, pp. 165–187.

Gunningham, Neil (2009). "The New Collaborative Environmental Governance: The Localization of Regulation", *Journal of Law and Society*, 36(1), pp. 145–166.

Hayırsever Topçu, Ferhunde (2007). Globalization and International Environmental Policies: The Problem of the Shift from Government to Governance, Unpublished Ph.D. Thesis, 2007, Ankara.

Jessop, Bob (2005). "The Entrepreneurial City: Re-imaging Localities, Re-designing Economis Governance, or Re-structuring Capital?", in ed. Betül Yarar, Alev Özkazanç (eds.), Hegemony, Post- fordism and the Capitalist State on the Axis Globalization. İstanbul: İletişim, pp. 379–404.

Karkkainen, B. (2004). "Post-Sovereign Environmental Governance", *Global Environmental Politics*, 4(1), pp. 72–96.

Kaypak, Şafak (2013). "The Global Environmental Politics for the Solution of Environmental Problems", *Muğla Sıtkı Koçman Üniversity The Journal of Institute for Social Sciences*, 31, pp. 17–34.

Lemos Maria, Carmen ve and Arun, Agrawal (2006). "Environmental Governance", *Annual Review of Environmental and Resources*, 31, pp. 297–325.

Levy, D. L., and Newell, P. (2005). "Introduction: The Business of Global Environmental Governance", in. D. L. Levy and P. Newell (eds.), Business of Global Environmental Governance. Cambridge, MA: MIT Press, pp. 1–20.

Newell, Peter (2008). "The Political Economy of Global Environmental Governance", *Review of International Studies*, 34, pp. 507–529.

Newig, Jens, and Oliver, Fritsch (2009). "Environmental Governance: Participatory, Multi-Level – and Effective?", *Environmental Policy and Governance*, 19, pp. 197–214.

Ostrom, Elinor (2005). *Understanding Institutional Diversity*. Princeton: Princeton University Press.

Paavola, Jouni (2007). "Institutions and Environmental Governance: A Reconceptualization", *Ecological Economics*, 63, pp. 93–103.

Sanwal, Mukul (2004). "Trends in Global Environmental Governance: The Emergence of a Mutual Supportiveness Approach to Achieve Sustainable Development", *Global Environmental Politics*, 4(4), pp. 16–22.

Schreurs, Miranda A. (1999). *An Analytic Framework for a Comparative Study of Environmental Governance in Asia,* IGES Environmental Governance, Country Reports on Environmental Governance in Four Asian, Countries. Japan: Shoman, IGES.

Sipahi, Esra Banu (2010). "Collective Solutions for Global Environmental Problems and Governance", *Selçuk Üniversity Journal of Institute for Social Sciences*, 24, pp. 331–344.

Speth, James Gustave (2002). "The Global Environmental Agenda: Origins and Prospects", in. Daniel C. Esty and Maria H. Ivanova (eds.), Global Environmental Governance: Options & Opportunities. New Haven, CT: Yale School of Forestry & Environmental Studies, Publications Series, pp. 11–30.

Streck, Charlotte (2002). "Global Public Policy Networks as Coalitions for Change", in. Daniel C. Esty and Maria H. Ivanova (eds.), Global Environmental Governance: Options & Opportunities. New Haven, CT: Yale School of Forestry & Environmental Studies, Publications Series, pp. 121–140.

Swyngedouw, Erik (2004). "Globalisation or 'Glocalisation'? Networks, Territories and Rescaling", *Cambridge Review of International Affairs*, 17(1), pp. 25–48.

Thornton, Joe (1991). "Risking Democracy", *Greenpeace*, March-April, pp. 14–17.

Uzel, Esra (2006). Global Environmental Governance (Good Governance), Unpublished Master Thesis, Ankara Üniversitesi Institute for Social Sciences, 2006.

Young, O. R. (1997). "Rights, Rules and Resources in World Aaffairs". in Oran Young (ed.), Global Governance: Drawing Insights from the Environmental Experience. Cambridge, MA: MIT Press, pp. 1–23.

Young O. R., and Les Gasser (2002). The Institutional Dimensions of Environmental Change: Fit, Interplay, and Scale, Global Environmental Accord. Cambridge, MA: MIT Press.

Kamber Güler

Climate Change and Migration: Positions of the Political Groups in the European Parliament on Climate Refugees

Introduction

Climate change is one of the most serious phenomena of the 21st century with its devastating impacts on various areas of living beings from politics to economics, and even to existence and survival. These impacts are not limited to a particular geography, species, demographics or identity. On the other hand, people who leave their lands to avoid negative effects of climate change and to survive are one of the most vulnerable groups that require closer scrutiny. Above all, these people do not have a legal status protected under any binding international agreement. Who are these people? Are they migrants, refugees or just *fake refugees* as commonly denominated by anti-immigration political circles? The fact is that the term 'climate refugee' is still not involved in the vocabulary of current international law though it is used more than ever in today's political discourse. This study aims at understanding and exposing the positions of political groups in the European Parliament (EP) regarding the legal status of these people fleeing their countries as a result of climate change and its negative impacts.

In the light of the premises of critical discourse analysis (CDA), the study analyses the discourses delivered during the parliamentary debates by the members of the EP political groups during the 7th (2009–2014), 8th (2014–2019) and 9th (2019–2024) parliamentary terms. These political groups are the European People's Party (EPP), Progressive Alliance of Socialists and Democrats (S&D), European Conservatives and Reformists (ECR), Alliance of Liberals and Democrats for Europe (ALDE), European United Left/Nordic Green Left (GUE/NGL), Greens/European Free Alliance (Greens/EFA), Europe of Freedom and Direct Democracy (EFDD) and Europe of Nations and Freedom (ENF). In the 9th parliamentary term, the ALDE and ENF are renamed as the Renew Europe (Renew) and Identity and Democracy (ID), respectively. Furthermore, the EFDD of the 8th parliamentary term does not exist anymore while it is known as Europe of Freedom and Democracy (EFD) in the 7th parliamentary term. It should be noted that each discourse in the study is given under the name of the

Tab. 1: Number of Debates and Speeches Reviewed on Climate Change and Migration

	Debate	EPP	S&D	ECR	ALDE (Renew)	GUE/ NGL	Greens/ EFA	EFDD (EFD)	ENF (ID)	Total
7th Parliamentay	614	1,063	800	69	166	145	134	108	—	2,485
Term (2009–2014)		38	33	3	5	7	5	5		96
8th Parliamentary	496	486	570	65	137	155	83	73	17	1,586
Term (2014–2019)		35	68	9	23	6	12	6	8	167
9th Parliamenty	133	81	85	14	42	23	41	—	16	302
Term (2019–2024)		5	9	0	4	1	5		1	25
Total	1,243	1,630	1,455	148	345	323	258	181	33	4,373
		78	110	12	32	14	22	11	9	288

political group to which the member affiliates when s/he delivered the relevant discourse. Therefore, for example, it is possible to see the names of ALDE and Renew together in the section analysing the discourses of these political group members.

The official website of the EP[1] was used for the data of this study. The number of debates and speeches reviewed for the study is shown in Tab. 1. As given in the table, the number of reviewed debates is 1,243 in total, and the total number of reviewed speeches involving the term 'climate change' is 4,373. The numbers given in the second row of each parliamentary term shows the speeches involving not only the term 'climate change' but also the term(s) '(im)migration', 'migrant(s)', 'refugee(s)' and/or 'asylum'. So, the number of speeches involving both 'climate change' and one or more of these terms are 288 in total. The most relevant speeches in various official EU languages were translated from the original language to English literally as much as possible when required, and analyzed in the context of the relevant groups' positions on the legal status of climate refugees.

1. Climate Refugees and Discourse

It has probably been sixty thousand years since the first people, *Homo sapiens*, migrated from East Africa to other parts of the world so as to survive (Harzig and Hoerder 2009: 8; Manning, 2013: 1–2). The International Organization for Migration (IOM) (2004: 41) officially defines migration as 'a process of moving, either across an international border, or within a State'. As for 'forced migration',

1 See (EP, 2021b).

it is 'a migratory movement in which an element of coercion exists, including threats to life and livelihood, whether arising from natural or man-made causes' (IOM, 2004: 25). Climate change is one of these causes resulting in forced migration, regardless of the debate on whether climate change is natural or a result of human action. Then, who is migrant, who is refugee? The persons that move to another country or region so as to improve their social conditions for a better life are called 'migrant' (IOM, 2004: 40) whereas the term 'refugee' is a legally recognized status under the Convention and Protocol Relating to the Status of Refugees and referred as follows:

> As a result of events occurring before 1 January 1951[2] and owing to wellfounded fear of being persecuted for reasons of race, religion, nationality, membership of a particular social group or political opinion, is outside the country of his nationality and is unable or, owing to such fear, is unwilling to avail himself of the protection of that country; or who, not having a nationality and being outside the country of his former habitual residence as a result of such events, is unable or, owing to such fear, is unwilling to return to it. (UNHCR, 2010: 14)

At this point, it should be noted that the European Union (EU) takes the Convention and Protocol Relating to the Status of Refugees as its starting point for a common asylum policy throughout the EU, and the EP and Council are the two EU institutions which are responsible for adopting measures for a common asylum system and a common immigration policy in accordance with the ordinary legislative procedure (EU, 2012b: 76–77). Furthermore, the legal bases of the EU's migration and asylum policy are Articles 67(2), 78 and 79 of the Treaty on the Functioning of the European Union (TFEU) and Article 18 of the Charter of Fundamental Rights of the European Union, which envisages that '[t]he right to asylum shall be guaranteed with due respect for the rules of the Geneva Convention of 28 July 1951 and the Protocol of 31 January 1967 relating to the status of refugees' in accordance with the TFEU (EU, 2012a: 399). As the single directly elected body of the EU, the EP has a key role in the legally recognition of climate refugees in the EU. Therefore, the discourses delivered by the Members of the European Parliament (MEPs) require close attention and follow-up in this context.

What makes these discourses delivered by the MEPs so important? The premises of CDA, theoretical framework of this study, can answer this question. As the forerunners of CDA, Fairclough and Wodak (1997: 258) argue that

---

2 The 1967 Protocol removed the geographical and time limitations that were previously involved in the 1951 Convention.

discourse is constitutive in terms of sustaining and reproducing the social status quo as well as contributing to the transformation of this social status quo; and thus, 'it gives rise to important issues of power'. In other words, discourse not only represents and signifies the world but also constitutes and constructs it in meaning (Fairclough, 1992: 64). This is also why discourse is power that needs to be seized (Foucault, 1981: 52–53). In this context, the political texts and talks are instruments of the politicians through which they can hold or seize the power. These discursive instruments for doing politics contribute to the public agenda and public opinion while also legitimizing political decisions that may not be legal or moral in the eyes of international law and human right principles (Van Dijk, 1997b: 39–40). Moreover, Van Dijk (1997a: 44) claims that 'who controls public discourse, at least partly controls the public mind'. Considering all these aspects of discourse, CDA can be defined as 'a type of discourse analytical research that primarily studies the way social power abuse, dominance, and inequality are enacted, reproduced, and resisted by text and talk in the social and political context' (Van Dijk, 2001: 352), and is employed to make 'the ideological loading of particular ways of using language and the relations of power' more visible for people (Fairclough and Wodak, 1997: 258). The positions of the EP political groups on climate refugees are reviewed within this theoretical framework in the following section.

2. Positions of the Political Groups on Climate Refugees

This section involves one main excerpt from each political group in the EP, and the excerpts are analyzed chronologically as much as possible within the aims and scope of the study. It is aimed that each excerpt analysis not only has coherence within itself but also completes the others in order to be able to expose the big picture. Also, some other relevant quotations are given within the analyses of the excerpts to make the positions of the political groups on climate refugees clearer.

> Madam President, the basic challenge which we have before us seven weeks before the Copenhagen Summit is whether or not we shall manage to reach agreement in terms of taking responsibility for the global financing of policies for the moderation of climate change on the part of developing countries. Europe has made important steps by defining sources of financing and ways of organising it, but now the time has come for us to persuade other developed countries to take their share of responsibility, bearing in mind that support for efforts by developing countries to combat climate change also affords an opportunity to combat global inequalities and to narrow the divide between developed and developing countries.

> There is something else which we must not forget, especially here in the European Union. We are on the point of creating a new order of refugees, climate refugees who are not protected today under any international convention, and, as a result, they have no rights. Closing this legal loophole and substantially supporting climate refugees is a basic obligation of the international community in which the European Union must take a leading role. (Anni Podimata, S&D, 20 October 2009)

The S&D, the leading left-wing political group in the EP, is one of the most pro-immigration political groups, and the research for this study reveals that its members mostly deliver moderate discourses regarding migrants and refugees. Starting with some self-criticism on the developed countries along with some assumed positive steps by the EU, Anni Podimata calls on 'other developed countries to take their share of responsibility' so that developing countries can also combat 'global inequalities' by combatting 'climate change'. For Podimata, this burden-sharing will finally 'narrow the divide between developed and developing countries' as well. While there is a common tendency particularly among right-wing political groups in the EP to denominate newcomers from the least developed or developing countries to Europe for various reasons 'fake refugees' (Güler, 2019), Podimata's call on the EU to create 'a new order of refugees, climate refugees' partly reveals S&D's willingness to take these people under international protection with the leadership of the EU. Aware of the fact that 'climate change will lead to an enormous number of refugees fleeing the poorest areas of the Earth', Vittorio Prodi (S&D, 15 December 2010) also favors the inclusion of the term 'climate refugee' into the vocabulary of current international law. Moreover, 'active participation in the debate on the term "climate refugee", including its possible legal definition in international law or in any legally binding international agreement' is seen as another step in this direction by the members of S&D (Claudette Abela Baldacchino, S&D, 3 April 2014; also see Miriam Dalli, S&D, 21 January 2016; Gilles Pargneaux, S&D, 3 October 2017). However, there is also an S&D member who tackles the issue of climate change on the basis of not only 'immigration' but also 'security, economic recovery' and 'even combating terrorism' (Edite Estrela, S&D, 20 October 2009).

> Regardless of the debate on the causes of climate change, and on verifying whether human action has caused and can reverse it, it is now clear that this issue has very serious implications in extremely diverse areas of human life, and that it is threatening to cause imbalances at global level. Therefore, we cannot fail to monitor it closely and with concern. In particular, climate change has caused the worrying rise in sea level, forced migrations, and the fight for access to waterways and more fertile land, as in Sudan, pitting nomadic herdsmen against settled farmers. The EU must actively participate in this global effort and do its best to monitor this problem and seek lasting solutions, which

> will ideally be able to reconcile scientific and technological progress, and the development of populations with environmental quality and respect for nature. The Cancún climate change conference is an excellent opportunity to pursue this objective in order to establish more ambitious targets and reach a more solid and comprehensive collective commitment to combating the problem. (Diogo Feio, EPP, 25 November 2010)

As the most populous right-wing political group in the EP, the EPP has more moderate discourses on immigration in general compared to other right-wing political groups of the parliament. Accepting the 'very serious implications' of climate change 'in extremely diverse areas of human life' and its threats 'at global level', Diogo Feio does not think that the EU has done its best on the issue up to now, and considers the Cancún climate change conference as an 'excellent opportunity' for a global effort in this respect which 'the EU must actively participate in'. In addition, at first sight, Feio's referring to 'forced migrations' within the results of climate change is of importance in the context of the EPP's attitude on involvement of the term 'climate refugee' within international law. Likewise, Françoise Grossetête (EPP, 20 October 2009) and Axel Voss (EPP, 24 November 2009) also regard 'migratory flows' and 'future damage in the form of migration', respectively, as consequences of climate change. Whereas Elena Băsescu (PPE, 20 April 2012) uses the term 'environmental refugees' for these people during a parliamentary debate, José Manuel Fernandes (EPP, 22 November 2012) emphasizes its direct and indirect effects on everyone and argues that 'climate change has a direct impact on security and economy, as it can cause people to migrate to other parts of the globe'. However, in spite of the EPP members' accepting the impacts of climate change on immigration in general (Peter Liese, PPE, 16 September 2015; José Manuel Fernandes, PPE, 14 October 2015; Françoise Grossetête, PPE, 4 October 2016; József Nagy, PPE, 4 October 2016; Andrea Bocskor, PPE, 6 October 2016; Dubravka Šuica, PPE, 6 October 2016; Bogdan Brunon Wenta, PPE, 18 January 2018; Janina Ochojska, PPE, 11 February 2020), there is still divergence among the members on 'the recognition of a status protection for climate refugees' as seen during a parliamentary debate and voting on a recommendation[3] related to the issue (Cristian Dan Preda, EPP, 2 July 2018).

> The Commissioner's speech on climate change did not leave much room for a satisfactory result in Durban. She more or less said that an internationally binding agreement was pie in the sky and that this was because of others, not because of us. Contrary to this pessimistic climate, all of us who voted in favour of the resolution on climate change[4]

3 See (EP, 2018).

4 See (EP, 2016).

> did so in order to send a strong message of political will concerning certain objectives: to adopt a global, integrated, legally binding framework that includes a strict implementation timetable for containing the rise in temperature of the planet to below 2°C compared with pre-industrial values; to bridge the yawning gap between the ambitions of the parties and the scientific data, by stopping dirty developments; to reduce greenhouse gas emissions by 80–95% by 2050 compared with 1990 levels; to offer developing countries proper financing and technological assistance; to protect the planet's tropical forests; to put an end to the millions of climate refugees. The economic crisis should not be used as an alibi for a Copenhagen-type failure. The climate cannot wait, nor can mankind. (Nikolaos Chountis, GUE/NGL, 16 November 2011)

The GUE/NGL is one of the two green and left-wing political groups in the EP. As expected, the group attach more importance to the issues related to environment. For the GUE/NGL (2021), '[t]ime is running out for strong measures to save the planet and deal with the massive challenge of climate change', and there is need for 'sustainable' and 'environmental' policies. On the same page of the group's official website, the GUE/NGL (2021) does not refer to climate refugees or migrants but to the 'minorities' who should be defended from 'attacks by the far right'. In the excerpt above, in a similar context, Nikolaos Chountis blames 'others' for the lack of 'an internationally binding agreement' on climate change. His reference to 'developing countries' in the framework of climate change, and then, to 'the millions of climate refugees' can give clues about the group's position regarding the relation between climate change and refugees. Furthermore, Chountis states that climate change should be priority of the EU without any 'alibi' such as 'economic crisis' because '[t]he climate cannot wait, nor can mankind'. Another member of the GUE/NGL, Eva-Britt Svensson (14 July 2009) criticizes the EU because of its policy on many issues including climate change and immigration, and adds as follows: 'We have a climate crisis that has already resulted in climate refugees.' Similarly, Xabier Benito Ziluaga (GUE/NGL, 5 October 2016) uses the term 'climate refugee' while referring to the people living on an island in Alaska and holding a referendum whether to migrate to the mainland because of the rising sea levels. During a more recent parliamentary debate, Merja Kyllönen (GUE/NGL, 2 July 2018) focuses on 'the effects of climate change on the rights of indigenous people' giving reference to the Sami people living in the Northern Europe. For the GUE/NGL, as clearly seen with the subjects of these two examples, climate change is not limited to well-known disadvantageous lands of the world but affects many people from various parts of the world, and eventually force them to leave their lands for a better option just to survive.

> Madam President, ladies and gentlemen, I hear about climate change still using the future: 'it will happen', 'it will occur', 'we will'. In reality, the effects of global warming are an emergency already underway and the term 'climate refugees' is sadly topical.
> Next week's summit will be held in New York. Well, it is a few months ago, in March 2014, a worrying figure that concerns the United States: 65 percent of the respondents to a survey know that global warming is taking place, but half of them do not believe it will involve serious risks or consequences. We call for the European Union to be a leader in combating climate change, also by interacting productively with the world of science, with the world of scientific dissemination, information and with the involvement of the public.
> We have heard in this House that there is a need for correct scientific information, as some still do not believe in climate change. We call for the European Union to speak with a unanimous voice and to participate as a protagonist in international climate negotiations. A new agreement must be found by the next Paris summit, otherwise next year's summit will end like the previous ones: many promises and few facts. (Marco Affronte, EFDD, 16 September 2014)

The EFDD was one of the right-wing Eurosceptic political groups, and could not survive in the current parliamentary term because of the Brexit. In other words, it requires at least 25 MEPs coming from at least one-quarter of the Member States to form a political group in the EP, and the 24 out of 48 members of the EFDD were coming from the UK in the 8th parliamentary term of 2014–2019 (EP, 2021a, c). In the excerpt above, as a member of one of the anti-immigration political groups in the EP, Marco Affronte asserts that 'the term "climate refugees" is sadly topical' though he accepts 'the effects of global warming' as an 'emergency' issue. And then, Affronte persistently emphasizes the importance of the issue with such words: 'global warming is taking place', 'serious risks or consequences', 'combating climate change', 'climate change', 'international climate negotiations'. Calling for the EU to 'speak with a unanimous voice' and become 'protagonist' in these negotiations, Affronte is of the opinion that the EU cannot go beyond 'many promises' on climate change. Dario Tamburrano (EFDD, 16 September 2014), taking the floor during the same parliamentary debate, also criticizes the EU with similar discourses: 'We have been sitting here for years, comfortable, discussing, while outside this change is a serious reality'. Compared to Affronte, Tamburrano is more overt on the relation between climate change and migration, and claims that climate change 'takes victims, unleashes conflicts for resources, increases migratory flows'. On the other hand, Oreste Rossi (EFD, 8 March 2011) denominates these peoples 'illegal migrants', and questions 'equal access to healthcare' for them. Furthermore, Laura Ferrara (EFDD, 14 October 2015) considers climate change as a 'global threat' and the reason of 'migratory flows' whereas Jonathan Arnott (EFDD, 21 January 2016) rejects the suggestion that '"climate change" is a major cause of the current refugee crisis'. Taking all these discourses into consideration, it is possible to argue that the EFDD did not have a clear or settled position on climate refugees.

> I would like to ask my colleague – it is of course a trick that is often used here, namely to link everything together. We are talking about refugees and we include the climate because those people come here because the climate is deteriorating. We need to give more development aid, because the climate is deteriorating and we need to give more development aid, because the refugees are coming here, all over the place so that nobody understands it anymore. But when we talk about climate change: I come from the Netherlands, the country that is the most vulnerable because it is almost entirely below sea level. So perhaps this is an opportunity – and I would like your answer to that – that the Netherlands will finally get money back from all those billions it has pumped into this circus. (Olaf Stuger, ENF, 2 December 2015)

As one of the anti-immigration political groups in the EP, the ID is mostly known with its overt and fierce discourses on immigration during the parliamentary debates (Güler, 2009). The research conducted for this study also re-exposes its well-known anti-immigration stance despite the existence of some rare moderate discourses on the issue. In the excerpt above, Olaf Stuger sarcastically criticizes the MEPs in 'this circus' for the correlation established between 'refugees' and 'climate'. Instead of talking about climate refugees, Stuger calls on these MEPs to talk about the Netherlands as 'the most vulnerable' country in the context of climate change 'because it is almost entirely below sea level'. On the other hand, in his speech on 'combating climate change', Laurențiu Rebega (ENF, 14 October 2015) accepts the existence of 'a new category of refugees', i.e. 'climate refugees', though they are 'not legally recognized'. However, Rebega's referring to 'climate refugees' as 'a new category' along with 'war refugees' in the same speech makes one think that these people may not have the same rights with those already protected by the international agreements even if they are 'legally recognized'. What is clear in his speech is that '[c]limate change is a threat to global stability and security in all respects'. During another debate on an EP resolution dated 28 September 2016 on climate change, the members of ENF are seen delivering speeches similar to each other and voting against the resolution (EP, 2016). Dominique Martin (ENF, 6 October 2016) argues that 'the resolution expresses unreasonable wishes' such as 'welcom[ing] more migrants because of climate change'. Marie-Christine Arnautu (ENF, 6 October 2016) and Sophie Montel (ENF, 6 October 2016) are skeptical of the resolution as it again means 'more migrants to be welcomed because of climate change'. Lastly, Jean-François Jalkh (ENF, 6 October 2016) is also against the resolution because he believes that it will result in 'ever more immigration linked to climate change'.

These opposing views on the issue demonstrate that the ID principally does not support the 'serious recognition of the issue of climate refugees, and the scope thereof, resulting from climate disasters caused by global warming' (EP, 2016).

> Climate change and global warming are creating climate refugees. Of these, women are the most vulnerable population precisely because of the lack of measures to consolidate gender equality. For this reason, climate justice requires measures to be taken to achieve social, employment and wage equality for men and women.
> It is well known that gender equality remains the greatest challenge of our time. The gender gap has narrowed significantly in recent years, but progress varies between Member States, and inequalities persist in various areas. An extremely large number of women continue to be discriminated against, without equal opportunities in education and the labor market. Particularly in developing countries, where women are particularly affected by climate change, although the vast majority work in agricultural work, a very small percentage of them own agricultural land.
> In addition, access to water in the same countries is particularly difficult and those most affected in this case are also women who, among other things, are in charge of household chores and food preparation. (Notis Marias, ECR, 15 January 2018)

Though it is another anti-immigration political group in the EP, the discourses of the ECR members on climate refugees are more moderate when compared to the ones delivered by the ID members. Just at the beginning of the excerpt above, Notis Marias claims that '[c]limate change and global warming are creating climate refugees'. In his speech that focuses on 'climate change' in general, Marias also refers to 'climate justice' in the context of 'gender equality' as 'the greatest challenge of our time'. He tackles the issue not only in the framework of 'Member States' but also 'developing countries' where he argues that 'women are particularly affected by climate change'. During another parliamentary debate held years ago, Marias (26 November 2014) describes 'climate change' as 'an immediate threat' that 'creates new migratory flows'. Richard Ashworth (ECR, 4 October 2016) also regards 'climate change' as one of the reasons of 'migrants all over the world'. That is why the efforts on migration should be directed to 'the cause, not just to symptoms' (Richard Ashworth, ECR, 4 October 2016). Finally, Marias (ECR, 4 October 2016) criticizes Paris Agreement for making no reference to the 'status of a refugee or migrant' in terms of 'climate migration'. Such moderate discourses delivered by its members on people affected by climate change reveal that the ECR is prone to legally recognition of a status protection for climate refugees.

> Madam President, Commissioner Oettinger, every time we discuss climate change in this House I look over there at the gallery at the young people because actually that's

> what we're discussing about. I want to give you a message today: the European Union is a climate mitigation giant but the European Union is also a climate adaptation dwarf. Climate change is here and is happening now, but we are doing so little to adapt to it. We must adapt to climate change by changing the way we build houses, by preventing climate migration, by building dykes to prevent floods, by managing forests to prevent wildfires, by greening the roofs in our cities.
> There is no contradiction between mitigation and adaptation. In France, insulating homes to reduce greenhouse emissions is also an adaptation measure preparing the homes for climate change. But in the current MFF [Multiannual Financial Framework], only 3% of our EU Structural and Investment Funds on climate are related to adaptation. In the next MFF, Mr Oettinger, let's put our money where our mouth is. (Nicolae Ştefănuţă, Renew, 23 October 2019)

The Renew is a left-wing pro-European political group in the EP. As the reviewed speeches reveal, the Renew members generally believe that there is a direct or indirect relation between climate change and migration (Andrea Zanoni, ALDE, 20 April 2012; Ramon Tremosa i Balcells, ALDE, 16 December 2015; Sophia in 't Veld, ALDE 12 September 2017; Urmas Paet, ALDE, 2 July 2018). In the excerpt above, Nicolae Ştefănuţă directly uses the term 'climate migration' while talking about climate change in a criticism of the EU, which he calls 'climate mitigation giant' and 'climate adaptation dwarf'. In the speeches of the group members, it is also possible to see the use of 'climate change and migration' together to list 'the great challenges facing the EU' (Susana Solís Pérez, Renew, 10 March 2020). Likewise, Malik Azmani (Renew, 27 November 2019) argues that the EU must, among others, 'tackle climate change' and 'gain control on migration' in order to overcome 'huge challenges'. Fredrick Federley (ALDE, 26 November 2014) claims that climate change 'will cost a lot in refugee flows' while Louis Michel (ALDE, 26 November 2014) states that it has already resulted in 'several thousand "refugees"' during the same debate. Lastly, speaking on the aforementioned resolution of 28 September 2016, Louis Michel (ALDE, 6 October 2016) uses the term 'climate refugees' during his speech, quoted as follows: 'The EP rightly urges all countries to take the issue of climate refugees and the social consequences of climate change seriously and to genuinely support developing countries in their pursuit of climate resilience.' As seen in the discourses of its members, the Renew is aware of the consequences of climate change on people who are forced to leave their own lands and to move, and has a positive stance on the rights of climate refugees.

> Downpours, droughts, tornadoes, extreme heat, rising sea and ocean levels, species extinctions, hunger, forced migration, epidemics. These are just some of the effects of the climate crisis. Decades of ruthless exploitation of the planet's resources have brought

> us to the brink of the abyss. We will not be able to reverse many losses, but we can and are still obliged to take steps to protect the Earth and its inhabitants from catastrophe. According to the UNEP report[5] published in 2019, meeting the goal of limiting climate change to 1.5 °C, which was identified in the Paris Agreement as a desirable state, will require the EU to reduce emissions by 2030 by at least 65%. Scientific studies clearly show that the effects of increasing the average temperature by even 0.5 °C more than 1.5 °C will be incomparably more severe. In the first case, it is estimated that approximately 37% of the population will be exposed to extremely high temperatures every 5 years, while in the second, it is 14%. An increase in temperature by 2 °C also means, inter alia, the loss of about 99% of the coral reefs or the rise in sea levels by 0.46 m. The stakes are high. The EU does not compromise and follow the current scientific knowledge, which is clear in this regard – therefore, it is important that an ambitious reduction target for 2030 is necessary and we must start implementing it today. (Sylwia Spurek, Greens/EFA, 6 October 2020)

The Greens/EFA is another green and left-wing political group in the EP, and the group members are, in general, overt in their discourses related to environment. In the excerpt above taken from a recent parliamentary debate, Sylwia Spurek mentions the general framework of climate change issue in the light of a report published by the United Nations Envrionment Programme (UNEP), and wants to draw attention to the current challenges resulting from climate change. According to Spurek, 'forced migration', among others, is one of 'the effects of the climate crisis' which is the result of '[d]ecades of ruthless exploitation of the planet's resources'. Besides, the emphasis of 'epidemics' in the excerpt revokes Coronavirus starting in late 2019 and spreading to the world in a very short time by claiming the lives of more than 4 million people until now (Worldometer, 2021). Taking these points into consideration, Spurek argues that '[t]he stakes are high' if the EU and other counterparties do not fulfill the requirements for 'limiting climate change'. In addition, with reference to the 'migrants' drown there, Jordi Solé (Greens/EFA, 15 December 2020) asserts that '[the Mediterranean] will be hardest hit by climate change'. Similarly, Raül Romeva i Rueda (Greens/EFA, 11 September 2012) warns the MEPs during another debate by claiming that 'climate change will become the biggest driver for population displacement in the coming years', and uses the term 'climate refugees' in the same speech (also see Florent Marcellesi, Greens/EFA, 28 November 2018; Jean Lambert, Greens/EFA, 15 January 2019). More importantly, Igor Šoltes (Greens/EFA, 6 October 2016) overtly states that 'I think it is very important that the resolution[6] also contains

5 See (UNEP, 2019).

6 See (EP, 2016).

serious recognition of the existence of so-called climate refugees.' Šoltes believes that migration due to climate change is 'a real problem today' which cannot be ignored. Linnéa Engström (Greens/EFA, 3 October 2017) is also one of the MEPs who considers climate change as the reason of 'escalation of refugee flows', and asks for the others to take 'migration of people as a result of climate disasters seriously'. With its overt discourses on climate change and migration together, the Greens/EFA seems considerably clear about its favoring position on climate refugees.

Conclusion

Forced migration as one of the negative impacts of climate change is a crucial phenomenon the world faces today. Within the cause-and-effect relation between climate change and migration, the politicians have begun to use the term 'climate refugee' more and more in their political speeches, which sometimes turns into the main subject of debates on whether it should be involved in international law or whether the persons leaving their countries as a result of the impacts of climate change should be called 'climate refugees'. The analysis of the discourses in this study reveals that the EP political groups do not have a uniform opinion on these people though some of them resemble each other to an extent in their stances on the issue. Furthermore, there is not always uniformity within the political parties in this respect as seen in the examples of the members of the EPP and partly the S&D. The GUE/NGL stands out with its emphasis on the globality of the issue of climate refugees with the examples of the people living on an island in Alaska and the Sami people living in the Northern Europe. As the former political group of the EP, the EFDD's position on climate refugees was not clear enough to have an argument on whether the group supported the term's involvement in current international law or not. The ID seems to be the only political group clearly opposing the legally recognition of climate refugees whereas the ECR has a more moderate approach within this framework. As for the Renew, the group overtly appreciates the negative consequences of climate change on these people and exhibits positive stance on the rights of climate refugees. Finally, the Greens/EFA is the most supportive group in this context with its clearly favoring position on climate refugees. Considering the general tendency of the EP political groups as important actors of the legislation in the EU and the fact that discourse is a constitutive and constructive power, it is not hard to envisage the legally recognition of climate refugees at the level of the EU in the foreseeable future, even if not at global level yet.

References

Abela Baldacchino, Claudette (2014). "69th Session of the United Nations General Assembly (A7-0250/2014 – Alexander Graf Lambsdorff)", 3 April <https://www.europarl.europa.eu/doceo/document/CRE-7-2014-04-03-ITM-009-04_EN.html> (Accessed 17 February 2021).

Affronte, Marco (2014). "UN Climate Summit 2014 (23 September 2014 – New York) (Debate)", 16 September <https://www.europarl.europa.eu/doceo/document/CRE-8-2014-09-16-ITM-017_EN.html> (Accessed 17 February 2021).

Arnautu, Marie-Christine (2016). 2016 UN Climate Change Conference in Marrakesh, Morocco (COP22) (B8-1043/2016), 6 October <https://www.europarl.europa.eu/doceo/document/CRE-8-2016-10-06-ITM-006-03_EN.html> (Accessed 20 February 2021).

Arnott, Jonathan (2016). "EU Priorities for the UNHRC Sessions in 2016 (RC-B8-0050/2016, B8-0050/2016, B8-0052/2016, B8-0056/2016, B8-0063/2016, B8-0064/2016, B8-0065/2016, B8-0066/2016)", 21 January <https://www.europarl.europa.eu/doceo/document/CRE-8-2016-01-21-ITM-009-05_EN.html> (Accessed 20 February 2021).

Ashworth, Richard (2016). "Situation in Calais (Debate)", 4 October <https://www.europarl.europa.eu/doceo/document/CRE-8-2016-10-04-ITM-014_EN.html> (Accessed 20 February 2021).

Azmani, Malik (2019). "Presentation by the Commission President-elect of the College of Commissioners and Their Programme (Debate)", 27 November <https://www.europarl.europa.eu/doceo/document/CRE-9-2019-11-27-ITM-003_EN.html> (Accessed 24 February 2021).

Băsescu, Elena (2012). "Explanations of Vote", 20 April <https://www.europarl.europa.eu/doceo/document/CRE-7-2012-04-20-ITM-011_EN.html> (Accessed 15 February 2021).

Benito Ziluaga, Xabier (2016). "2016 UN Climate Change Conference in Marrakesh, Morocco (COP22) (Debate)", 5 October <https://www.europarl.europa.eu/doceo/document/CRE-8-2016-10-05-ITM-019_EN.html> (Accessed 20 February 2021).

Bocskor, Andrea (2016). 2016 UN Climate Change Conference in Marrakesh, Morocco (COP22) (B8-1043/2016), 6 October <https://www.europarl.europa.eu/doceo/document/CRE-8-2016-10-06-ITM-006-03_EN.html> (Accessed 20 February 2021).

Chountis, Nikolaos (2011). "Explanations of Vote", 16 November <https://www.europarl.europa.eu/doceo/document/CRE-7-2011-11-16-ITM-007_EN.html> (Accessed 14 February 2021).

Dalli, Miriam (2016). "EU Priorities for the UNHRC Sessions in 2016", 21 January <https://www.europarl.europa.eu/doceo/document/CRE-8-2016-01-21-ITM-009-05_EN.html> (Accessed 20 February 2021).

Engström, Linnéa (2017). "2017 UN Climate Change Conference in Bonn, Germany (COP23) (Debate)", 3 October <https://www.europarl.europa.eu/doceo/document/CRE-8-2017-10-03-ITM-013_EN.html> (Accessed 21 February 2021).

EP (2016). Motion for a Resolution on the Implementation of the Paris Agreement and the 2016 UN Climate Change Conference in Marrakesh, Morocco (COP22) (2016/2814(RSP)), 28 September <https://www.europarl.europa.eu/doceo/document/B-8-2016-1043_EN.pdf> (Accessed 20 February 2021).

EP (2018). Report on a European Parliament Recommendation to the Council on the 73rd Session of the United Nations General Assembly (2018/2040(INI)), 27 June <https://www.europarl.europa.eu/doceo/document/A-8-2018-0230_EN.html> (Accessed 22 February 2021).

EP (2021a). "European Parliament: 2014–2019. Constitutive Session", <https://www.europarl.europa.eu/election-results-2019/en/european-results/2014-2019/constitutive-session> (Accessed 12 March 2021).

EP (2021b). "European Parliament Plenary: Debates and Videos", <https://www.europarl.europa.eu/plenary/en/debates-video.html> (Accessed 12 February 2021).

EP (2021c). "Results by National Party: 2014–2019. United Kingdom – Final Results", <https://www.europarl.europa.eu/election-results-2019/en/national-results/united-kingdom/2014-2019/constitutive-session> (Accessed 12 March 2021).

Estrela, Edite (2009). "Climate Change and Developing Countries in the Framework of the UN Conference on Climate Change in Copenhagen (Debate)", 20 October <https://www.europarl.europa.eu/doceo/document/CRE-7-2009-10-20-ITM-005_EN.html> (Accessed 12 February 2021).

EU (2012a). "Charter of Fundamental Rights of the European Union", *Official Journal of the European Union*, C 326, 26 October <https://eur-lex.europa.eu/legal-content/EN/TXT/PDF/?uri=CELEX:12012P/TXT&from=EN> (Accessed 23 March 2021).

EU (2012b). "Consolidated Version of the Treaty on the Functioning of the European Union", *Official Journal of the European Union*, C 326, 26 October <https://eur-lex.europa.eu/legal-content/EN/TXT/PDF/?uri=CELEX:12012E/TXT&from= EN> (Accessed 23 March 2021).

Fairclough, Norman (1992). *Discourse and Social Change*, Polity Press, Cambridge.

Fairclough, Norman and Wodak, Ruth (1997). "Critical Discourse Analysis". In: A. Teun Van Dijk (Ed.), *Discourse as Social Interaction: Discourse Studies: A Multidisciplinary Introduction*, Vol. 2, SAGE, London, pp. 258–284.

Federley, Fredrick (2014). "2014 UN Climate Change Conference – COP 20 in Lima, Peru (1–12 December 2014) (Debate)", 26 November <https://www.europarl.europa.eu/doceo/document/CRE-8-2014-11-26-ITM-007_EN.html> (Accessed 17 February 2021).

Feio, Diogo (2010). "Explanations of Vote", 25 November <https://www.europarl.europa.eu/doceo/document/CRE-7-2010-11-25-ITM-009_EN.html> (Accessed 13 February 2021).

Fernandes, José Manuel (2012). "Explanations of Vote", 22 November <https://www.europarl.europa.eu/doceo/document/CRE-7-2012-11-22-ITM-014_EN.html> (Accessed 15 February 2021).

Fernandes, José Manuel (2015). "Towards a New International Climate Agreement in Paris (A8-0275/2015 – Gilles Pargneaux)", 14 October <https://www.europarl.europa.eu/doceo/document/CRE-8-2015-10-14-ITM-021-08_EN.html> (Accessed 19 February 2021).

Ferrara, Laura (2015). "Towards a New International Climate Agreement in Paris (A8-0275/2015 – Gilles Pargneaux)", 14 October <https://www.europarl.europa.eu/doceo/document/CRE-8-2015-10-14-ITM-021-08_EN.html> (Accessed 19 February 2021).

Foucault, Michel (1981). "The Order of Discourse". In: Robert Young (Ed.), *Untying the Text: A Post-Structuralist Reader*, Routledge and Kegan Paul, London, pp. 51–78.

Grossetête, Françoise (2009). "Climate Change and Developing Countries in the Framework of the UN Conference on Climate Change in Copenhagen (Debate)", 20 October <https://www.europarl.europa.eu/doceo/document/CRE-7-2009-10-20-ITM-005_EN.html> (Accessed 12 February 2021).

Grossetête, Françoise (2016). "Conclusion on Behalf of the EU of the Paris Agreement Adopted under the UN Framework Convention on Climate Change (Giovanni La Via (A8-0280/2016))", 4 October <https://www.europarl.europa.eu/doceo/document/CRE-8-2016-10-04-ITM-008-01_EN.html> (Accessed 20 February 2021).

GUE/NGL (2021). "What We Stand for", <https://left.eu/what-we-stand-for> (Accessed 7 March 2021).

Güler, Kamber (2019). "Discursive Construction of an 'Anti-immigration Europe' by the Right-wing Political Groups in the European Parliament", *Marmara Journal of European Studies*, 27(2), pp. 347–369.

Harzig, Christiane and Hoerder, Dirk (2009). *What is Migration History?* Polity Press, Cambridge.

in 't Veld, Sophia (2017). "Recent Developments in Migration (Debate)", 12 September <https://www.europarl.europa.eu/doceo/document/CRE-8-2017-09-12-ITM-014_EN.html> (Accessed 21 February 2021).

IOM (2004). *International Migration Law: Glossary on Migration*, IOM, Geneva.

Jalkh, Jean-François (2016). 2016 UN Climate Change Conference in Marrakesh, Morocco (COP22) (B8-1043/2016), 6 October <https://www.europarl.europa.eu/doceo/document/CRE-8-2016-10-06-ITM-006-03_EN.html> (Accessed 20 February 2021).

Kyllönen, Merja (2018). "Violation of Rights of Indigenous Peoples in the World (Debate)", 2 July <https://www.europarl.europa.eu/doceo/document/CRE-8-2018-07-02-ITM-017_EN.html> (Accessed 22 February 2021).

Lambert, Jean (2019). "Reform of the EU Asylum and Migration Policy in Light of the Continued Humanitarian Crisis in the Mediterranean and Africa (Debate)", 15 January <https://www.europarl.europa.eu/doceo/document/CRE-8-2019-01-15-ITM-002_EN.html> (Accessed 24 February 2021).

Liese, Peter (2015). "Decision Adopted on 15 July 2015 on the Energy Summer Package (Debate)", 16 September <https://www.europarl.europa.eu/doceo/document/CRE-8-2015-09-16-ITM-014_EN.html> (Accessed 19 February 2021).

Manning, Patrick (2013). *Migration in World History*, 2nd ed., Routledge, London and New York.

Marcellesi, Florent (2018). "Strategy for Long-term EU Greenhouse Gas Emissions Reduction in Accordance with the Paris Agreement (Debate)", 28 November <https://www.europarl.europa.eu/doceo/document/CRE-8-2018-11-28-ITM-018_EN.html> (Accessed 22 February 2021).

Marias, Notis (2014). "2014 UN Climate Change Conference – COP 20 in Lima, Peru (1–12 December 2014) (B8-0251/2014)", 26 November <https://www.europarl.europa.eu/doceo/document/CRE-8-2014-11-26-ITM-013-03_EN.html> (Accessed 17 February 2021).

Marias, Notis (2016). "Conclusion on Behalf of the EU of the Paris Agreement Adopted under the UN Framework Convention on Climate Change (Giovanni La Via (A8-0280/2016))", 4 October <https://www.europarl.europa.eu/doceo/document/CRE-8-2016-10-04-ITM-008-01_EN.html> (Accessed 20 February 2021).

Marias, Notis (2018). "Women, Gender Equality and Climate Justice (Short Presentation)", 15 January <https://www.europarl.europa.eu/doceo/document/CRE-8-2018-01-15-ITM-018_EN.html> (Accessed 22 February 2021).

Martin, Dominique (2016). "2016 UN Climate Change Conference in Marrakesh, Morocco (COP22) (B8-1043/2016)", 6 October <https://www.europarl.europa.eu/doceo/document/CRE-8-2016-10-06-ITM-006-03_EN.html> (Accessed 20 February 2021).

Michel, Louis (2014). "2014 UN Climate Change Conference – COP 20 in Lima, Peru (1–12 December 2014) (Debate)", 26 November <https://www.europarl.europa.eu/doceo/document/CRE-8-2014-11-26-ITM-007_EN.html> (Accessed 17 February 2021).

Michel, Louis (2016). 2016 UN Climate Change Conference in Marrakesh, Morocco (COP22) (B8-1043/2016), 6 October <https://www.europarl.europa.eu/doceo/document/CRE-8-2016-10-06-ITM-006-03_EN.html> (Accessed 20 February 2021).

Montel, Sophie (2016). 2016 UN Climate Change Conference in Marrakesh, Morocco (COP22) (B8-1043/2016), 6 October <https://www.europarl.europa.eu/doceo/document/CRE-8-2016-10-06-ITM-006-03_EN.html> (Accessed 20 February 2021).

Nagy, József (2016). "Conclusion on Behalf of the EU of the Paris Agreement Adopted under the UN Framework Convention on Climate Change (Giovanni La Via (A8-0280/2016))", 4 October <https://www.europarl.europa.eu/doceo/document/CRE-8-2016-10-04-ITM-008-01_EN.html> (Accessed 20 February 2021).

Ochojska, Janina (2020). "The New Comprehensive EU-Africa Strategy (Debate)", 11 February <https://www.europarl.europa.eu/doceo/document/CRE-9-2020-02-11-ITM-012_EN.html> (Accessed 25 February 2021).

Paet, Urmas (2018). "Climate Diplomacy (Debate)", 2 July <https://www.europarl.europa.eu/doceo/document/CRE-8-2018-07-02-ITM-019_EN.html> (Accessed 22 February 2021).

Pargneaux, Gilles (2017). "2017 UN Climate Change Conference in Bonn, Germany (COP23) (Debate)", 3 October <https://www.europarl.europa.eu/doceo/document/CRE-8-2017-10-03-ITM-013_EN.html> (Accessed 21 February 2021).

Podimata, Anni (2009). "Climate Change and Developing Countries in the Framework of the UN Conference on Climate Change in Copenhagen (Debate)", 20 October <https://www.europarl.europa.eu/doceo/document/CRE-7-2009-10-20-ITM-005_EN.html> (Accessed 12 February 2021).

Preda, Cristian Dan (2018). "73rd Session of the UN General Assembly (Debate)", 2 July <https://www.europarl.europa.eu/doceo/document/CRE-8-2018-07-02-ITM-020_EN.html> (Accessed 22 February 2021).

Prodi, Vittorio (2010). "Human Rights in the World 2009 and EU Policy on the Matter (Debate)", 15 December <https://www.europarl.europa.eu/doceo/document/CRE-7-2010-12-15-ITM-014_EN.html> (Accessed 13 February 2021).

Rebega, Laurenţiu (2015). "Towards a New International Climate Agreement in Paris (Debate)", 14 October <https://www.europarl.europa.eu/doceo/document/CRE-8-2015-10-14-ITM-014_EN.html> (Accessed 19 February 2021).

Romeva i Rueda, Raül (2012). "Explanations of Vote", 11 September <https://www.europarl.europa.eu/doceo/document/CRE-7-2012-09-11-ITM-011_EN.html> (Accessed 15 February 2021).

Rossi, Oreste (2011). "Explanations of Vote", 8 March <https://www.europarl.europa.eu/doceo/document/CRE-7-2011-03-08-ITM-010_EN.html> (Accessed 14 February 2021).

Solé, Jordi (2020). "25 Year Anniversary of the Barcelona Process and the Southern Neighbourhood (Debate)", 15 December <https://www.europarl.europa.eu/doceo/document/CRE-9-2020-12-15-ITM-013_EN.html> (Accessed 25 February 2021).

Solís Pérez, Susana (2020). "Conclusions of the Special European Council Meeting of 20 February 2020 on the Multiannual Financial Framework (Debate)", 10 March <https://www.europarl.europa.eu/doceo/document/CRE-9-2020-03-10-ITM-008_EN.html> (Accessed 25 February 2021).

Šoltes, Igor (2016). 2016 UN Climate Change Conference in Marrakesh, Morocco (COP22) (B8-1043/2016), 6 October <https://www.europarl.europa.eu/doceo/document/CRE-8-2016-10-06-ITM-006-03_EN.html> (Accessed 20 February 2021).

Spurek, Sylwia (2020). "European Climate Law (Debate)", 6 October <https://www.europarl.europa.eu/doceo/document/CRE-9-2020-10-06-ITM-011_EN.html> (Accessed 25 February 2021).

Ştefănuţă, Nicolae (2019). "Climate and Ecological Emergency (Topical Debate)", 23 October <https://www.europarl.europa.eu/doceo/document/CRE-9-2019-10-23-ITM-016_EN.html> (Accessed 24 February 2021).

Stuger, Olaf (2015). "Implementation and Legacy of the European Year for Development (Debate)", 2 December <https://www.europarl.europa.eu/doceo/document/CRE-8-2015-12-02-ITM-015_EN.html> (Accessed 19 February 2021).

Šuica, Dubravka (2016). 2016 UN Climate Change Conference in Marrakesh, Morocco (COP22) (B8-1043/2016), 6 October <https://www.europarl.europa.eu/doceo/document/CRE-8-2016-10-06-ITM-006-03_EN.html> (Accessed 20 February 2021).

Svensson, Eva-Britt (2009). "Election of the President of the European Parliament", 14 July <https://www.europarl.europa.eu/doceo/document/CRE-7-2009-07-14-ITM-007_EN.html> (Accessed 12 February 2021).

Tamburrano, Dario (2014). "UN Climate Summit 2014 (23 September 2014 – New York) (Debate)", 16 September <https://www.europarl.europa.eu/doceo/document/CRE-8-2014-09-16-ITM-017_EN.html> (Accessed 17 February 2021).

Tremosa i Balcells, Ramon (2015). "Preparing for the World Humanitarian Summit: Challenges and Opportunities for Humanitarian Assistance (A8-0332/2015 – Enrique Guerrero Salom)", 16 December <https://www.europarl.europa.eu/doceo/document/CRE-8-2015-12-16-ITM-012-10_EN.html> (Accessed 19 February 2021).

UNEP (2019). Emissions Gap Report 2019, November, <https://wedocs.unep.org/bitstream/handle/20.500.11822/30797/EGR2019.pdf?sequence=1&isAllowed=y> (Accessed 25 February 2021).

UNHCR (2010). Convention and Protocol Relating to the Status of Refugees, <http://www.unhcr.org/3b66c2aa10.html> (Accessed 21 March 2021).

Van Dijk, Teun A. (1997a). "Political Discourse and Racism: Describing Others in Western Parliaments". In: Stephen H. Riggins (Ed.), *The Language and Politics of Exclusion: Others in Discourse*, SAGE, Thousand Oaks, CA, pp. 31–64.

Van Dijk, Teun A. (1997b). "What is Political Discourse Analysis?". In: Jan Blommaert and Chris Bulcaen (Eds.), *Political Linguistics*, Benjamins, Amsterdam, pp. 11–52.

Van Dijk, Teun A. (2001). "Critical Discourse Analysis". In: Deborah Schiffrin et al. (Eds.), *The Hanbdbook of Discourse Analysis*, Blackwell, Malden, MA, pp. 352–371.

Voss, Axel (2009). Preparation of the Copenhagen Summit on Climate Change (Debate), 24 November <https://www.europarl.europa.eu/doceo/document/CRE-7-2009-11-24-ITM-003_EN.html> (Accessed 12 February 2021).

Wenta, Bogdan Brunon (2018). "Nigeria", 18 January <https://www.europarl.europa.eu/doceo/document/CRE-8-2018-01-18-ITM-004-01_EN.html> (Accessed 22 February 2021).

Worldometer (2021). "Covid-19 Coronavirus Pandemic", 14 July <https://www.worldometers.info/coronavirus> (Accessed 14 July 2021).

Zanoni, Andrea (2012). "Women and Climate Change (Debate)", 20 April <https://www.europarl.europa.eu/doceo/document/CRE-7-2012-04-20-ITM-006_EN.html> (Accessed 15 February 2021).

Candan Yılmaz Ugur

Environmental Policies, Climate Change Perception and Trust

Introduction

In recent years, the goal of reducing greenhouse gases in the atmosphere; although it creates great difficulties for countries, it also brings financial and economic measures with it. Even though tax comes to mind first within the scope of financial instruments in combating environmental problems, the increasing problems over the years also bring new intervention tools to the agenda. In addition to the environmental taxes applied in many countries today, the use of financial instruments such as incentives/subsidies, funds, pricing, penalties, prohibitions, etc. is gradually expanding. However, it may be useful to accurately measure the attitude of the public towards environmental policies in order to determine environmental policies in a country. In this way, it can be ensured that the environmental policies to be implemented are sustainable and reach their targets in a healthy way.

Based on the climate change perception and political trust, this study empirically examines whether it affects individuals' attitudes towards policies such as increasing taxes on fossil fuels, subsidizing renewable energy and banning household appliances with the lowest energy efficiency, and if it does, the direction of this effect. In the study under consideration, it is important in terms of trying to explain the climate change perception and the element of political trust and the support given to environmental policies. Because very few studies have included the use of individual level data to examine support for environmental policies, thus this study will assist to fill the gap in the literature. In addition to this, the absence of a study to measure the relationship between the environmental policies in Turkey and the element of trust-at least as far as we know- it will provide a valuable contribution to the literature on this subject.

The study is designed as five parts, including the introduction and conclusion parts. In this context, theoretical background and literature review are included in the second part of the study, and quantitative analysis and findings are included in the third part. The fourth part of the study ends with the evaluation of the results and empirical findings.

1. Theoretical Background and Literature Review

1.1. Theoretical Background

It is clear that in the face of global warming and accompanying natural disasters, which accelerate as a result of increasing greenhouse gas emissions, governments will have to take some measures to eliminate the negative consequences of climate change (Otto and Gugushvili, 2020: 1; Ugur, 2019: 84; Yılmaz and Çiftçi, 2013: 6; Cengiz, 2019: 77). Just as all environmental problems, climate change is a market failure where individuals, households and firms pay only a fraction of the pollution costs and social costs are not taken into account (Fairbrother, 2019: 2). These costs are defined as "negative externalities" and they damage the whole society and even the whole universe in a global sense. For this reason, governments are struggling with increasing environmental problems with taxes, sanctions for pollution-intensive activities and/or policies to promote a sustainable environment (Uğur and Doğan, 2015: 48). Fossil fuel taxes, which are frequently adopted by governments within these policies, reduce the amount of carbon dioxide (CO2) emissions of the country in a certain period, on the other hand, provide tax revenue. However, increasing the rate of fossil fuel taxes or expanding their scope puts pressure on the income of citizens living in the country (Klenert et al., 2018; 669). That being said, as long as fossil fuel taxes are unfairly financed and not effectively enforced for most citizens, policies to combat climate change are likely to add a new dimension to existing social conflicts. As an example, the "yellow vests" protests triggered by the French government's decision to increase fossil fuel taxes to reduce carbon emissions can be given (Otto and Gugushvili, 2020: 1).

Low public support for policies adopted in combating climate change constitutes an obstacle to the policies in question (Kulin and Seva, 2020: 2). As a matter of fact, previous studies show that there is a relationship between policies to be implemented in combating climate change and citizens' trust in various state institutions and actors (Fairbrother, 2016; Harring and Jagers, 2013; Konisky et al., 2008).

On the other hand, the focus of studies on climate change is to define climate change attitudes and beliefs. Accordingly, individuals can deny that the climate actually changes, accept that the climate has changed, but deny that human activity is responsible, or accept the reality of climate change and support the necessary policies. A great number of studies in the literature show that individuals in three different positions are distributed among the populations of different countries (Cook et al., 2013). Therefore, it is seen that the perception of climate change will increase the support given to environmental policies.

This study examines the relationship between political trust and climate change perception's support for environmental policies with Fairbrother et al. (2019), Kulin and Seva (2020), and Sivonen and Kukkonen (2021) models. In this context, when viewed from a theoretical point of view, it is seen that the perception of climate change and political trust will increase the support given to environmental policies. In this study, which one (s) of the theoretical effect occurs empirically is investigated.

1.2. Literature Review

In the literature, there are many studies on the factors that support the increase in carbon taxes at certain periods and for certain country groups. However, it is seen that the empirical literature studies on political trust's carbon tax increases have emerged predominantly in 2000 and afterward. In these studies, the effects of many variables such as ideology at the country level (Yılmaz, 2013: 4), political trust, political trust, trust in political actors and the perception of climate change on the increase of carbon taxes are investigated. For this purpose, the factors affecting the increase in carbon taxes, the period, country or country group, the method used and the findings obtained are included in Tab. 1.

Tab. 1: Literature Summary

Author	**Period**	**Country**	**Method**
Hammar ve Jagers (2006)	2002	Sweden/1270 Observations Based on Random Sampling	Logistic Regression Method
Results; – If the political trust is high, it is 0.062 times more likely to support the CO_2 tax increase. – Supporters of the green party are 0.146 times more likely to support the CO_2 tax increase.			
Konisky vd. (2008)	2007	Cooperative Congressional Election Study/ California	OLS regression models
Results; – Individuals with high trust in the state have high support (0.22) for the government addressing pollution and global environmental issues.			
Harring (2013)	2000	International Social Survey Programme/ 25 Countries	Multilevel Regression Analysis
Results; – Countries with higher levels of political confidence are more willing to make economic sacrifices to protect the environment (0.065).			
Harring ve Jagers (2013)	2009	Sweden/1057 Observations Based on Random Sampling	Least Squares (OLS) Regression
Results; – Political trust increases the attitude to increase carbon (CO_2) tax by 0.16; interpersonal trust increases the attitude of increasing carbon (CO_2) tax by 0.05. – The attitude of those who adopt the left ideology to increase the carbon (CO_2) tax is 0.21.			
McCright vd. (2015)	2008	Eurobarometer Survey/14 Western European countries and 11 former Communist countries	Least Squares (OLS) Regression
Results; – It has been observed that those with leftist ideologies in 14 Western European countries stand stronger against climate change (0.009) and are more willing to pay environmental taxes (0.007) to mitigate the effects of climate change. – There was no such ideological division against climate change and environmental taxes in 11 former Communist countries.			

Tab. 1: Continued

Author	Period	Country	Method
Davidovic (2018)	ISSP was collected in 2010; WVS was collected during the time period 2005–2009	World Values Survey/ International Social Survey Programme.	Multilevel Regression Analysis
Results; – Both survey results show that the relationship between social and political trust and support for environmental taxes is positive and strong			
Kollmann ve Reichl (2016)	2015	35 Countries/45,000 Observations	Cross Country Analysis
Results; – In the study, the probability of accepting new environmental taxes is 17 %, the probability of being indifferent is 21 % and the probability of not accepting environmental taxes is 62 %. – However, it has been concluded that a 1 % increase in the trust level will increase the probability of accepting new environmental taxes from 17 % to 23 %.			
Harring (2018)	Sweden	Sweden/1800 University Students	Ordered Logit Regressions
Results; – Furthermore, trust in business actors is negatively linked to the acceptance of environmental taxes targeting people in general (–0.36). – If political trust is high, it is 0.21 times more likely to support the CO2 tax increase. – The higher the penalty, the higher the probability of supporting the CO2 tax increase by 0.16 times.			
Fairbrother vd. (2019)	2016	European Social Research Data/23 European Union Members	Multilevel Regression Analysis
Results; – It has been observed that there is a strong relationship between the reality and dangers of climate change and fossil fuel taxes in European countries with high political trust. – In 23 European countries, the countries that most support high taxes on fossil fuels are those with the highest levels of political trust.			
Davidovic vd (2020)	2012	ISSP/30 Countries	Multilevel Regression Analysis

(*continued on next page*)

Tab. 1: Continued

Author	Period	Country	Method
Results; – Individuals concerned about environmental problems were found to be more likely (0.37) to be willing to pay higher environmental taxes. – Those closer to the left ideology were found to be more likely to be willing to pay higher environmental tax (0.29). – Higher public quality at the country level was found to be associated with stronger support for environmental taxes (0.15).			
Kulin ve Seva (2020)	2016	European Social Research Data/23 European Union Members	Multilevel Regression Analysis
Results; – There has been seen a positive and strong relationship (direct effect = 0.216, indirect effect = 0.212) between the concerns about climate change and the increase in the carbon tax. – A positive correlation (direct effect = 0.178, indirect effect = 0.136) has been found between trust in parties and the increase in carbon tax. – There has been had a negative relationship (direct effect = –0.042, indirect effect = –0.042) between those who were closer to the right ideology and the increase in the carbon tax. – A positive correlation (direct effect = 0.022, indirect effect = 0.022) has been determined between general confidence at the country level and the increase in carbon tax.			
Sivonen (2020)	2016	European Social Survey (ESS) Round 8	Least Squares (OLS) Regression
Results; – The relationship between stronger left orientation, higher confidence and higher political trust and support for fossil fuel taxation has been found to be positive and strong.			
Sivonen ve Kukkonen (2021)	2016	European Social Survey (ESS) Round 8	Multilevel Regression Analysis
Results; – There is a positive relationship between political trust and increased carbon (CO2) tax, the ban on renewable energy and non-energy efficient household appliances. However, the strongest instrument of this relationship is related to the carbon (CO2) tax increases.			

As can be seen in the studies in the literature, although their methodologies, country groups and periods are different, it is seen that the results are generally common. Political trust appears to have a significant impact on carbon tax increases in most studies. In the next part of the study, SEM will be included and the obtained empirical findings will be evaluated.

2. Economic Analysis and Findings

2.1. Data Set

The main body of the study consists of associate, undergraduate, graduate and doctoral students studying at Gümüşhane University. Although there are various formulas and methods in determining the sample size, Schumacker and Lomax (2004) state that 250–500 observations are sufficient to reach healthy results in studies based on structural equation modeling. In the selection of the sample, simple (random) probabilistic sampling, which is one of the non-probabilistic sampling methods representing the population, was used. The questionnaire forms were answered between 25/12/2020 and 15/01/2021, and statistical analyzes were completed with the remaining 255 questionnaires after eliminating the questionnaire forms with incomplete and incorrect answers and contradictory answers among the questionnaires.

2.2. Methodology

In this study, in order to determine the factors affecting the support to environmental policies, the SEM, which has been expanded with environmental policies, climate change perception and political trust factors, which have been frequently used in previous similar studies (see Fairbrother et al., 2019; Kulin and Seva, 2020; Sivonen and Kukkonen, 2021), was used. Accordingly, 2 basic hypotheses were created with the SEM shown in Fig. 1.

H_1: Belief in climate change positively affects the attitude towards environmental policies.

H_2: Political trust positively affects the attitude towards environmental policies.

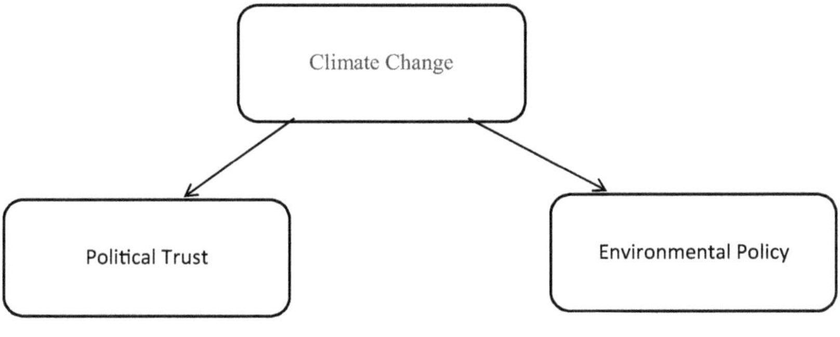

Fig. 1: Structural Equation Model

Among the research tools, the environmental policy scale were taken from Kulin and Seva (2020), the climate change scale were taken from Fairbrother et al. (2019) and the political trust scale were taken from the Kulin and Seva (2020) study, and the statements were adapted in accordance with the research topic. The questionnaire form of the research consists of 2 parts. While the first part of the form consists of questions about determining the demographic characteristics of the participants, the second part includes questions about the variables in the research model. The research includes 3 statements for attitude towards environmental policies, 5 statements for belief in climate change, and 5 statements for political trust. Participant responses of the statements were measured with a 5-level Likert-type scale ranging from 1 (= strongly disagree) to 5 (= strongly agree).

2.3. Findings

The frequency findings that give the general characteristics of the sample are shown in Tab. 2. When the distribution of the participants according to their gender is examined, 71 % of the participants are women and 29 % are men. In terms of age group, the majority of the sample (91 %) constitutes the 18–24 age group. It is observed that a significant proportion of the participants are university graduates (approximately 49 %), while 79 % of the participants do not indicate their political ideology.

Tab. 2: General Characteristics of the Sample

Group	Subgroup	Frequency	Percent (%)
Gender	Woman	181	71
	Man	74	29
Age	18–24	232	91
	25–34	21	8,2
	35–44	2	0,8
Education level	High school	111	43,5
	Associate's degree	13	5,1
	Undergraduate Degree	125	49
	Graduate Degree	6	2,4
Political view	Right	19	7,5
	Left	39	15,3
	Unspecified	197	77,3
Total		255	100

SEM validity was tested in order to examine the validity of the research scale consisting of 13 statements and 3 variables, and Cronbach's Alpha coefficient analyzes were applied to examine the reliability level of the scale consisting of 12 statements. According to the first DFA solution, it was seen that model-data fit could not be achieved and modification suggestions were applied to increase the goodness of fit. Accordingly, when the goodness of fit values obtained with the DFA solution and the suggested acceptance level values for the model are compared (see Tab. 3), it can be stated that model-data fit is acceptable.

Tab. 3: Model Goodness of Fit

Criteria	Model	Model Fit	
		Perfect Fit	Acceptable Fit
χ^2/df	2,438*	$0 \leq \chi^2/df \leq 2$	$2 < \chi^2/df \leq 5$
RMSEA	0,075*	< 0,05	< 0,08
RMR	0,104*	< 0,05	< 0,10
NFI	0,859	> 0,95	> 0,90
CFI	0,910	> 0,97	> 0,95
GFI	0,921*	> 0,90	> 0,85
AGFI	0,880*	> 0,90	> 0,85
IFI	0,912*	> 0,95	> 0,90
TLI	0,883	> 0,95	> 0,90
RFI	0,817	> 0,95	> 0,90

Source: Doll et al. (1994), Forza and Filippini (1998), and Hu and Bentler (1999).

In order for the estimation results to be reliable in the structural equation model, the fit between the data and the structural model should be at acceptable levels. Hereby, too, goodness of fit indices were used to examine the level of model-data fit. According to the index findings of goodness of fit, it (X2/df = 2.438; RMSEA = 0.075; GFI = 0.921; IFI = 0.912; and AGFI = 0.880) is seen that there is an acceptable goodness of fit between the data and the model.

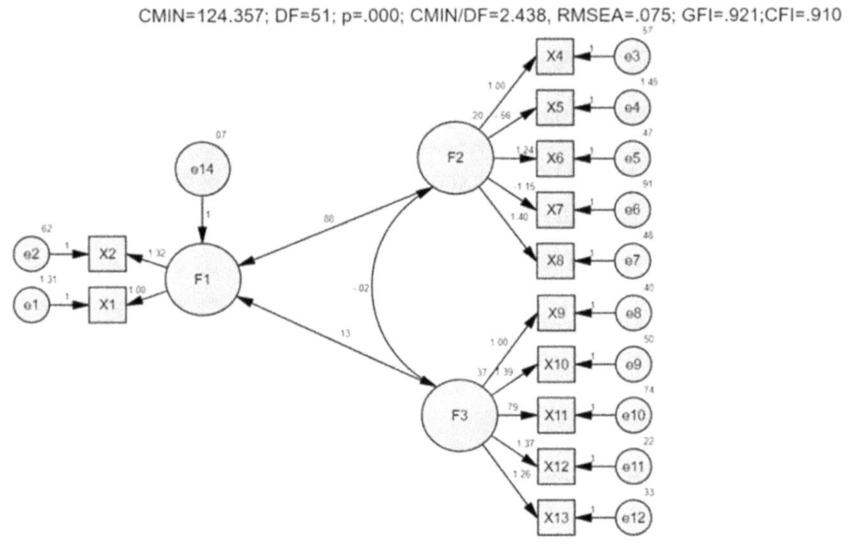

Fig. 2: Measurement Model Path Diagram

Tab. 4 shows the results of the applied DFA. The standardized regression coefficients representing the relationship between the expressions and the factors considered to be related take values between 0.621 and 0.708. According to these results, it is seen that the construct validity of the research scale with 12 statements and a structure with 3 variables was verified by DFA. In addition, reliability analysis was applied for the scale with 11 expressions and it was determined that the calculated Cronbach's Alpha coefficient was 0.681. According to this finding, it can be stated that the research scale is reliable.

Tab. 4: Construct Validity of the Research Scale

Factors	**Code**	**Mean**	**Cronbach's Alpha**
Environmental Policies	X1	I support increasing taxes on products that pollute the environment, such as coal, to reduce climate change.	,666
	X2	I support the subsidization of renewable energy sources such as solar energy and wind energy to reduce climate change.	,688
	X3	I support the ban on the sale of household appliances such as refrigerators, vacuum cleaners and ovens that are the least energy efficient in order to reduce climate change.	-
Climate Change	X4	I believe that the climate is changing in the world and in our country.	,681
	X5	I think that climate change is caused by natural processes in the world and in our country.	,698
	X6	I think that climate change in the world and in our country is caused by human activities.	,668
	X7	I think the effects of climate change will be good in the world and in our country.	,708
	X8	I think the effects of climate change will create negative consequences in the world and in our country.	,686
Political Trust	X9	I trust the parliament in my country and the decisions taken by the parliament	,629
	X10	I trust the legal system in our country	,621
	X11	In my country, I trust law enforcement agencies such as police, gendarmerie and watchmen.	,631
	X12	I trust politicians and decisions made by politicians in my country	,620
	X13	I trust political parties being active in my country and decisions taken by political parties.	,625

The Structural Equation Model Path Diagram formed as a result of the analysis of the Structural Equation Model prepared in the light of the hypotheses in the AMOS program is given in Tab. 5. According to the findings, it is seen that the two hypotheses established are statistically significant at a confidence interval of at least 90 % ($p < 10$ %), and the hypotheses regarding the effect of climate change perception on environmental policies and the hypotheses regarding the effect of political trust on environmental policies are statistically verified. Likewise, the climate change perceptions of the participants positively and significantly increase the support for environmental policies ($\beta = 0.825$; $p < 0.001$). On the other hand, it is seen that there is a positive, significant but relatively weak relationship between political trust and support for environmental policies (= 0.162; $p < 0.010$).

Tab. 5: Measurement Model

Hypotheses	Variables	β_1	β_2	S.E.	C.R.	p
H_1	F1<--- F2	.825	.881	.231	3.811	< 0,001
H_2	F1<--- F3	.162	.127	.076	1.675	< 0,010

Conclusion

This study aims to determine the relationship between the climate change perception and political trust factors of Gümüşhane University students and the support given to environmental policies. Statements regarding environmental policies in the study are "fossil fuel taxes", "subsidies" and "prohibitions", and statements about political trust are "parliament" and "politician", "political parties", "legal system", "law enforcement" and "political parties" criteria, and political trust has been addressed within the framework of trust in institutions involved in the legislature, the executive and the judiciary. Climate change perception is evaluated in the context of "belief in climate change", "process of climate change" and "consequences of climate change". In statistical terms, it is observed that there is a strong relationship between climate change and support for environmental policies, and a relatively weak relationship between political trust and support for environmental policies.

As the research results of many studies point out, it is seen that the climate change perception and political trust factors increase the support for environmental policies in the fight against climate change. The most striking result of this study emerges at this point. First of all, it should be stated that the perception of climate change and political trust in Turkey increase the support for environmental policies, and with increasing environmental awareness and political confidence, the support to be given to these policies will be accepted by wider circles. Having say that, it is also noteworthy that there are question marks on the extent to which this is internalized by individuals. For example, should income from fossil fuel taxes be used as a new tax source? Or should it be transferred to projects such as green infrastructure investments and renewable energy facilities? with questions such and the conditions under which the public's support to environmental policies will increase can be measured. On the other hand, knowing whether subsidies to be given to renewable energy fields or fossil fuel taxes are supported by wider circles, as well as supporting it with practices other than financial measures will also increase the support given to environmental policies.

However, we also have some limitations in the study. First of all, the field research of the study is evaluated on the students of Gümüşhane University, which is located in a small city of our country. Therefore, the statistical results obtained may differ for different provinces/countries. Although the study provides a general idea, it is thought that laboratory, questionnaire and field experiments and more research based on broader data will contribute to the study we present herein. Secondly, the support given to environmental policies was discussed in terms of political trust and the perception of climate change, and the structural equation method was used when examining the influential factors. There are many more factors that can increase support for environmental policies. In subsequent studies, the study can be expanded with different factors. Thirdly, in this study, individuals' views on environmental policies, their level of knowledge on climate change and political trust are not taken into account. In studies where these limitations are taken into account, it may be possible to design and implement environmental policies that will be created with the support of individuals. As a matter of fact, it is important for governments to take the support of the public and take into account the wishes of the people while creating their environmental policies in terms of the sustainability of the policies.

References

"Arktika Bölgesi'nin Siyasal Önemi ve Siyasal ve Hukuksal Statüsünün Karşılaştırmalı Değerlendirmesi", **Muğla Sıtkı Koçman Üniversitesi Sosyal Bilimler Enstitüsü Dergisi**, Vol: 31, No: 2013 Güz, pp: 1–16.

Cengiz, Emre, Mega Etkinlikler ve Yerinden Edilme Olimpiyat Oyunları Etkisi, On İki Levha Yayıncılık, İstanbul, 2019.

Cook, J., Nuccitelli, D., Green, S. A., Richardson, M., Winkler, B., Painting, R., Skuce, A. (2013), "Quantifying the Consensus on Anthropogenic Global Warming in the Scientific Literatüre", **Environmental Research Letters**, Vol: 8, pp: 1–7.

Davidovıc, D. (2018), Trust, Values, and Qualıty of Government: Exploring The Interaction Between Individual and Contextual Level Determinants of Environmental Tax Support, QoG Working Paper Series 2018: 4, ISSN: 1653-8919.

Davidovic, D., Harring, N., ve Jagers, S. (2020), "The Contingent Effects of Environmental Concern and Ideology: Institutional Context And People's Willingness to Pay Environmental Taxes", **Environmental Politics**, Vol: 29, No: 4, pp: 674–696.

Fairbrother, M. (2016), "Trust and Public Support for Environmental Protection in Diverse National Contexts", **Sociological Science**, Vol: 3, pp: 359–382.

Fairbrother, M., Sevä, J., ve Kulin J. (2019), "Political Trust and the Relationship Between Climate Change Beliefs and Support for Fossil Fuel Taxes: Evidence from a Survey of 23 European Countries", **Global Environmental Change**, Vol: 59, pp. 1–15.

Hammar, H., ve Jagers S. (2006), " Can Trust in Politicians Explain Individuals' Support for Climate Policy? The Case of CO_2 Tax", **Climate Policy**, Vol: 5, No: 6, pp: 613–625.

Harring, N. (2013), "Understanding the Effects of Corruption and Political Trust on Willingness to Make Economic Sacrifices for Environmental Protection in a Cross-National Perspective", **Social Science Quarterly**, Vol: 94, No: 3, pp. 660–671.

Harring, N. (2018), "Trust and State Intervention: Results from a Swedish Survey on Environmental Policy Support", **Environmental Science & Policy**, Vol: 82, pp: 1–8.

Harring, N., ve Jagers, S. (2013), "Should We Trust in Values? Explaining Public Support for Pro-Environmental Taxes", **Sustainability**, Vol:5, No:1, pp: 210–227.

Klenert, D., Mattauch, L., Combet, E., Edenhofer, O., Hepburn, C., et al. (2018), "Making Carbon Pricing Work for Citizens", **Nature Climate Change**, Vol: 8, No: 8, p: 669–677.

Kollmann, A., ve Reichl, J. (2016), "How Trust in Governments Influences the Acceptance of Environmental Taxes", In F. Schneider, A. Kollmann ve, J. Reichl (Eds.), Political Economy and Instruments of Environmental Politics, The MIT Press.

Konisky, M. D., Milyo, J., Richardson, Lilliard, E. (2008), "Environmental Policy Attitudes: Issues, Geographical Scale, and Political Trust", **Social Science Quarterly**, Vol: 89, No: 5, pp: 1066–1085.

Kulin, J., ve Sevä, J. (2020), "Who Do You Trust? How Trust in Partial Andimpartial Government Institutions Influences Climate Policy Attitudes", **Climate Policy**, https://doi.org/10.1080/14693062.2020.1792822.

McCright, A., Dunlap, R., ve Marquart-Pyatt S. (2015), "Political Ideology and Views About Climate Change in The European Union", **Environmental Politics**, ISSN: 0964-4016 (Print) 1743-8934 (Online).

Otto, A., ve Gugushvili, D. (2020), "Eco-Social Divides in Europe: Public Attitudes towards Welfare and Climate Change Policies Adeline", **Sustainability**, Vol: 12, No: 1, pp: 1–18.

Schumacker, R. E., Lomax, R. G. (2004), **A Beginner's Guide To Structural Equation Modeling**, Second Edition, Lawrence Erlbaum Associates Publishers, Mahwah, New Jersey, United States.

Sivonen, J. (2020), " Predictors of Fossil Fuel Taxation Attitudes Across Post – Communist And Other Europe", **International Journal of Sociology and Social Policy**, Vol: 40, No: 11/12, pp: 1337–1355.

Sivonen, J., ve Kukkonen, L. (2021), "Is there a Link between Welfare Regime and Attitudes toward Climate Policy Instruments?", **Sociological Perspectives**, Vol:40, No: 11/12, pp: 1–21.

Ugur, Omer (2019), "Climate Change in Global Politics in the Postmodern Era: A New Challenge and Responses", In Ömer uğur, Kadir Caner Doğan (Eds.), Contemporary Debates on Politics and Public Administration in the Postmodern Era, Peter Lang, Berlin, ss. 83–99.

Uğur, Ömer, ve Kadir Caner Doğan (2015), "Avrupa Birliği'nin Sürdürülebilir Kalkınma Stratejisi: İklim Değişikliği Çerçevesinde Teoriden Pratiğe", Doğu Karadeniz Bölgesi Sürdürülebilir Turizm Kongresi Bildiriler Kitabı, 14–16 Mayıs, Gümüşhane.

Yılmaz, N. (2013). "Sosyalleşme Sürecinin Siyasallaşma Boyutu", **Int. Journal of Management Economics and Business**, Vol. 9, No. 19, pp: 1–14.

Gökhan Zengin

Wind as a Renewable Energy Resource: The Outlook and Incentive Policies in Turkey

Introduction

Global destructive effects of COVID 19 Pandemic, which we are currently experiencing, have poignantly brought forward many controversies about 6th great extinction since the end of Anthropocene has been reached. Human-induced nature destruction, which has reached its peak nowadays, is seen as the reason of great disasters. During Holocene Era, which is conceived to have started approximately 11,700 years ago, disturbance of nature by humans in a growing rate in correlation to social life and development has reached to the point of breaking ecological balance. Therefore, appellation of Anthropocene Era (new human), which contains a negative connotation, has been conjured up with the aim of finding an alternative terminology to Holocene Era (Çalışır, 2020:1).

In an important research published in the journal of Science Advances in 2015, it is stated that, even in optimistic predictions, extinction paces of species are 100 times greater than the percentages during the periods when mass extinctions[1] slowed down. According to Ceballos, a member of the research team, if we let the course of events be, self-repair of life will take millions of years; and probably our own species will extinct even at the beginning of this process (Ceballos and Eirlich et al., 2015: 4). Again, according to the study, as the species continue to extinct, ecosystem balances are broken. For example, pollination of agricultural plants by bees is increasing, and the capacity of wetlands to re-clean water is decreasing (Ceballos and Eirlich et al., 2015: 4–6).

In the study titled as "Anthropocene Extinction" published in the journal Nature Communication in 2020, 6th mass extinction has been brought up for discussion. The conclusion drawn in the study is that CO_2 levels of today may bring about consequences similar to those of the extraordinary magma-induced

1 According to the fossil records, there have been 5 major mass extinctions. While the Permian extinction almost ended life, the Cretaceous destroyed the dinosaurs and led to the proliferation of mammals (Gürdilek, https://kurious.ku.edu.tr/buyuk-yokoluslar/).

rise in CO_2 levels during Triassic extinction period, which occurred around 250 million years ago. According to the study, the fact that the use of fossil fuels, in particular, has increased CO_2 in atmosphere by more than 40 % in only 200 years resembles to the increase in Triassic Era in terms of ratio (Capricolo, Marzoli et al., 2020: 2–3).

According to the latest World Energy Outlook Report global energy demand will decrease by 5 %, Co_2 emission by 7 %, and energy investments by 18 %. Oil and coal demands will also decrease. Furthermore, despite lower oil and gas production, first signs indicate that the greenhouse effect, which methane emitted by the energy sector causes, will not decrease. Again, according to one of the scenarios provided in the report, the negative effects of the pandemic upon economic growth will probably vanish only in 2023. And global energy demand will experience its lowest since the 1930s (IEA, 2021).

In the peak period of the pandemic, nearly 50 % decrease in emissions from automobile and air transportation has created a change, even if slightly, in the carbon density in the atmosphere. However, it is stated that the amount of global emission is still at the levels of 2012 despite the historic decrease in 2020, and the decreasing amount is insignificant compared to the amount of carbon dioxide emitted in the last few centuries. While the highest measurable decreases in carbon emissions were seen in the USA by 12 % and in the EU by 11 % in 2020, the decrease in China came about as only 1.7 % (WEC Turkey, 2020).

It is accepted that the most important method to fight against global temperature increase is to reduce greenhouse gas emissions. The long-term goal of the Paris Climate Agreement, which replaced the Kyoto Protocol that expired in 2020, is to keep the global average temperature rise below 2°C compared to the pre-industrial level, and below 1.5°C if possible. The states that signed the agreement give various declarations of intent to reduce these emissions and develop policies accordingly. Turkey has not yet signed this agreement. In this document, the EU set its target as reducing greenhouse gas emissions by at least 40 % in every part of its economy for the year of 2030. This target, which was set according to global predictions, is also compatible with the medium-term target of the Paris Agreement (Avrupa.info, 2: 2019).

In accordance with the Paris Climate Agreement, the European Union has committed to reduce its emissions 40 % below the levels of 1990s by 2030 but has not set a certain target for 2050. European Green Deal (EGD), signed in 2019, set the target for the year 2030 as 50–55 % (compared to 1990) and 100 % for 2050. In other words, in 2050 a carbon-neutral (net-zero) Europe will be achieved. EGD plan, which aims to put EU on the path of a new sustainable growth, is introduced as the new growth strategy of the EU. In the new action plan to be adapted to the Green Deal, there are also so many important issues such as re-determining the previously determined targets such as renewable energy and energy efficiency; identifying new sectors and activities to be included in the European Emissions Trading System (EU ETS); new industrial strategy and action plan for transition to circular economy; agriculture policy of farm to fork strategy and, the implementation of carbon limit regulation (Karakaya, 2019: 2).

Wind energy, one of the renewable energy sources, constitutes the subject of this study. Among the renewable energy options, wind energy is the type of energy that does not create pollution and has the second lowest environmental impact after solar energy. In the world (2020), wind energy has increased at an unprecedented level in its history. Throughout the world, the capacity of wind energy installed on land, by increasing its power to 743 GW, was raised by 53 % compared to the previous year (GWEC, 2021: 8). The study consists of 4 parts. In the first part, information on the use of renewable energy in the world is given. Secondly, some activities of the cities that have exemplary practices on renewable energy are addressed. In the third part, the profile of renewable energy resources of Turkey is presented. In the fourth part of the study, wind energy and wind energy incentive systems in the world and in Turkey are examined.

1. Renewable Energy Outlook in the World

The results of the fact that the economic growth mindset, which directs the world economy, uses nature as a consumable and endless commodity, come out as ecological destruction. The increase in global temperature stands out as the most evident indicator of the deteriorated ecological balance. In the background of scientific and economic developments, which are produced by consuming natural resources (energy, mines) shared by the developed capitalist countries of the world population, to a great extent, the energy generated by burning fossil fuels is observed to be used. Carbon dioxide and other similar gases released into the atmosphere as a result of the use of fossil fuels also create a greenhouse effect, briefly causing an increase in global temperature.

The ever-increasing population rate in the world, increasing consumption rates in the developed capitalist countries and economic inequalities cause destruction of nature, which can mainly be summarized under the following points (Delibalta, 2015):

1. Forestlands deteriorated for agriculture,
2. Migration of invasive species from their natural habitats,
3. Climate change and CO_2 emissions leading to ocean acidification,

4. Increased use of toxic substances for faster production,

Increasing the capacity of renewable energy sources (RER) and developing incentive policies to reduce CO_2 emissions caused by fossil fuel use are of great importance for the future of our world. The rapidly rising CO_2 concentrations after the year of 1950 have reached levels exceeding 400 PPM, unprecedented in Earth's cyclical processes (Çalışır, 2020: 2).

The COVID 19 pandemic has caused mankind to contemplate even more alarming scenarios about the future of the world. Although problems such as the ongoing decrease of biodiversity, global warming and food security have been on the agenda of the world for a long time, the pandemic has caused these problems to be felt more. It is now clearly seen that the use of fossil fuel-based energy is now irreversibly disrupting the ecological balance. The decreasing greenhouse gas emissions caused by the downward energy demand due to pandemic has shown that a world with clean air is actually possible. The COVID 19 pandemic has caused cuts in energy demand at unprecedented scales in recent events.

Global greenhouse gas emissions dropped by 7 % behind the level in 2019 by decreasing 2.4 billion tons in 2020. The most significant decreases have been recorded to date as; 0.9 billion tons in 1945, 0.5 billion tons in 1981, 0.7 billion tons in 1992 and 0.5 billion tons in 1999. According to a research by a UK-based university, this situation is the highest drop that has been recorded so far. Upon predicting that carbon emissions will increase in 2021 once again, researchers warned governments to prioritize clean energy transition policies as well (Global Carbon Budget, 2020; UEA, 2020). According to the latest figures, upon increasing again in 2021, carbon dioxide concentrations in the atmosphere have reached record levels despite the decline in emissions during the COVID 19 pandemic. CO_2 concentrations, reaching up to an average of 420 PPM, are about 50 % higher than those before the Industrial Revolution (İklim Haber, 2021).

Energy demand in the world is continuously increasing. This increase is proportional to population and economic development. For the continuation of economic activities and social life without compromising the level of welfare achieved, it is necessary to reach energy in an uninterrupted, easy, environmentally friendly and sustainable way. However, the energy resources in the world are not distributed to countries equally. With the invention of the engine during the Industrial Revolution, natural energy sources such as wood became inadequate, and thus other energy sources were sought. Owning energy resources has been seen as the most important strategy for economic development and world domination. Especially for oil, countries even take the risk of war. Henry Kissinger's aphorism in 1974, "*If you control the oil, you control the nations; if you control the food, you control the people*"[2] emphasizes the importance of energy resources and policies.

It is known that fossil fuels bring about serious health[3] and environmental problems, their reserve life is gradually depleting and they are used as a tool for political pressure. Fossil fuels, which meet most of the world's energy needs, are getting depleted. This issue is put on speculations especially by the big oil companies. Apart from various estimates being made in the published energy reports, the common opinion is fossil fuel resources have reserves enough to fulfill the needs of humanity for a maximum of another 50–100 years. However, scientists with different opinions argue that fossil resources have decreased more than expected in the last 10–20 years due to the unforeseen increase in consumption, and that if alternative resources are not obtained, great difficulties will soon be faced. In particular, the reliability and sustainability of oil supply stems from the unstable Middle East (where 65.4 % of global oil reserves are located). Global oil reserves are at a level that will last approximately 25–30 years with current oil production. Reserves are depleting but consumption demand is increasing (Özekicioğlu, 2008: 81–83).

Energy resources are commonly classified according to their use or whether being convertible. The form of energy that has not undergone any change or transformation is the primary energy source. These resources are; oil, coal, natural gas, nuclear, hydraulic, wave, solar, biomass and wind. Electricity, gasoline, diesel, air gas and Liquefied Petroleum Gas (LPG), which are obtained by transforming primary sources, are secondary energy sources (Koç and Kaya, 2015: 37). The energy resources that remain unchanged in a natural cycle process and do not deplete despite being used are named as renewable energy sources. Hydraulic, solar, wind, geothermal, biomass, tidal wave, hydrogen are renewable energy sources. Energy sources that cannot renew themselves when used are

2 https://en.wikiquote.org/wiki/Henry_Kissinger#cite_note-1. National Security Survey Report 200: Impact of World Population Growth on US Security and Overseas Interests. 10.12.1974.

3 More than 10μM of the particulate matter PM taken into the respiratory tract is retained in the nose, while those less than 10 microns accumulate in the bronchi, and those with a diameter of 1–2 microns are collected in the alveoli. All these cause lung cancer as well as serious respiratory tract infections. It is seen that the annual SO_2 and PM concentrations of air pollution in cities of Turkey are far above the target limit values determined by the Turkish Air Quality Protection Regulation and the values determined by the World Health Organization (Bayram, Dörtbudak et al., 2006:107).

Tab. 1: Renewable Energy Capacity in Selected Countries (2020)

Electricity Capacity (MW)	Total Renewable Capacity	Wind[a]		Solar
		Onshore	Offshore	
China	894 879	273.003	8.990	254.355
USA	292 065	117.715	29	75.572
Germany	131 739	54.437	7.747	53.783
Spain	59 108	27.084	5	14.089
France	55 365	17.380	2	11.733
Turkey	*49.398*	8.832	-	6.668
UK	47 676	14.282	10.383	13.563
Denmark	9.607	4.534	1.701	1.300

Source: Compiled from IRENA 2021 Database.

a Wind energy turbines are installed in two different types as onshore and offshore.

called non-renewable energy sources. Natural gas, coal, oil are primary examples of these resources (Koç and Kaya, 2015: 37).

Surely, renewable energy production will differ according to the natural resources and technologies of the countries. However, sometimes the political preferences of country governances and various incentives can exceed the limitations brought about by natural resources. Germany is the best example to this situation.

In Tab. 1, the leading countries in electricity generation from renewable energy in the world and Turkey are given. China is by far the world leader in this regard. At the same time, China is the leading country in greenhouse gas emissions into the atmosphere because of fossil fuel use. Renewable energy capacity of Turkey is not very low. 10 % of the total installed renewable energy capacity of EU28 countries is in Turkey (IRENA, 2021). However, the share of hydraulic energy, which is not a sustainable resource, in the installed power is high in Turkey. Today, electricity generation from renewable energy sources is supported due to such benefits as "energy supply security", "diversification of energy", "reducing import dependency in energy", "combating climate change" and "creating employment".

2. Cities and Renewable Energy

So many countries are providing examples on how to make a transition to a sustainable energy system. Cities play a critical role in combating climate change. The total surface area of cities covers only 2–3 % of the earth. Nonetheless, cities are the center of social and economic life with their population, production, and consumption activities. Also, more than half of the global population lives in places defined as cities. Cities are somehow both perpetrators and victims of climate change. Cities are responsible for 60–75 % of natural energy use and 70 % of greenhouse gas emissions. Urban heat islands, floods and overflows, and the destruction of coasts due to rising sea levels are the negative effects of climate change on cities (350Turkiye, 2019). 30 % of the global population is exposed to heat waves for about 20 days in 1 year. If greenhouse gas emissions continue to be released as they are today, it is expected that 74 % of the global population will be exposed to heat waves in 2100 (Mora et al., 2017: 5–7). In addition, climate change causes various problems such as social (climate migration), economic, infrastructural and environmental issues in cities.

Measures to be taken in transportation, heating, construction of buildings, planning and green space arrangements will protect cities from the negative effects of global climate change. These measures can be summarized under the following headings (350Turkey, 2019): What needs to be done in cities until 2050 to reach the goal of keeping the earth temperature increase at the 1.5°C limit are briefly as follows (350Turkey, 2019):

1. Lowering greenhouse gas emissions given out from buildings by 80–90 % below today's total level,
2. Minimum 30 % reduction of energy use in transportation,
3. Obtaining minimum 75–80 % of the total electricity production from renewable resources.

The most fundamental condition for preventing climate change in cities is transition to renewable energy. All areas where energy is in use, especially buildings and transportation, need to be freed from fossil fuel dependence, and run on renewable resources. Apart from the transition to renewable energy sources, the improvement of energy efficiency and the development of energy savings are also the main targets. Solar energy is the simplest way to obtain renewable energy to be used in cities (350Turkey, 2019: 30). It is not only a decentralized system where energy is directly produced and used with such applications as rooftop solar energy panels, but also a centralized system where the energy produced in renewable energy facilities in or outside of the city is distributed through the general grid network. The use of rooftop solar PV panels and planar solar collectors is the easiest solution to be applied. According to a study, Frankfurt, which has a target of 100 % renewable energy in 2050, will be able to meet 50 % of its energy needs from urban renewable energy production activities, and the other 50 % from the ones in the vicinity of the city by 2050 (Elliot, 2018).

Geothermal, biofuels and hydro resources should be used in the process of transition to 100 % renewable energy, but only in places and areas where they are essential, with necessary controls and practices that will minimize damage. Methane gas emission, deforestation, loss of agricultural lands, soil pollution are its problematic aspects. To achieve the target of transition to 100 % renewable energy, the participation of the entire public in all processes related to energy such as production, distribution and consumption is an important element. One of the best methods for this is energy cooperatives. Thanks to the energy cooperatives, the barriers between the producer and the consumer are removed, and collective decisions on such issues as determining the energy need, the amount of energy production, and the areas of use of energy can be made with the participation of everyone (350Turkey, 2019).

Energy cooperatives, which transform consumers into producers at the same time, enable such practices as providing economic, environmental and social benefits, as well as public and voluntary participation. As of the year 2016, there are a total of 1024 energy cooperatives across Germany (Borchert, 2018). In Turkey, on the other hand, the first renewable energy cooperative was established in 2014 and their number amounted to 22 in 2018. The first wind energy cooperative, which was founded in Denmark in the late 1970s, is one of the best examples for renewable energy communities. In addition, three fourths of the 900 MW wind power capacity in Denmark is half owned by individuals, and half by wind energy cooperatives. In an empirical study on the subject, it is expected that the total installed capacity of Turkey's unlicensed electricity generation will increase thanks to the establishment of renewable energy cooperatives. To achieve this development, it is necessary to provide state supports/incentives such as the extension of 10-year electrical energy purchase guarantee, system integration of renewable energy facilities, increase in transmission capacity, the improvement of grid connections and management (Özgül et al., 2018: 5–6)

For energy efficiency, smart grids in cities are used to optimize electricity supply, demand and management. With the help of advanced remote sensing and monitoring technologies, smart grids provide a regular and bi-directional flow of information between demands of consumers and supply from manufacturer. Thus, by providing real-time operations and flexibility between supply and demand, it facilitates the inclusion of renewable energy in the existing system, which can be interrupted, as well as increasing energy efficiency and reliability of the system. Such improvement activities as adding new generation technologies to existing traditional networks are being carried out (IRENA, 2015). Transition from fossil fuels to sustainable energy sources for stopping the climate crisis offers humanity a different option. Now the power plants that produce electricity are getting smaller and energy can be produced with local resources wherever it is needed. 30.2 % of renewable energy sources (2019) installed in Germany are privately owned. The share of farmers who own ¼ of the biogas facilities in the country is 10 % (Gürbüz WWF, 2021).

Cities around the world now prepare action plans against climate change by forging collaborations among themselves, without waiting for national governments to take action. The Carbon Neutral Cities Pact and C40 Cities are the best examples of such collaborations. A total of 27 cities that are members of the C40 Climate Leadership Group have so far been able to achieve their targeted reduction in carbon emissions, despite the increase in their populations and growth in their economies. While maintaining the economic growth, there has been an annual average of 2 % decrease in greenhouse gas emissions (350Turkey, 2019: 67). The most prominent action of Barcelona, one of these cities, has been the "Superblocks Project". This project, which functionally transforms the streets without any physical changes, has increased the areas where non-motorized vehicles do not enter by up to 23 hectares. In this way, dwellers of Barcelona have turned to such vehicles without carbon footprints as bicycles and electric bicycles (C40 Cities, 2017).

Paris has come to the fore with its energy transformation plans and efforts to reduce the carbon footprint in transportation. It has made the necessary legislative amendments to achieve its goal of installing solar panels on minimum 20 % of roofs in Paris by 2050. It has been determined that approximately three fourths of the energy need must be supplied from non-urban sources to effectuate the transition to 100 % renewable energy in 2050. Especially for wind energy, it was decided to establish and support energy cooperatives in rural areas around Paris. In the field of transportation, the city of Paris managed to reduce greenhouse gas emissions by 39 %, traffic congestion by 30 %, and the quantity of particles in the air by 50 %, thanks to various measures taken between 2004 and 2014. In the new climate action plan; in 2050, use of electricity produced from biogas and renewable resources in all urban transportation is aimed (Cities 100: 2016).

15 world cities that are members of the Carbon Neutral Cities Pact have revised their carbon neutral targets until 2050 in the form of an emergency action plan. They suggested urgent action on energy, green building technologies, transportation and waste; and announced their short and long-term plans. They have formed different roadmaps for carbon neutral targets in their urban zones in 2030 and 2050. For example, for a carbon-neutral London in 2030, 70 % of all buildings must achieve energy efficiency performance. In addition, by 2050, motorized road transport in the entire city must turn to battery-electric or fuel-cell vehicles. Oslo has committed to achieve a net zero carbon target for all public

Tab. 2: Development of Turkey's Installed Capacity According to Primary Energy Sources (2009–2019)

MW	Thermic (Coal)	Hydraulic	Geothermal	Wind	Solar	Total
2009	29.339,1	14.553,3	77,2	791,6	-	44.761,2
%	65,55	32,51	0,17	1,77	-	100,00
2019	47.663,0	28.503,0	1.514,7	7.591,2	5.995,2	91.267,0
%	52,22	31,23	1,66	8,32	6,57	100,00

Source: (TEİAŞ, 2019)

transportation, including buses and ferries, by 2030. Iowa, on the other hand, has planned to generate electricity entirely from wind energy by the end of 2021 (CNCA, 2021: 6–12). The fact that a very rapid transition to renewable energy sources is required for zero carbon cities is a clear fact.

3. Outlook of Renewable Energy in Turkey

Renewable energy capacity in Turkey has significantly increased in the last 10 years. Apart from the fact that renewable energy production capacity of Turkey has substantially risen since 2002, the share of renewable energy sources other than hydroelectric, especially wind and solar energy, in the total installed power has also increased as of 2010.

The figures of the installed power obtained from primary sources in Turkey are given in Tab. 2. The share of wind and solar has increased in the last 10 years, and their share in total energy is around 14–15 %. In most of the thermal power plants, coal is used. Coal-fired power plants still constitute half of the installed energy power.

In Tab. 3, it is observed that 40 % of the electricity energy in Turkey is met from renewable resources. Unlicensed power plants are not included in these rates. An average of 7.5 % (6,824 MW) of the total installed power belongs to unlicensed power plants. 91 % of unlicensed power plants are solar power plants (EMO, 2021). The use of natural gas and imported coal in domestic heating is still very high and foreign dependency for these resources is another important problem as well as the high use of hydraulic energy.

Thermal and natural gas power plants, which run on fossil fuels, hold the first two ranks in energy production in Turkey. In Tab. 3 the development of natural gas, coal and renewable energy resources in Turkey over the course 20 years is presented. To simplify the comparison, these two major fossil sources have been included alongside renewable energy sources, and other fossil energy sources are

Tab. 3: Annual Development of Turkey's Renewable Energy, Thermic and Natural Gas Total Installed Capacity (2000–2019)

Years	Wind+ Geothermal+ Solar[a]		Hydraulic		Thermic		Natural Gas	
	MW	Share %	MW	Share %	MW	Share %	MW	Share %
2000	36	0.1	11.175	41.0	16.053	58.9	4.905	18.0
2001	36	0.1	11.673	41.2	16.623	58.7	4.851	17.1
2002	36	0.1	12.241	88.4	19.569	61.4	7.247	22.8
2003	34	0.1	12.579	35.3	22.974	64.6	8.862	24.9
2004	34	0.1	12.645	34.3	24.145	65.6	10.131	27.5
2005	35	0.1	12.906	33.2	25.902	66.7	10.976	28.3
2006	82	0.2	13.063	32.2.	27.420	67.6	11.462	28.3
2007	169	0.4	13.395	32.8	27.272	66.8	11.467	28.5
2008	394	0.9	13.829	33.1	27.595	66.0	10.657	25.5
2009	869	1.9	14.553	32.5	29.339	65.5	11.826	26.4
2010	1.414	2.9	15.831	32.0	32.279	65.2	13.302	26.9
2011	1.843	3.5	17.137	32.4	33.931	64.1	13.144	24.8
2012	2.423	4.2	19.609	34.4	35.027	61.4	14.116	24.7
2013	3.071	4.8	22.289	34.8	38.648	60.4	17.171	26.8
2014	4.075	5.9	23.643	34.0	41.802	60.1	18.704	26.9
2015	5.376	7.3	26.868	36.2	41.903	56.5	18.528	25.0
2016	7.405	9.4	26.681	34.0	44.412	56.6	19.564	24.9
2017	11.001	12.9	27.273	32.0	46.926	55.1	23.206	27.2
2018	13.333	15.1	28.291	32.0	46.902	53.0	25.675	29.0
2019	15.101	16.5	28.503	31.2	47.663	52.2	25.904	28.4

Source: Türkyılmaz and Bayrak, 2020: 24.

[a] Although it is a renewable energy source, hydroelectric energy is not included in this table because it is not a sustainable resource.

excluded. When the annual distribution of installed power at regard of thermal power plants and power plants running on renewable resources is taken into account especially after 2001, due to the increase in the total capacity of natural gas fired power plants, the share of thermal power plants in the total installed power has considerably increased, and after 2011, there has been a significant increase in the share of renewable resources. The reduction of natural gas prices after 2001, as well as the fact that natural gas power plants could be installed more easily and in a shorter time, caused a rapid increase in natural gas related capacity. However, after 2011, not only increase in natural gas prices, but also the development in wind turbine technologies and the unit power investments becoming more economical, as well as the fact that important incentives were given for small hydraulic power plants, led to a greater inclination to wind and hydraulic power plant capacity. Therefore, the proportion of those running on renewable resources within the total installed power has increased significantly after the year of 2011 (Türkyılmaz and Bayraktar, 2020: 25–26). In terms of fossil fuel, Turkey is highly dependent on foreign resources. 90 % of oil, 99 % of natural gas and 95 % of anthracite are imported. This foreign dependency affects the security of supply, the balance of international payments and, of course, consumer prices. Against this dependency, Turkey has increased its initiatives towards domestic and renewable resources, although not very high for now. The Ministry of Energy and Natural Resources (MENR) put a relatively greater emphasis on hydroelectricity in the RE Action Plan, which they prepared in 2014. For wind and solar energy, even a concrete strategic target has not been set (MENR, 2014):

- Benefiting from hydroelectric generation capacity in maximum and continuing to use mechanisms to encourage private sector investment in this field,
- Establishing the necessary cooperation and coordination in the determination and development of water resources suitable for hydroelectric production, with a holistic approach based on the basin and considering the changing consumption demands.
- Evaluation of economic analysis criteria for hydroelectric power plants according to current conditions.
- Fortifying the energy transmission and distribution systems with technical equipment enabling higher use of solar and wind power plants that produce intermittent energy,
- In the use of geothermal resources, following the conservation principles for maintaining the reusability properties through regeneration.
- Speeding up the initiations to open geothermal areas that are suitable for electricity generation at economically investable level to the private sector.
- Concentrating on studies about domestic technology development for every stage in the field of conversion technologies for renewable energy resources.

Considering that Turkey is not in a suitable region in terms of water resources, and also existing water resources are mainly located in the Black Sea Region, it is a fact that incentives and policies for hydraulic energy are unsustainable. Especially the damage caused by hydroelectric power plants to the environment

Tab. 4: Distribution of Electricity Generation by Resources in Turkey (2018–2020)

Resource	2018 (%)	2019 (%)	2020 (%)
Hydroelectric (dam + stocks)	20.08	29.22	25.8
Naturel Gas	29.53	18.59	22.5
Imported Coal	21.07	19.86	20.7
Coal, Lignite and Asphaltite	12.7	17.34	14.5
Wind	10.81	7.15	8.1
Solar	2.59	3.16	3.7
Geothermal	1.83	2.94	3.1
Biofuel	0.7	1.49	1.4
Fuel-Oil and Diesel	0.69	0.24	0.1
Total	100	100	100

Source: Compiled from Energy Atlas Data and EMO

is another issue. When the last 3 years of electricity generation resources in Turkey are taken into account, it is clearly seen that the proportion of hydroelectricity (HEPP) holds the first position. This ratio is an ironic indicator of the strategy being loyally followed.

In Turkey, the rate of hydroelectric power plants built on rivers is 8 % on average (EMO, 2021). Hydroelectricity is a renewable energy source, but its harmful effects on the environment and people during its construction and after the operation unfolds later. In addition, HEPPs with a capacity of over 10 MW are classified as non-renewable energy sources (Ermiş, 2019: 75). 339 (equal to 49.4 % of all) of a total of 685 HEPPs in Turkey are below 10 MW capacity (Enerji Atlas, 2021). It can be seen from these ratios that half of the HEPPs in Turkey are not actually renewable energy sources. In addition, considering that 71 % of HEPP projects in Turkey are exempt from Environmental Impact Assessment, the harmful effects of HEPPs can be summarized as follows (WWF, 2013):

- Thousands of trees are cut down during the construction of HEPPs,
- In some HEPP projects, water is transported by pipes for kilometers. Therefore, wild animals cannot access water resources,
- The natural flow paths of surface water are interrupted or altered. This causes the rivers to dry up and some of the living species around them to die,
- Excavation soil that comes out during the construction phase are dumped into the stream beds,

In the strategy document of the Ministry of Energy and Natural Resources (2019–2023), the most important ones among the goals and objectives that include the issue of increasing the proportion of clean energy and RE in energy consumption are as follows (MENR, 2019):

- Increasing the installed electricity capacity (shifting up from 59 % to 65 %) running on domestic and renewable energy sources so as to ensure sustainable security of energy supply.
- To uprise the energy efficiency, an energy system will be planned for electric vehicles.
- Initiations to raise the rate of domestic production of the equipment used in the field of energy and natural resources will be maintained.
- In renewable energy, endeavors will be made to combine the dispersed system.

When the strategy document is broadly examined, objectives and targets related to mining and natural gas are more prominent than RE. This shows that Turkey will not give up the use of fossil resources soon. Although some RE-related goals are set, concrete measures on how to achieve them are not included in the plan.

The following 2023 targets are included in The Strategy Plan regarding the evaluation of domestic and renewable energy resources (MENR, 2019):

- Rising the installed power of HEPPs to 32.037 MW,
- Installed power of WEPPs to 11.883 MW,
- Installed power of GEPPs and BEPPs to 2. 884MW
- Installed power of SEPPs to 10.000 MW
- Installed power of the plants running on domestic coal to 14.664 MW.

In addition to renewable resources, it is controversial how realistic the targets are. Establishing a new capacity of 4,460 MW from domestic coal resources until 2023 means an 44 % increase in the existing 10,101 MW installed power. Total installed power of all licensed domestic coal power plant projects is 3,281 MW, and realization rates of 26 % of these power plant investments are unknown. The other 25 % has a realization rate below 10 %. As in Eskişehir Alpu, people living in the power plant areas resist the power plant projects, and thus they receive annulment decisions from the judiciary. Many developed countries deactivate coal-fired power plants according to certain programs. International financial institutions also report that they will not finance coal-fired power plant investments (Türkyılmaz and Bayrak, 2020: 57).

4. Wind Energy

Wind, which is the current that low and high pressure form against each other in the atmosphere, is an endless source in the natural system and a force that influences climate, precipitation and vegetation. Since wind has certain effects on living and non-living entities, it holds a position in the fields of such sciences as climatology, meteorology and geography. Since B.C., wind power has been utilized in a wide variety of fields ranging from milling grain to extracting water. Since the 1900s, in Europe, it has gradually started to be used in electricity generation as well. Electricity generation from wind power generally consists of the stages of converting the kinetic energy carried by the wind during its flow in the atmosphere to mechanical energy by revolving the turbine blades; and converting this mechanical energy into electrical energy by means of the generator in the core. Although they deploy a similar technique in terms of their working principle, it is possible to see many examples where the setup of the mechanisms and the propeller systems, in which kinetic energy of the wind is transferred to the mechanic energy (Ermiş, 2018: 50–54). In a study (2008), greenhouse gas emissions that are produced were calculated at regard of energy sources. For 1 kWh, greenhouse gas emissions are 66 grams from nuclear power plants, 9–10 grams from wind, 13–32 grams from solar, 10–13 grams from hydroelectric, 11 grams from biogas, and 14–41 grams from biomass (Sovaccol, 2008: 2948–2950). From the study, it is seen that wind energy is the cleanest energy source.

Wind energy also has some certain advantages and disadvantages (EMO, 2021):
Advantages of Wind Energy:

1. No emission of gases polluting the atmosphere,
2. Being a clean energy source,
3. Not running out of resources
4. Wind energy facilities are easier to install; also, operation and maintenance costs are lower than other facilities: Since wind turbine operation and maintenance contracts can be concluded for up to 15 years, the common terms in the market are 15 years. Although the operation and maintenance costs of wind power plants vary according to the turbine type and size, the average total operating maintenance cost per MWh is less than 10 Euros.
5. Low energy production costs,
6. Increasing reliability,
7. Being regional and thus locals can produce their own electricity.

Disadvantages of Wind Energy:

1. Since wind lacks stability, energy production figures are changeable,

2. Large area coverage of wind turbines,
3. Causing noise pollution,
4. Low energy production compared to the energy obtained from fossil and nuclear fuels
5. High investment costs: For example, hydroelectric power plants have the average installation costs 750,000–1,200,000 US$, lignite based thermal power plants 1,600,000 US$, natural gas based thermal power plants 680,000 US$ while wind power plants have 1,450,000 US$ installation cost.
6. Maintenance costs are low. Wind turbine operation and maintenance contracts can be made up to 15 years. Although the operating maintenance costs of wind power plants vary according to the turbine type and size, the total operating maintenance cost per MWh is around 10 Euros.
7. Composite parts that have reached the end of their lifespan cannot be recycled in nature.

Also, there are studies on environmental and social problems that wind power plants created. It has been seen that the direct effects of the wind facilities on environment, socially, have 4 basic domains of sensitivity. These are the environmental, economic, sensory, and technological domains. It is observed that for the environmental domain, within or near the wind energy production area, water resource products, marine life and forest-based species have changed; they have moved away from the feeding areas of wildlife; and the migration routes of birds have changed. It has been emphasized that agricultural activities stopped due to the installations on the cultivation fields, and land ownership problems were experienced after the installations. For the emotional domain, effects such as headache and noise disturbance have been observed in those living close to the turbines (Demir and Ataöv, 2021: 6–7).

No restriction by legislation has been made in Turkey on how far wind turbines can be installed from residential areas. Therefore, wind facilities can choose sites very close to natural, cultural and socio-economic activity areas. When Turkey and countries such as Denmark and Germany are compared in terms of where a sensitive selection of site is required, the following results are obtained (Yetiş et al., 2015):

- ✓ While wind facilities can select sites minimum 300–2000 m away from residential areas, or a minimum distance of 200–500 m from forest areas, WPP installation in forest areas is allowed in Turkey as long as the fees for the trees being cut down is paid by the investor.
- ✓ In Turkey, facilities are allowed to be established at a minimum distance of 300 m from sensitive natural sites that are strictly protected. Facilities can be

located in national parks, in special environmental protection zones, upon the positive opinion of state institutions.

✓ Although wind facilities must select a site at least 3 km away from the sea; a distance of 300 m to lakes and rivers, and 100 m to the seashore are stipulated in Turkey.

✓ While wind facilities can be established 1000 m away from cultural heritage sites in the world, wind facilities are not allowed only in 1st and 2nd degree cultural heritage sites in Turkey.

Wind potential represents the strength of the wind. Wind turbines, on the other hand, can only use 20–30 % of the current potential. The wind potential of countries differs according to their geographical location, distance and proximity to pressure centers, and changes in the atmosphere. Speed of the wind varies according to the roughness classes in the topography (EMO, 2021). According to this:

1. Settlements, forests, agricultural lands with many windbreaking areas are considered as high roughness class.
2. Open lands and inland areas with few breakers, smooth coastal areas, and very few land surfaces without any breakers are 1st class in terms of roughness,
3. In open seas at least 10 km from the coast, the roughness class is 0.

The installation and distribution costs of WPPs to be built on the sea are high. According to the report prepared by the Global Wind Energy Council (GWEC), 17 separate and full-time lines of work are required in order to obtain 1 megawatt capacity from offshore wind farms with an average lifetime of 25 years (offshore). (GWEC, 2021: 7–8). Today, almost all of offshore wind turbines in Europe are connected to the grid. This situation brings along the need for extra investments and technologies and increases the unit energy costs. Considering that, in terms of technologies, energy is carried from the sea to the land, offshore wind turbines have been included in the same category as the energy obtained from wave energy and have also been considered as ocean energy in some studies (Esteban and Leary, 2012).

Although Denmark (374 MW) is currently behind the UK (932MW), which is the world leader in offshore wind energy, it will produce 1400 MW of electricity with its two offshore energy farms, Thor and Vattenfall, which it will complete in 2021. This will make Denmark the world leader in this regard. The reasons why Denmark's offshore wind turbine investments are so high are as follows (Şahin, 2020: 5):

1. Denmark has a good wind potential in offshore and onshore areas.
2. Wind turbine distribution brings advantages along.
3. Significant employment is created, and wind turbine components contribute to exports.
4. Onshore wind farm areas of Denmark are small and relatively densely populated.
5. Denmark has a 7300 km coastline which consists of shallow waters.

It is stated that Turkey has an offshore potential apart from the calculated one, especially on the Aegean coasts and Çanakkale. It is an advantage in this respect that the waters are not at the depth of the ocean. However, the number of projects, investments and legal regulations are close to none in Turkey. One offshore WPP is expected to be completed in İzmir by the end of 2021. In the next part, the incentive mechanisms developed by some countries that have a significant share in global wind energy will be discussed.

4.1. Wind Energy Incentives in the World

Owing to their contribution to sustainable energy, many countries in the world support energy production from renewable energy sources, especially wind energy. Apart from encouraging widespread use of the resources, these countries are also endeavoring to develop policies appropriate for the development of domestic technology production in order to meet this demand. Even though there were a few countries such as Denmark and Germany that implemented support policies in the early 1980s and 1990s, the number of countries that embarked on and adhibited renewable energy increased after 2005. These incentives have spread up to city administrations. The top 5 countries in wind energy production in the world are China, USA, Germany, India, and Spain. However, the top 5 countries in wind energy production per capita are Denmark, Sweden, Ireland, Germany, Norway. Although China is the leading country in wind energy, it can only meet 5.3 % of its electricity need from wind energy (GWEC, 2021: 8). Denmark, which started wind energy production since the 1970s and is an example with the incentive systems it has developed, is one of the first countries that bears in mind when it comes to wind energy.

Denmark has developed one of the first grid specifications related to interconnection lines to integrate its increasing wind and solar capacity into the system in the late 1980s. Thanks to the hydroelectric energy imported from Norway and the strong interconnection lines, which it has established with other Northern European countries, Denmark has become the country that produces approximately 44 % of its electricity from wind in 2017 (SHURA, 2018: 21–23).

Denmark[4] has been advancing forward in clean energy since the 1980s. It started this transformation with the installation of small wind turbines. Local markets have emerged by supplying the electricity from these small turbines to the interconnected system under market conditions. Depending on these markets, a local industry has been established that generates significant incomes for local municipalities as well as citizens of the country and farmers (SHURA, 2018: 21–23). Denmark have used various financial supports, regulations, voluntary agreements, planning tools and economics. Two most important methods Denmark used for renewable energy investments are; guaranteed purchase and guaranteed fixed premium above market prices. General financing method was the Public Service Obligation item reflected on the electricity bills (Gyekye, 2018).

Spain has an interconnection capacity of less than 10 % of its total installed generation capacity (10 % is the minimum level set by the European Union). However, Spain overcame this challenge by developing a real-time control system for all wind farms. And now, its biggest source for electricity generation is wind. Germany is a unique example of the energy transition. It has been continuously transforming the energy system since the 1990s with its pioneering "Energiewende"[5] strategy that sets standards for other countries. Energy efficiency also plays a major role in this strategy. In 2017, electricity generation from renewable energy sources started to constitute one third of the total production. Offshore wind turbines play a significant role in these increases (SHURA, 2018: 53). The US gives way to strategies and technologies for clean energy, such as developing smart grids and modernizing grid reliability. Brazil is an example of how long-term cooperation between government and private sector can create the world's largest biodegradable ethanol industry, and then how to lower the costs so that this industry can compete with fossil fuels (SHURA, 2018: 61). Incentive mechanisms, used for expanding the use of wind and other renewable energy, are basically divided into two categories as direct financial support and indirect financial support (see Figure 1).. Among the direct financial supports, the most widely used ones are fixed price incentive and premium guaranteed systems, green certificate and tender systems based on quota applications, and

4 Denmark is the first country to use financial incentives for wind energy in 1979. The program started with direct support to 30 % of the total investment, continued for 10 years at a decreasing rate and ended in 1989 when the subsidy decreased to 10 % (Altuntaşoğlu, 2011: 3).

5 Energiewende: An advanced policy approach based on national consensus, applying both the energy efficiency and renewable energy pillars, and targeting all sectors of the energy system.

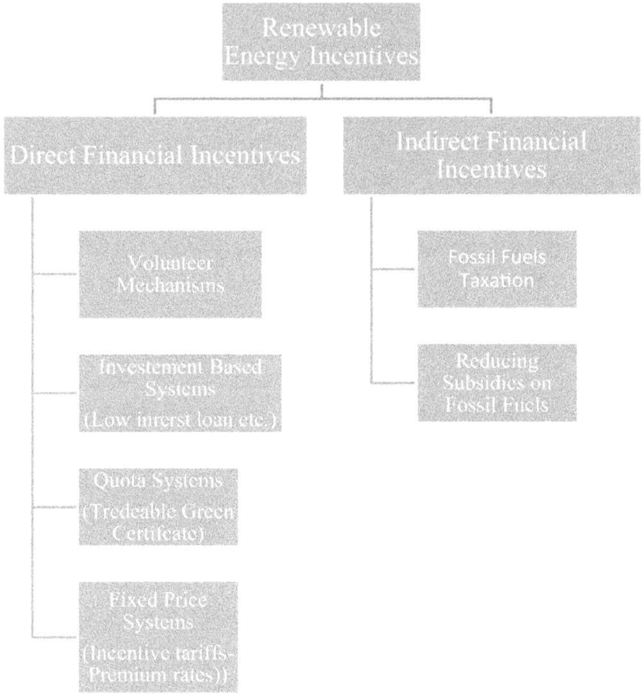

Fig. 1: Types of Incentives Used for Renewable Energy. Source: Adapted from Altuntaşoğlu, 2011: 2.

investment-based systems. Indirect financial supports used in dissemination are implemented in the form of taxing fossil fuels and reducing the subsidies applied to these fuels (Altuntaşoğlu, 2011: 1).

These incentives are used for electricity generation from all renewable energy sources in a mixed manner. The weight of the incentives provided for wind, solar and hydraulic power plants varies according to the natural resource diversity and abundance of the countries. Mechanisms that directly support domestic wind power technology have separately been developed for wind energy. These are (Altuntaşoğlu, 2011: 2–3):

1. *Domestic Production Obligation:* Wind power plant components part or all must be domestic production,
2. *Financial Incentives:* Low interest credits, tax credits, VAT and income tax discounts, domestic Labor,

Tab. 5: Supports Applied to Wind Energy in Some EU Countries

State	Basic Incentive Mechanisms	Explanation
Denmark	Fixed price and Premium Guarantee (onshore), Tender for offshore	For onshore additional to market price premium, plus refund for balancing costs. For offshore market price plus premium
Germany	Fixed price guarantee	For onshore 83 €/MWh for at least 5 years, backwards 52.8 €/MWh for the remaining 15 years (2 % reduction in tariff per year from 2007) For offshore 91 €/MWh for at least 12 years, 61.9 €/MWh for the remaining 8 years (2 % reduction in tariff per year from 2007)
Spain	Fixed price guarantee premium rate with choose between	Premium guarantee system with ceiling and floor price application being implemented. During the day thanks to the intraday market with a total of 6 sessions the resulting imbalances are reduced and the wind energy producers are advantage is provided
U.K.	With a quota requirement green certificate tax exemptions	There is obligation to electricity suppliers based on green certification. There are penalties for companies that do not comply with the obligation. In addition, tax on renewable energy producers have exemptions from the climate change tax exemptions certificates
Bulgaria	Forced purchase price	12 years for power plants established after January 2006 prices applied: 79.8 for effective operating time > 2250 hours/year €/MWh, 89.5 €/MWh for effective operating time < 2250 hours/year

Source: Applied from Altuntaşoğlu, 2011.

3. *Ease of Customs Tax,*
4. *Export Credit Aids,*
5. *Quality Certification,*
6. *Research and Development.*

Obligation for domestic production, financial and tax incentives, aids for export credit, quality certification as well as research and development supports. Not all the mechanisms utilized to encourage domestic production are focused on the same target. Some provide comprehensive support for domestic production of both international and domestic companies, while others provide various supports to domestic wind turbine or turbine component manufacturers. Today, many countries (Germany, Denmark, Spain, China, etc.) that are leaders in energy, particularly, have used or are using these supports in a mixed way.

4.2. Outlook of Wind Energy and Incentives in Turkey

Turkey is seen as a country which has been described to have a high potential to generate energy from wind in Europe. Turkey ranks 6th in Europe and 13th in the world in terms of installed capacity of wind power plants. It generates an average of 8 % of its electricity out of wind energy. The first wind farm in Turkey was established in Izmir in 1998 (Energy Atlas, 2021). In terms of wind energy in Turkey, especially Çanakkale-İzmir, Balıkesir and Hatay, as well as Bozcaada and Gökçeada, are some of the regions with high wind potential in our country. In Turkey, it has been assumed that 5 MW wind power plants per square kilometer can be established in areas 50 m above ground level and with wind speeds above 7.5 m/s. In the light of these assumptions, the Wind Energy Potential Atlas (WEPA) has been prepared, in which wind resource information produced by using a medium-scale numerical weather forecast model and a micro-scale wind flow model are presented (Caliskan-MGM: 10–12). Turkey is located in the south of the middle belt, where the most active atmospheric structure is dominant. This location has 2 advantages, one of which is, among the global winds, the westerly wind is effective in Anatolia; and the other is that the pressure centers that are effective in the belt in which it is located affect the country at varying rates and times throughout the year (Ermiş, 2019: 186). With WEPA[6], which was put forward within the scope of the joint project of the General Directorate of Meteorology and the Electricity Works Survey Administration, it has been proven that Turkey has a rich wind resource, and the production from this resource will be an important tool in the country's energy independence and environmental protection.

As shown on chart 1, a wind speed of 7 m/s or more is required for an economical WPP investment. When the map is analyzed, it is seen that especially the North Aegean coasts and the coasts of the Marmara Sea have a very serious potential for WPP construction. Again, according to the report, for the connection of the electrical energy produced from the wind to the electricity grid, the

---

6 REPA is the Wind Energy Potential Atlas that gives wind resource information generated using a medium-scale numerical weather forecast model and a micro-scale wind flow model (Çalışkan-MGM).

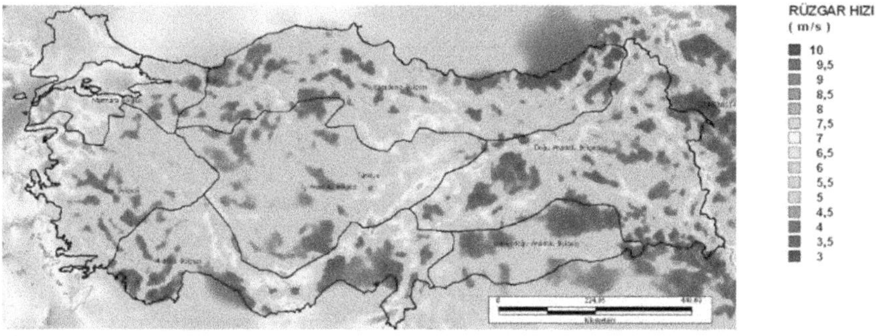

Chart 1: Distribution of Average Annual Wind Speeds in 50-meter Height Over Turkey. Source: Çalışkan-MGM: 11.

variability feature necessitates the availability of backup power due to limitations in terms of the continuity and quality of the electricity. New technologies applied on wind turbines, information technologies, as well as integrated management of wind farms and the use of wind forecasting techniques gradually reduces these problems and ensures that larger amounts of wind electricity are supplied to the grid (Çalışkan-MGM: 14).

Turkey's wind energy potential has been determined as 47,895 MW. 37,836 MW of this potential is onshore and 10,013 MW is offshore (MENR, 2021). Considering that the installed power of electricity based on wind energy is 9.305 MW as of May 2021, it is understood that only 1/4 of the onshore potential can be used. There is currently no WPP installed on any sea in Turkey. Wind turbines are generally installed collectively in the form of a windfarm. However, installments with windfarm model are not very common in Turkey. Today, there are 252 licensed and 17 unlicensed WPPs in Turkey (Energy Atlas, 2021). When WPPs are analyzed by region (see Table 6), the Aegean Region stands out. Within the Aegean Region, the province of İzmir covers half of the regional potential; in the Marmara Region, Balıkesir province constitutes 39 % of the regional potential (TUREB, 2021).

Countries of origin of wind turbines used in wind farms operating in Turkey are German Nordex and Enercom, Danish Vestas, USA General Electric (GE), and German-Spanish partnership Siemens-Gamesa. The only Turkish company is the Milres wind turbine, which is not yet operational. The first tribune with 500 kW power, developed by TÜBİTAK within the scope of the Milres project (Development of National Wind Energy Systems), will, in a while, be installed

Tab. 6: Distribution of Wind Power Plants by Region

Region	Cumulative Installation MW/m
Aegean	3.511
Marmara	3.291
Mediterranean	1.121
Central Anatolia	921
Black Sea	354
Southeast Anatolia	93
East Anatolia	15

Source: TUREB 2021.

in Istanbul on the shore of the Terkos Dam and operated by İSKİ (Enerji Atlası, 2021). When the investor profile is observed, it is seen that foreign energy companies do not operate wind power plants in Turkey. The companies that have installed the power plants are domestic energy companies. Tenders were held by TEIAS for wind power plants with thousands of MW, but they did not attract the attention of foreign investors. It is thought-provoking that foreign investors who took all the tenders when it comes to gold mines and nuclear power plants were not interested in this issue. The problem is either in the incentive system or in the investment potential of the country.

In Turkey, where no significant renewable energy investment was made until 1998 after the first geothermal power plant (Kızıldere Power Plant) operating with geothermal resources and opened in 1975, with the first law on renewable resources in 2005 and the support and regulatory amendments and laws that followed in the sequent years, it showed significant progress. Installed power capacity of wind energy of Turkey has increased rapidly after 2005 mainly with the adoption of the Law No. 5346 "Electricity Market Law" dated 10/05/2005, as well as "Electricity Market Law" dated 3/3/2001 and numbered 24335, the "Electricity Market License Regulation" dated 04/08/2002 and numbered 24836. In Turkey, as well as 5 basic laws and 3 regulations, some other regulatory processes and production and incentive mechanisms are in effect for the generation of electricity from wind energy and other renewable energy sources. These legal regulations are:

1. Law No. 4628 (2013) "On the Duties of the Energy Market Regulatory and Supervision Board",
2. Law No. 5346 (2005) "On the Use of Renewable Energy Resources for the Purpose of Electricity Generation" (YEK-e),
3. Law No. 5627 (2007) "Energy Efficiency Law",

4. Law No. 5784 (2001) "Electricity Market Law",
5. Law No. 6094 (2010) Amendment of the Law on the Use of Renewable Energy Resources for the Purpose of Electricity Generation"
6. YEKDEM- "Regulation on Certification and Support of Renewable Energy Resources" (2013) Official Gazette: 28872.
7. "Regulation on Connecting Wind Power Plants to Wind Power Monitoring and Forecasting Center" (2015), OG: 29278.
8. "Electricity Market License Regulation" (2013) OG: 28809

The purpose of the Law No. 5436 is to expand the use of energy resources for electrical energy production; to bring these resources to the economy in a reliable, economical and high quality manner; to increase the diversity of resources, to reduce greenhouse gas emissions; to recycle wastes; to protect the environment; and to develop the manufacturing sector needed for the realization of these goals. The support system provided according to the Law No. 5436 is the "fixed price with incentives" mechanism. Legal entities with retail sales license are obliged to purchase RES (renewable energy source). If the total amount of RES Certified RES-E supplied in the country is sufficient, the purchase obligation cannot be less than 8 % of the sales of license holders of the retail sales in the previous calendar year (Altuntaşoğlu-EMO: 257)

- *Fixed Price with Incentive*: Incentive rates vary according to the renewable energy source to be used. The tariff validity period will be put into operation until the end of 2025 and will be applied for electricity generation facilities with RES (renewable energy source) certificate[7] (PD 3453: 2021). The validity period was previously applied as 10 years. Presidential Decree for the amount of incentives are issued in accordance with the Law No. 5346. According to this decree, the purchase guarantee for wind energy was 32 KW/h per 0.01 lira. The highest incentive (54 cent) in RE was given to geothermal energy (PD 3453: 2021). However, giving 90 cents incentive for nuclear energy is thought-provoking. The upper limit to be taken in the update is 5.10 dollars/cent. In addition, to encourage the formation of domestic technology according to the 4th article of the Law No. 5436, an additional price will be applied for the electrical energy to be produced in these facilities on condition that the mechanical and/or electro-mechanical components used are domestic production.

7 A "Renewable Energy Source Certificate" (RES Certificate) is given by EMRA to the legal entity holding the generation license in order to determine and follow the source type in the domestic and international markets of the electrical energy produced from renewable energy sources.

- *Land Rental Fee:* Within the scope of this Law, which will be operational until 31/12/2025, 85 % discount is applied to permit, rent, easement and usage permit fees for 10 years following the date of license from generation facilities based on renewable energy sources, and from transportation routes and from energy transmission lines up to the connection point to the system specified in their licenses, including those to be transferred to TEİAŞ and distribution companies.
- *Production Facilities*: An additional share of domestic contribution is given for WPP production to be executed in the country. Financial support is provided for the components of the wind farm in US dollar cents/kWh. 0.8 for the blade, 1.0 for the generator and power electronics, 0.6 for the turbine tower, 1.3 dollars for the entire mechanical equipment in the rotor and nacelle groups.

Supported components are produced in Turkey. However, the engine, which is the most basic part for a WPP, cannot be produced in Turkey unfortunately. Incentives provided in accordance with Law No. 4628 and Electricity Market License Regulation:

- 99 % discount on license application fee,
- Exemption from the annual license fee for the first 8 years
- Priority to RES facilities in connecting to the system,
- Preemption liability of TETAŞ to retail sales companies if there is no other source of supply equal to or cheaper than its hourly price,
- In addition, there is no obligation to obtain a license for WPPs below 500 kW. The surplus electricity produced by these facilities must be purchased by energy companies.

Hitherto, 927 RE power plants benefiting from YEKDEM have been installed. Of these, 448 are hydraulic, 98 are wind, 153 are geothermal, 184 are biomass, and 44 are solar power plants. The low number of the Wind and Solar power plants is remarkable (Final RES List: 2021). VAT exemption and customs tax exemption have been granted to 5 projects (Datça, Muğla, Balıkesir, İzmir, Aydın) by the Ministry of Economy (Energy Atlas-Incentives, 2021). Apart from this, only stamp duty exemption is applied as a tax incentive. In order for a RE plant to generate electricity, it must complete the phases of project development, pre-license, license, ministry acceptance procedure and commissioning. In RE production, a long bureaucratic path is followed until the plant starts operating. The tender[8] process in the project development stage, the pre-license stage, and

8 If there is more than one application for the same region and/or the same substation, TEİAŞ will announce a tender and determine the one to be connected to the system.

the permissions obtained from different institutions are the predominant aspects of the heavy bureaucracy. The RE incentive system implemented in Turkey has some financial, legal and judiciary problems. It is thought that a successful incentive system should have the following principles (Altuntaşoğlu, 2011: 8–9):

1. It should be simple and easy to implement,
2. It should be a temporary mechanism,
3. It should create safe conditions for potential investors
4. It should be cost-effective
5. It should be able to direct to efficient technologies
6. It should include factors that will provide economies of scale,
7. It should be able to lay the foundation for the development of different technologies,
8. It should comply with national conditions.

The fact that the price incentives in the first version of Law No. 5436 were not attractive and did not give different prices according to different sources drove the investor away. However, fixed prices with incentives being foreseen with the changes made, and the additional tariff application to be implemented on condition that domestic production components are used have been positive changes. However, making purchase guarantees in TL in 2020 is a factor that can shake up the safe conditions again. Because excessive fluctuations in exchange rates have a distorting effect on price risks in the electricity market. More tax and financial instruments should be deployed to support RE investments in Turkey.

Green energy support in Turkey is executed with fixed tariff guarantee and premium payment as "regulatory policies". Other than that, such "regulatory policies" as green certificate quotas and renewable energy portfolio standards are not implemented. As financial incentives, stamp duty and domestic production incentives as well as, to some companies, customs tax and VAT incentives are applied. There is also no such implementation as "carbon tax", which is a deterrent factor from fossil fuels. Turkish tax incentive portfolio is also very narrow and insufficient. The following arguments, which are not used in Turkey in terms of tax incentives for green energy, are used in the world (Ulusoy and Daştan, 2018: 7):

- Tax reduction (income or corporate tax discount until the amount of contribution planned for the investment is reached),
- Premium support for general health insurance to employer and/or employee,
- Withholding support for income tax,

- Income or corporate tax exemption (for 1–5 years corporate and/or income tax exemption for renewable energy income).

An incentive system that attracts investors should be used for wind energy, which is an expensive technology in terms of installation costs. More effective tax incentives should be implemented to use the existing advantage of Turkey, which has an above-average natural potential in terms of solar, geothermal and wind resources. In addition, political decision makers should withdraw their support from fossil fuels as soon as possible. Practices causing deterrence from fossil energy investments are another step for promoting green energy. Exchange-related price increases in oil and natural gas are also factors that decrease supply security and increase consumer costs.

Conclusion

The COVID 19 has slowed both energy production and demand. Unemployment rate has increased in both equipment production and related sectors. On the other hand, the pandemic underlined the importance of the transition to renewable energy in the world. For this, of course, countries that have developed technology in renewable energy should support other countries with methods such as funds, credits, and technology transfer. However, developments show that the transition to green energy in the world is not at the desired level at all. Although the green order, Paris Agreement, energy specifications, incentives and other international agreements have brought many regulations on the transition to renewable energy, the use of fossil fuels in the world has not decreased much. According to the REN21, "2021 Renewable Energy Global Status Report", while renewable energy investments commissioned in the world in 2020 increased by 30 % compared to 2019, the share of fossil fuels in total energy consumption remained the same as it was 10 years ago with 80 % (REN 21: 15). With the development plans created within the scope of combating the COVID-19 pandemic, unfortunately, six times more resources than renewable energy have been allocated to fossil fuels. Despite the historic decline in energy demand due to the COVID-19 pandemic, G20 countries have not been able to meet their renewable energy targets. Fifteen of these countries did not have a clean energy target, but 5 of them approached the targets (REN 21: 15).

According to the current data in the world (2018), only 17.1 % of the total energy consumption in the world is met from renewable resources. In 2010, this rate was 10.6 %. It is not possible to deem this increase as sufficient considering the situation that the world is facing. The resources allocated to developing countries for the use of clean energy have been increased by 32 % (IRENA, 2021: 2). According to the IPCC scenario, to limit the global temperature increase, it is necessary to reduce coal consumption by 97 % and oil consumption by 87 % in 2050 compared to 2010. Also, the share of renewables should be increased by 77 %. Although the number of incentives used for fossil fuels in the world is four times that of renewable energy, investments in wind and solar energy continue to increase rapidly. In fact, the countries that use renewable energy sources the most are the countries that pollute the world the most, such as China, the USA, and Germany. Especially in the aforementioned industrialized countries, RE should be determined as a performance criterion in all economic activities as soon as possible. It is also necessary not to give incentives and credits to power plants that use fossil fuels such as coal and natural gas. Since wholesale electricity prices remain at very low levels, it is necessary to maintain incentives for wind and solar energy in this process. At the same time, it is clear that the green finance required for a partial solution to the economic crisis and energy transformation will take a priority place on the agenda (Acar and Değer, 2020). The issue of energy security and supply, as well as sustainable and efficient energy, remains on the agenda.

Today, Turkey meets approximately 50 % of its electricity needs from RE sources. However, the share of hydraulic energy in renewable resources at the level of 30–35 % is not a sustainable situation. The rapid depletion of water resources and the damage caused by HEPPs to the environment means that we cannot evaluate this resource in the clean energy category. The share of wind and solar, which are real renewable energy sources, in electricity generation is around 10 % in Turkey. Turkey has the world's leading natural resources in Solar and Geothermal. Aegean coasts for offshore wind, Central and Southeastern Anatolia Regions for solar energy are very important source regions. The offshore wind power plant is not used at all. The solar source is used very limitedly.

Electricity generation technologies using local and renewable energy sources can contribute to reducing energy import dependency. According to a report, it is predicted that by increasing the share of renewable energy in electricity generation, harmonizing its transmission system with renewable resources, Turkey can save 2.1 billion USD annually from reducing fossil fuel imports by 2028 (IPM, 2021: 10). Natural resources of Turkey are rich in terms of solar and wind. Turkey benefit very little from solar and geothermal energy potential just as its wind energy potential. Turkey has the potential to produce solar energy thousands of times more than its installed power. Although it has a capacity to produce 10,000 times the electricity produced, today it has an installed power of only 5.063 MW. As for geothermal resources, although the water temperature is suitable for direct use, it is stated in some studies that ten times the installed power (1,238) could be produced with different methods to be developed (Ermiş, 2019: 184).

Differences based on the potential and the cost structure, as well as technological opportunities, make it difficult for a single incentive type for renewable energy sources to be successful. Therefore, countries can provide support for the field of renewable energy with more than one mechanism instead of a single incentive type. Examples in the world show that the incentive system is very important in RE investments. Incentives implemented in Turkey that are provided as guaranteed purchase, besides those applied to domestic power plant components, are not enough. Just as multi-member energy cooperatives, green certificate applications based on quota enforcement are the most efficient implementation tools. The RE incentive system used by Denmark is an example in the world in this regard. Currently Denmark gets half of its electricity only from wind energy. Solar energy is very suitable for compact use. The panels to be installed in large estates will be an important alternative for heating and hot water supply, especially in the Southern Regions, where the winters are hot even if not for electricity production. In this regard, the State or the companies or organizations it will authorize will be able to fill a very important gap in the establishment and operation phases.

It is also necessary to simplify bureaucratic processes for wind and solar power plants in Turkey. Today, a WPP project must get the approval from 14 institutions and 50 units, which includes the licensing and commissioning phases and takes a period of 5–6 years. In Turkey, which carries out the WPP business by means of the private sector, this heavy bureaucracy draws the investors away. Despite the complications of these bureaucratic processes, the decision that "environmental impact assessment is not necessary", which can otherwise reveal the environmental damage of the power plant scientifically, is obtained very easily. Turkey is a new market for countries such as Denmark, which uses almost all of its resources efficiently, for investors and companies there. However, these market opportunities are likely to take many years due to such reasons as bureaucratic and legal regulations and insufficient technical infrastructure.

Turkey provides incentives for wind farm laterals. However, it has hardly any workers and engineers qualified to work in the maintenance and repair of these power plants. In order to increase the number of trained personnel who are experts in wind power plant operations and maintenance in Turkey, relevant departments should be opened in vocational high schools and vocational schools of higher education that provide training on this subject, and the qualified personnel shortage of the sector should thus be eliminated. Today, when smart cities are discussed, energy efficiency is also very important. It is very important that the energy to be obtained from wind and sun is given to the interconnected system without any loss. Directly supplying the surplus electricity produced in energy cooperatives or from solar panels to the system will also reduce the lost energy rate. Tax incentives for energy efficient buildings, smart grids and digital transformation in wind farms are other elements of energy efficiency.

References

Acar, Ahmet and Değer Saygın (2020). "COVID 19 Döneminde Dünya'da ve Türkiye'de Enerji Dönüşümüne Bakış", İPM-Mercator Politika. https://ipc.sabanciuniv.edu/Content/Images/CKeditorImages/20201124-20110342.pdf (Access Date: 26.06.2021).

Altuntaşoğlu, Zerrin Taç (2011). "Rüzgar Enerjisinden Elektrik Üretimine Sağlanan Teşvikler", İzmir Rüzgâr Sempozyumu ve Sergisi/23–24 Aralık, İzmir. http://www1.mmo.org.tr/resimler/dosya_ekler/6853480112fefb7_ek.pdf (Access Date: 12.05.2021).

Altuntaşoğlu, Zeynep Taş-EMO Elektrik Mühendisleri Odası (Date Unspocified). "YENİLENEBİLİR Enerji AB ve Türkiye Mevzuatı". https://www.emo.org.tr/ekler/6edc1cd1f36e45d_ek.pdf (Acces Date: 26.06.2021).

Bayrak, Hasan, Dörtbudak Zeynep, et al. (2006). "Hava Kirliliğinin İnsan Sağlığına Etkileri, Dünyada, Ülkemizde ve Bölgemizde Hava Kirliliği Sorunu", *Dicle Tıp Dergisi*, Cilt: 33, Sayı: 2, pp: 105–112.

C40 Cities Barcelona (2019). "Barcelona – The implementation of the Superblocks programme in Barcelona: Filling our streets with life". https://www.c40.org/awards/2017-awards/profiles/125 (Access Date: 19.06.2021).

Çalişir, Haluk (2020). "COVID-19 Salgınına Antroposen Penceresinden Bakmak", *Türk Tabipler Birliği Covid 19 Pandemisi Altıncı Ayı Değerlendirme Raporu.* https://www.ttb.org.tr/kutuphane/covid19-rapor_6/covid19-rapor_6_Part77.pdf, Pp. 1–11.

Çalişkan, Mustafa (Date Unspecified). "Türkiye'nin Rüzgar Enerjisi Potansiyeli". https://www.mgm.gov.tr/FILES/haberler/2010/retsseminer/2_Mustafa_CALISKAN_RITM.pdf (Access Date: 26.06.2021).

Capriolo, Manfredo, Marzoli, et al. (2020). "Deep CO_2 in the end-Triassic Central Atlantic Magmatic Province", *Nature Communications*, Vol: 11, No: 1670. https://doi.org/10.1038/s41467-020-15325-6, pp: 1–11.

Ceballos, Gerardo, Ehrlich, Paul, et al. (2015). "Accelerated modern human-induced specieslosses: Entering the sixth mass extinction", *Science Advances*, 19 Jun 2015: Vol. 1, No. 5, e1400253. https://doi.org/10.1126/sciadv.1400253, pp: 1–6.

Cities 100: Paris Renewed Plan Advances Climate Action (2016). https://www.c40.org/case_studies/cities100-paris-renewed-plan-advances-climate-action (Access Date: 19.06.2021).

CNCA (2021). "This is Not a Drill: How Communities Are Using the Climate Emergency to Make Big New Moves to Decarbonize Locally". http://carbonneutralcities.org/wp-content/uploads/2021/02/CNCA-Climate-Emergency-Report_This-Is-Not-a-Drill_Feb-2021.pdf (Access Date: 19.06.2021).

Delibalta, Feyza (2015). "Antropojen Kaynaklı Holosen Kitlesel Yok Oluşu: 6. Büyük Kitlesel Yok Oluşun İçerisindeyiz!". https://evrimagaci.org/antropojen-kaynakli-holosen-kitlesel-yok-olusu-6-buyuk-kitlesel-yok-olusun-icerisindeyiz-3715 (Access Date: 10.06.2021).

Demir, Başak and Ataöv, Anlı (2021). "Rüzgârdan Enerji Üretiminin Sosyo-Mekânsal Duyarlılık Alanları: İzmir Örneği", Planlama Dergisi-TMMOB, Şehir Plancıları Odası 31. https://doi.org/10.14744/planlama.2021.09226.

Elektrik Mühendisleri Odası-EMO-TMMOB (2021). "Enerji Bilgi Notu". https://www.emo.org.tr/ekler/914ffd4d04a8aab_ek.pdf (Access Date: 19.06.2021).

Elliot, David (2018). How close can cities get to 100% renewable energy? https://physicsworld.com/a/how-close-can-cities-get-to-100renewable-energy/ (Access Date: 19.06.2021).

Ermiş, Fevzi (2019). "Türkiye'de Rüzgar Enerjisi", İstanbul Üniversitesi Sosyal Bilimler Enstitüsü, Yayımlanmamış Yüksek Lisans Tezi, İstanbul.

Esteban, Miguel, and Leary, D. (2012). "Current developments and future prospects of offshore wind and ocean energy", *Applied Energy*, Vol: 90, No: 20121, pp: 128–136.

Geleceğe Dair Paris İklim Anlaşması (2019). https://www.avrupa.info.tr/sites/default/files/2016-08/brochure_4_v2.pdf (Access Date: 09.06.2021).

Global Carbon Budget (2020a). https://www.earth-system-science data.net/about/news_and_press/2020-12-11_global-carbon-budget-2020.html (Access Date: 08.04.2021).

Global Carbon Budget (2020b). https://www.earth-system-science-data.net/about/news_and_press/2020-12-11_global-carbon-budget-2020.html (Access Date: 08.04.2021).

Global Wind Energy Council-GWEC (2021). "Global Wind Report 2021". https://gwec.net/wp-content/uploads/2021/03/GWEC-Global-Wind-Report-2021.pdf (Access Date: 12.05.2021).

Gürbüz, Özgür (2021). "Güneş Cumhuriyeti", WWF. https://www.dunyasaati.org/2021/03/24/gunes-cumhuriyeti/ (Access Date: 26.06.2021).

Gyekye, Liz (2018). "Denmark Moves to Strengthen Renewable Energy Goals", https://www.windpowermonthly.com/article/1463710 (Access Date: 12.05.2021).

İklim, Haber (2021). "Atmosferdeki Karbondioksit Seviyeleri Rekor Seviyeye Ulaştı". https://www.iklimhaber.org/atmosferdeki-karbondioksit-seviyeleri-rekor-seviyeye-ulasti/ (Access Date: 08.04.2021).

International Renewable Energy Agency (IRENA) (2021). "*Tracking SDG7 The Energy Progress Report*". https://www.irena.org//media/Files/IRENA/Agency/Publication/2021/Jun/SDG7_Tracking_Progress_2021.pdf (Access Date: 12.05.2021), pp: 1–236.

IRENA (2015). "Smart Grids and Renewables". https://www.irena.org/-/media/Files/IRENA/Agency/Publication/2015/IRENA_PST_Smart_Grids_CBA_Guide_2015.pdf. (Access Date: 19.06.2021).

İstanbul Politikalar Merkezi- IPM (2021). "Türkiye'nin Yenilenebilir Enerjiyle, Enerji Arzının Güvence Altına Alınması". https://ipc.sabanciuniv.edu/Content/Images/CKeditorImages/20210623-19064168.pdf (Access Date: 12.05.2021).

Karakaya, Ethem (2019). "*Avrupa Yeşil Düzeni: Büyük Meydan Okuma ve Küresel Etkileri*" https://www.iklimhaber.org/avrupa-yesil-duzeni-buyuk-meydan-okuma-ve-kuresel-etkileri/ (Access Date: 09.06.2021).

Koç, Erdem and Kaya, K. (2015). "Enerji Kaynakları–Yenilenebilir Enerji Durumu," *Mühendis ve Makina*, Cilt 56, Sayı 668, pp. 36–47.

Mora, Camilio, et al. (2017). "Global Risk of Deadly Heat", Central Archive at the University of Reading Reading's research outputs online. http://dx.doi.org/10.1038/nclimate3322, pp: 1–14 (Access Date: 19.06.2021).

Nihai YEK Listesi.xlsx (2021). https://www.epdk.gov.tr/Detay/Icerik/3-0-0-122/yenilenebilir-enerji-kaynaklari-destekleme-mekanizmasi-yekdem (Access Date: 26.06.2021).

Özekicioğlu, Halil (2008). "Enerji ve Ekonomi İlişkisi Çerçevesinde Hidrojen Alternatifi: İzlanda ve Türkiye Uygulaması", İstanbul Üniversitesi Sosyal Bilimler Enstitüsü Yayımlanmamış Doktora Tezi, İstanbul.

Özgül, Sevim, et al. (2018). "Türkiye'de Yenilenebilir Enerji Kooperatiflerinin Mevcut Durumu". https://www.mmo.org.tr/sites/default/files/2%20 (Access Date: 19.06.2021).

REN 21 (2021). "Renewables 2021 Global Status Report". https://www.ren21.net/wp-content/uploads/2019/05/GSR2021_Full_Report.pdf (Access Date: 12.05.2021), pp: 1–371.

Şahin, Mustafa Ergin (2020). "Açık Deniz Rüzgâr Sistemleri Üzerine Bir İnceleme ve Danimarka Modeli", *Recep Tayyip Erdogan University Journal of Science and Engineering*, Vol: 1, No: 1, pp: 54–67.

SHURA Enerji Dönüşüm Merkezi (2018). "*Rüzgâr ve Güneş Türkiye'de EnerjiDönüşümü Nasıl Hızlandırabilir: Küresel Örnekler*". https://www.shura.org.tr/ruzgar-ve-gunes-turkiyede-enerji-donusumunu-nasil-hizlandirabilir-kuresel-ornekler/ (Access Date: 12.05.2021).

Sovaccol, Benjamin K. (2008). "Valuing the Greenhouse Gas Emissions from Nuclear Power: A Critical Survey", *Energy Policy*, Vol: 36, pp: 2940–2953.

Statistical Review of World Energy (2020). https://www.bp.com/content/dam/bp/business-sites/en/global/corporate/pdfs/energy-economics/statistical-review/bp-stats-review-2020-full-report.pdf, pp: 1–13 (Access Date: 11.06.2021).

T.C. Enerji ve Tabii Kaynaklar Bakanlığı-ETKB (2014). "T*ürkiye Ulusal Yenilenebilir Enerji Eylem Planı*". https://www.ebrd.com/documents/admin/trkye-ulusal-yenleneblr-enerj-eylem-plani.pdf (Access Date: 12.05.2021).

T.C. Enerji ve Tabii Kaynaklar Bakanlığı-ETKB (2019). "*2019–2023 Stratejik Plan*". https://sp.enerji.gov.tr/ETKB_2019_2023_Stratejik_Plani.pdf (Access Date: 12.05.2021).

T.C. Enerji ve Tabii Kaynaklar Bakanlığı-ETKB (2021). "Türkiye'de Rüzgar Enerjisi Kurulu Gücü". https://enerji.gov.tr/eigm-yenilenebilir-enerji-kaynaklar-ruzgar (Access Date: 09.06.2021).

Türkiye Elektrik İletim A.Ş.-TEİAŞ (2019). "*Türkiye'de Kurulu Gücün Yıllar itibariyle Değişimi*". https://www.teias.gov.tr/tr-TR/turkiye-elektrik-uretim-iletim-istatistikleri (Access Date: 12.05.2021).

Türkiye Elektrik İstatistikleri (2021). https://www.emo.org.tr/genel/bizden_detay.php?kod=88369 (Access Date: 09.06.2021).

Türkiye Elektrik Üretim (2021). https://www.enerjiatlasi.com/elektrik-uretimi/ (Access Date: 10.06.2021).

Türkiye Rüzgar Enerjisi Birliği (TÜREB) (2019). "Türkiye Rüzgar Enerjisi İstatistik Raporu" Temmuz 2019, Ankara.

Türkiye Rüzgar Enerjisi Birliği-TUREB (2021). "RES'lerin Bölgelere Göre Dağılımı". https://app.powerbi.com/view?r=eyJrIjoiNmFmYWY0MTYtNjUyNS00NzQ1LWIwMTMtOTI5ZTNkM2FlYWIxIiwidCI6ImU5YzY0NjU4LWFkMWQtNDUwOS1hODk0LTE2NWZhYjU2NjEyMyIsImMiOjl9 (Access Date: 19.06.2021).

Türkyilmaz, Oğuz and Bayrak, Yusuf (2020). "Türkiye'nin Enerji Görünümü Elektrik Üretimi: Mevut Durumu ve Analizi". https://www.mmo.org.tr/sites/default/files/TEG-20204.1_Elektrik%20%C3%9Cretimi_O%C4%9Fuz%20T%C3%BCrky%C4%B1lmaz%2BYusuf%20Bayrak%20_A.pdf (Access Date: 20.06.2021), pp: 1–30.

UEA University of East Anglia (2020). "COVID lockdown causes record drop in CO2 emissions for 2020", Release Date: 11.11.2020 (Access Date: 08.04.2021).

Ulusoy, Ahmet and Daştan, Ceyda Bayraktar (2018). "Yenilenebilir Enerji Kaynaklarına Yönelik Vergisel Teşviklerin Değerlendirilmesi", *HAK-İŞ Uluslararası Emek ve Toplum Dergisi*, Cilt: 7, Yıl: 7, Sayı: 17.

Uncu, Baran Alp (2019). "*İklim İçin Kentler: Yerel Yönetimler Eylem Planı*" https://world.350.org/iklimicinkentler/files/2019/05/350_booklet_2.pdf (Access Date: 22.05.2021).

University of East Anglia (2020). "COVID lockdown causes record drop in CO2 emissions for 2020". https://www.uea.ac.uk/news/-/article/covid-lockdown-causes-record-drop-in-co2-emissions-for-2020 (Access Date: 09.06.2021).

Wettengel, Julian (2018). "Citizens' participation in the energiewende". https://www.cleanenergywire.org/factsheets/citizens-participation-energiewende (Access Date: 19.06.2021).

World Energy Council Turkey (2020). "COVID19 2020'de Küresel Karbon Emisyonunda Rekor Düşüşe Yol Açtı". https://www.dunyaenerji.org.tr/covid19-2020de-kuresel-karbon-emisyonunda-rekor-dususe-yol-acti/ (Access Date: 09.06.2021).

WWF 10 Soruda HES (2013). https://www.wwf.org.tr/basin_bultenleri/raporlar/?1800/10sorudahes (Access Date: 12.05.2021).

Yetiş, Ülkü, et al. (2015). "Rüzgar Enerjisi Santralleri Raporu", Muğla Belediyesi.

3453 sayılı Cumhurbaşkanlığı Kararı 2021, R.G. 30.01.2021.

Merve Suna Özel Özcan

Rethinking Environment and Fossil Energy in COVID-19 Era

One of the most striking studies on environmental issues is Al Gore's "Inconvenient Truth " for which he won the Nobel Peace Prize. With this documentary, it has been revealed that global warming is an international problem. With this documentary that appeared in 2007, it can be said that environmental problems in the field of international relations became visible once again. In the face of the search for trust of international actors in the global arena, it is thought-provoking that we have encountered the coronavirus (Covid-19) epidemic, especially in recent years. Because in the system, it is seen that not only actors but also non-actor elements (pandemic, epidemic, earthquake, tsunami, etc.) affect international relations and states significantly. Like "Inconvenient Truth", we have to face with another global issues.

By 2020, besides the problems related to global warming and other environmental pollution, a new problem has emerged: Covid-19. Covid-19 is a diseases which suddenly emerge in China, and it spread all over the world. For centuries, diseases emerge as one of the security problems that human beings are faced with. In today's world, this situation shows itself again with Covid 19. The dimensions of the crisis created by Covid-19 on the global axis cause controversy in every sense. This has created the need for certain political steps to be avoided, not only on the basis of countries, but also globally. As it is known, the Covid-19 epidemic has created a great economic questioning against the market logic created by neo-liberalism and has put countries into crisis processes with health and environmental problems.

With the epidemic aspect carries matters directly to the mass death. Even terrorist attacks in the international arena or major global crises have not created such an intense perception of fear and threat. In this respect, Drezner (2020) stated that epidemics and politics are intertwined by their nature. According to him, this situation can be clearly seen in the progress of the process depending on the decisions of the political leaders. At the same time, a reflection of this emerges especially in the context of the policies of the states. Environmental policies, which will constitute our field of study within the scope of this study, is one of these policy areas.

Environment can be defined by defining a center. Here, people put themselves in the center. Herein environmental right is essentially a Human Right. The most important situation here is the protection of the environment and ensuring its continuity (Gemalmaz, 1987). Of course, it is also important to protect the ecological balance and accordingly the environment is suitable for human life. There are two different approaches to the global environment: cornucopians (Hornborg, 2003) and neo maltuhisans theories (Urdal, 2005). Among these approaches, cornucopia has a more positive approach, while neo malthusian approaches the environmental issue in a more pessimistic way. The Cornucopian view is that there are no adaptive and limited natural resources. It essentially rejects environmental boundaries (Dryzek, 2013, s. 52). Neo-Malthusians, on the other hand, argue that there are serious limits to growth and resourcs, and its focusing on pollution and environmental problems. In this respect, the approach focuses on environmental scarcity, limited agricultural and economic productivity. And it proceeds in a pessimistic picture, focusing on the problems of scarcity in the future (Urdal, 2005).

Despite such serious problems, can Covid-19 did conclude that the situation was not hopeless? The environmental issue has become one of the most important issues related to Covid-19. Despite all the negativities of Covid 19, there are important developments in the environmental problems. Although it is seen as simple, the decrease in hedgehog deaths in Poland or the decrease in the number of vehicles in the traffic (Huizen, 2021) can be seen as tiny steps of a certain change in the system in a sense. Individuals, states or systems can not exist without a healthy environment, so the effects of Covid 19 should be handled with a high level of security perception lately. We can see pandemic affects on security fields which not only environmental and health problems but also in Energy sectors. In addition to lockdown, Covid 19 has perhaps given us an advantage in terms of environmental problems. In this process, there was less carbon dioxide (CO_2) emission in the earth, people did not drive every day. In a sense, some steps to be achieved with the Kyoto protocol have taken place during the pandemic process. So, this study will be focused on energy consumption and environment.

In order to provide limitation in the study, I will focus on fossil fuels to understand the energy-environment relationship. There are environmental problems depending on energy consumption. In this study, the relationship between energy and environment during the pandemic period will be examined. From this point of view, the impact of the pandemic in the fields of energy and environment will be examined. Also, I will focus on air polutions and carbondioxide (CO_2) emissions . Beside aimed to create a short future vision. In this context, the main question in the study is whether this creates a win-win effect, especially in the context of environmental factors.

Energy and Overview of Fossil Fuel

According to the paradigm that sees nature as a mechanical machine rather than a living system, energy is the capacity to do work (Shiva, 2015, s. Introduction). As I mentioned in the introduction, energy sources are diverse. The situation here presents us an example in terms of the usage and consumption area of fuels. In this respect, we come across fossil and renewable energy types. In fact, although renewable energy is more advantageous than fossil energy sources, it can be seen as an important alternative among disadvantaged countries that do not have fossil energy sources in the system. Fossil energy sources are coal, crude oil, natural gas and nuclear fuel, which have been used as traditional energy sources since the past. These energy sources also appear as non-renewable energy sources that are depleted simultaneously. Natural gas, petroleum and coal, which stand out among the energy resources in this group, contain carbon (CO_2). They were formed as a result of geological processes. These non-renewable fuels constitute about 80 % of the world's energy and this energy is used in all sectors including industry and households, especially in fields such as electricity, heat and transportation (Nunez, 2019).

One of the areas where the effects of Covid-19 started to make itself felt in all areas of life since the beginning of 2020 has been the energy sector. It can be said that energy started to become one of the prominent areas in the international arena, albeit slowly, at the end of the 19th century. While the energy needs of the countries have increased with industrialization, the orientation to alternative areas has simultaneously revealed the search for alternative areas.The discovery of fossil fuels have had a big effect on development of technology. Also we can see its effects on environment.

Especially with the rapid developments in the field of technology and industry in the 20th century, the needs of developed countries have an important place in energy consumption. Considering the world wars or global crisis periods, it is seen that the speed of change in the fields of use of energy simultaneously becomes an important factor affecting the international system. Flavin and Dunn (1999) pointed out that the energy system is undergoing a major transformation and compared it to a kind of glasnost and perestroika transformation similar to that seen in the economic and political systems of the Soviet Union. According to them, the pre-millennium energy paradigm shift has also been the source of an important shift for the international system regarding both familiar

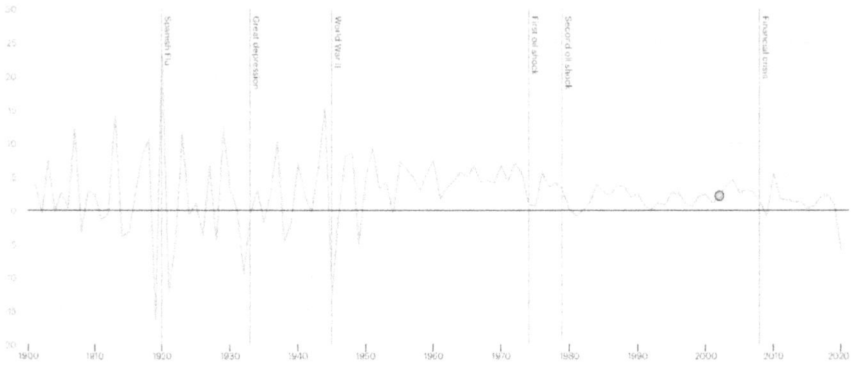

Tab. 1: Rate of change of global primary energy demand, 1900–2020.
Source: (IEA, 2020)

and new security threats, such as dependence on imported oil and climate destabilization (Flavin & Dunn, 1999).

It is important to reconsider the impacts on the environment and climate change within the Covid-19 process. Because there is a decrease in energy consumption in this period. Changes in energy consumption between 1900 and 2020 showed a remarkable decrease and increase, especially during crisis periods. These results can be seen in Tab. 1. If it is necessary to make a comparison at the point of the data in the table, we can look at the crises experienced in the last 2000s. Even in the 2008 economic global crisis, the energy consumption rate was less than the effect of Covid-19. This situation shows us that when the theoretical framework or historical background of energy security is considered, new problems have entered the field with the developments and globalization in the 21st century. The issue to be considered here is security.

The issue of energy security includes different elements as well as the context of states' power capacities. In terms of energy security, Yergin draws attention to the fact that the concept is an abstract concept (Yergin, 2011). Although significant progress has been made in terms of conceptualization until the 21st century, it can be said that the concept of Energy Security emerged with the establishment of the IEA (Scott, 1974). The main reason for this is that the needs of producer and consumer countries are not the same. In addition, threats and crises are also important in terms of energy security for producer and consumer countries (Fig. 1). This can be man-made or natural causes, as well as threats to the System (Gundel, 2005). While internal and external security threats are

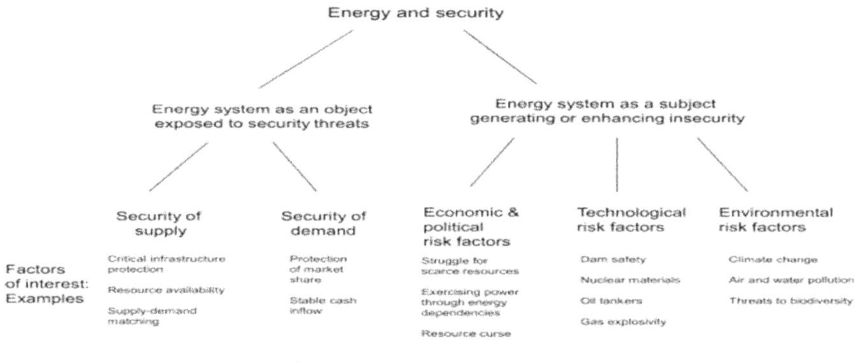

Fig. 1: The analytical structure used in this paper to study the relations between energy and security. Source: (Johansson, 2013, p. 200)

especially important, natural disasters and pandemics can also be considered as important topics at this security point (Johansson, 2013).

Basically, there are 4 factors related to energy. The first is the physical element. In other words, it is a problem of fossil fuels having a source and the right geopolitical basis. The second point is the cost of production. The costs and profits in accessing the resource are important for its inclusion in the system. For example, when the global oil price rises, drilling in many more difficult-to-reach places can also become profitable. The third point is technology. As mentioned before, although technology is the most important part of life, it is also effective in the field of energy to the extent that it provides ease of use and transportation. Indeed, the last factor is political developments. Developments such as war and internal conflict on a regional or global basis significantly affect the formation of resources and supply. In the Covid-19 process, the conceptualization of energy security is mostly based on the change in the supply-demand relationship in terms of production and use.

With the pandemic, many countries in the world have started to implement a closure policy. Of course, this policy has affected many areas, especially the industrial sector in developing and developed countries. In this context, the demand for oil among energy sources has also decreased. This decline and the stagnation in the oil market have reached such a level that oil exporting countries have received an unprecedented double blow. As a result of a global economic contraction caused by the COVID-19 epidemic, the oil market collapsed and in April 2020, for the first time in history, negative values were seen in oil prices, albeit for a short time ("The impact of Coronavirus…", 2020). Of course, this is only seen as the economic dimension of the process. Its impact on the environment may not be seen as such negative.

Environment and International Environmental Regimes

With the increase of many environmental problems such as pollution and natural destruction, people and states have begun to feel the need to approach the ecological system more carefully. The biggest consequence of environmental problems is undoubtedly climate Change (Shiva, 2015) and the destruction of the ozone layer. If the Covid 19 pandemic is taken as a milestone, certain elements will come to the fore in the relationship between energy and environment. In this respect, considering the pre-pandemic process, the carbon dioxide (CO_2) effect on the climate and soil is important. The main problem here is the use of energy resources and the problems created by these resources.

Starting from this short introduction, certain definitions of environmental problems should be included. The first thing to answer is what carbon dioxide gas is. Carbon dioxide is a greenhouse gas that absorbs and emits heat. So what greengases meanning. According to United Nations Framework Convention On Climate Change; "*"Greenhouse gases" means those gaseous constituents of the atmosphere, both natural and anthropogenic, that absorb and re-emit infrared radiation* (United Nations, 1992)". Thus greenhouse gases absorb this heat, but increases in greenhouse gases have upset the Earth's energy balance and raised the Earth's average temperature. In fact, the last time atmospheric CO_2 amounts were this high was more than 3 million years ago, when sea level was 15–25 meters (50–80 feet) higher than today. As seen in the Graphic 1, the change over time is increasing, especially in the post-industrial period. Thus, increases in atmospheric carbon dioxide today are responsible for about two-thirds of the total energy imbalance that is causing the Earth's temperature to rise (Lindsey, 2020). In fact, it is seen that the first research on climate change and global warming was made in the 19th century. In 1896, Svante Arrhenius published a study on the warming of the earth's surface. He was predicting how much the earth's surface would warm from changing concentrations of atmospheric carbon dioxide (Michaels, 2005, p. 14). Today, we see this prediction come true.

In addition to the destruction of carbon gas in the atmosphere, the environmental problem has always been one of the important issues. From this point environmental issue is not only one of the important agendas of today's international relations. Approximately 3621 environmental agreements were signed from 1800 to 2021. Some are bilateral and some are multilateral agreements. The first agreement in history is "Treaty between Britain and France concerning

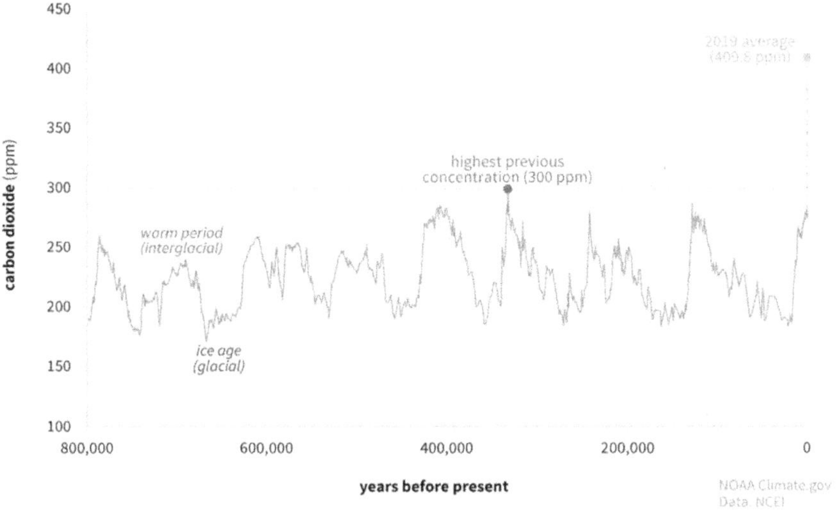

Graphic 1: Carbon dioxide over 800,000 years. Source: (Lindsey, 2020)

Access Rights to the American North Atlantic"[1], which was signed bilaterally in 1713. Therefore, it is possible to say that the problems in the atmosphere and the environment were noticed centuries ago. The destructive effect of this situation on an ecosystem surrounding the whole world, and therefore on the climate system, has led the states to take measures regarding the issue in the international arena.

The complex nature of environmental questions makes them borderless and nationalistic. At this point, we should see especially environmental problems as problems that concern the entire globe. The fact that it consists of interconnected problems necessitates the joint actions of the states, especially the interdependence that exists in the liberal approach. Because the environment is directly binding on states and the roles of international actors in the system. In addition, attention should be paid to environmental regulations regarding international regimes.[2] The term "regime" is sometimes used in a purely descriptive way.

1 Members: United Kingdom and France .

2 The debate between the competitive and zero-sum "anarchy" of international relations and the "authority" of domestic politics reveals in the system. This debate created by the interdependence, especially in international arena since the Second World War, have produced new forms of coordination and organization. The analysis of the

According to Krasner's (1982) accepted definition in the field of international relations; The explicit or implicit principles, norms, rules, and decision-making procedures in which the expectations of actors in a field converge (Krasner, 1982). Some of the international environmental regimes are based on prohibitive principles, while others are regulatory. The main problem here, whether prohibition or violation of regulations, is actually what the sanctions will be in case of non-compliance with the principles. Moreover, the sanctions for today are almost non-existent. Today, many international and regional organizations have initiatives to give importance to environmental problems. Organizations such as the United Nations, European Union, Organization for Economic Co-operation and Development, European Security and Cooperation Organization, World Bank, World Trade Organization, Food and Agriculture Organization, WHO (World Health Organization) are the leading ones (Sönmezoğlu & Bayır, 2021, pp. 248, 250).

The first example of multilateral participation of states in the international arena regarding environmental problems is the United Nations Stockholm Environment and Human Conference in 1972. This is the first important step towards seeking solutions to environmental problems at the international level. The Stockholm Declaration, contained 26 principles. Also according to The Action Plan there were 3 main categories: (a) *Global Environmental Assessment Program (watch plan)*; (b) *Environmental management activities*; (c) *International measures to support assessment and management activities carried out at the national and international levels* (United Nations, n.d.). This conference was convened with the slogan "Only One Earth" and subsequently The United Nations Environment Program (UNEP) was established. UNEP categorize their work into seven broad thematic areas: (i) *climate change*, (ii) *disasters and conflicts*, (iii) *ecosystem management*, (iv) *environmental governance*, (v) *chemicals and waste*, (vi) *resource efficiency, and* (vii) *environment under review* (UNEP, n.d.). Although these areas focus directly on environmental problems, it is important that a study area has been created on diseases such as covid 19. Because diseases, in a sense, are related to the environment and environmental problems.

International Regime is neither as broad as the international structure nor as narrow as the study of official organizations. The literature of regimes thus creates a space that reconciles idealist and realist traditions (Levy, Young, & Zürn, 1995). So in this study, the details and theoretical development of international regimes will not be included. For detailed information on the subject, see (Haggard & Simmons, 1987).

The UN Conference on Environment and Development held in Rio de Janeiro in 1992 has an important place in the development of UNEP. There has been an increasing awareness of the environment in the 1990s. The emergence of the Kyoto Protocol and the steps to create sustainable environmental awareness are remarkable. Again, the World Sustainable Development Summit held in Johannesburg in 2002 is important in this context. The transfer of environmental problems to the international arena has been thanks to the United Nations. In the context of sustainable development and environment, organizations such as the EU, WTO, WB, WHO, WMO emerge. However, according to Sönmezoğlu and Bayındır the environmental policies of these organizations have no direct sanction. Instead, it is tried to influence the behavior of the members of the organization regarding environmental problems (Sönmezoğlu & Bayır, 2021, p. 250).

Also On 21 March 1994 The UNFCCC entered into force and it has 197 members. These countries that have ratified the Convention are called Parties to the Convention which preventing "dangerous" human interference with the climate system (UNFCCC, n.d.). On the other hand, the most important environmental step we should mention is the Kyoto Protocol. Although it has been mentioned in the study from time to time, this Protocol focuses on climate change. In this sense, the Kyoto Protocol is the only important and only framework for dealing with and dealing with global warming and climate change issues. The protocol was signed within the United Nations Framework Convention on Climate Change in Kyoto in 1997 (UNFCCC, 2021). The Kyoto Protocol entered into force on 16 February 2005 and there are 192 Parties to the Kyoto Protocol.

On the other hand, actors who draw attention to environmental problems and seek solutions in the international arena are not only international organizations. The activities of international companies regarding environmental problems also draw attention. One such example is Exxon. Exxon has started to work on global climate and environmental problems since the 1970s. In this regard, Exxon has hired scientists to develop climate models. In 1982, the company even began creating programs and models with its own scientists to assess the impact of emissions on global temperatures. Exxon's research laid the foundation for an institutional book on carbon dioxide and climate change in 1982 (Banerjee, John H. Cushman, Hasemyer, & Song, 2015). Beside, British Petroleum's publishes annual reports on the environment. With these Sustainability reports, BP aims to *help the world reach net zero and improve people's lives* (British Petroleum, 2019) it should be included.

COVID-19 and Its Effects on Environment and Energy

The diseases and epidemics historically, one of the earliest examples appears in the Greek city of Athens in the summer of 430 BC. According to the Athenian historian Thucydides, this epidemic first affected the neighboring port region (Piraeus) and then moved to the centers. The epidemic was seen in the Athenian military forces in the years 430–427, and spread as much as Rome in later years. In this epidemic, 25–35 % of the population of Athens died (Hays, 2005). This is a high number when looking at the subject in the context of city states. The main issue in the context of coronavirus, it is seen as one of the most serious problems we encounter in the 21st century. This virus, which emerged in Wuhan, China, has become a global epidemic in a short time. And the world has begun to close rapidly. The World Health Organization (WHO) confirmed that this virus started to spread from person to person on January 22, 2020, and declared Covid-19 a global pandemic on March 11, 2020. Although most of the countries affected by the virus have gone to a nationwide closure to minimize the spread of the virus, it was not possible to see the extent of the first stage outbreak.

From the realistic approach pandemics are a crucial security problem for state. The problem in the context of security should not be considered only in the field of manpower and related defense. Especially in the context of Covid-19, it can be said that there is a safety problem in the field of hygiene and health. Especially the mask wars with Covid-19 are remarkable. In the first months of the pandemic, a global struggle for medical equipment such as masks and gloves has also started. Although there have been cases where the world has seen the north-south distinction again, especially depending on the purchasing power of developed countries, it has been observed that developed countries have also committed "modern piracy" against each other (Lister, Shukla, & Bobille, 2020). In this context, Covid-19 has been a process that has raised security problems for the EU as well as all over the world. However, this problem creates a security problem in the context of environmental problems and policies affecting the earth, not just the countries individually.

The connection of the health field with the environment and therefore energy makes it more prominent in security perceptions. In this respect, it can be said that a security problem has emerged within the health-environment-energy triangle with Covid-19. This situation draws more attention in the context of the limited resource perception of the neo-malthusian approach, especially in environmental approaches. Because after a while, states can produce policies with a more realistic approach rather than cooperation within the perception of security.

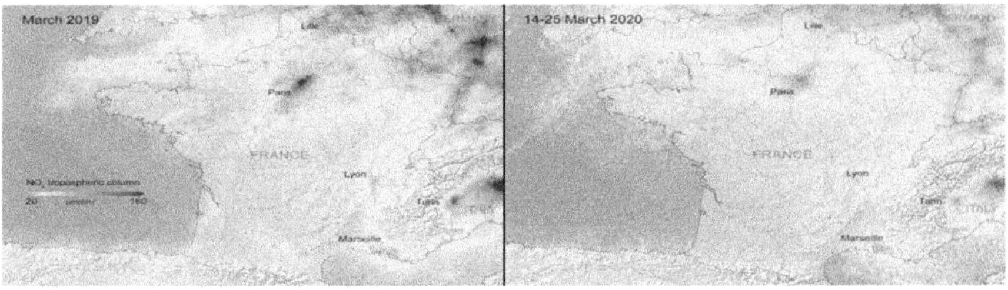

Picture 1: Coronavirus lockdown leading to drop in pollution across Europe.
Source: (NASA, 2020)

Since the impact of Covid-19 as a security problem is limited to the environment and energy, I will continue from these two areas. The COVID-19 pandemic led to restrictions that reduced pollutions. Because of the most countries shut down schools and businesses, and halted some industrial activity we could see a cleaner sky. So, what happened to the environment? PM 2.5[3] is a particle matter which refers to air pollution and these particles, contribute to their secondary formation in the atmosphere, as a *coal-burning power plants, industrial activities, waste burning, and many other human and natural sources* (The State of Global Air, 2020). The purpose of addressing the issue of air pollution is that more than 6.67 million deaths in 2019 were associated with this risk group. It is the 4th leading risk factor for premature death globally in 2019, accounting for approximately 12 % of all deaths (The State of Global Air, 2020).

According to NASA datas, in Picture 1 lockdowns leading to drop in pollution across Europe (NASA, 2020). It is important that this development took place in a very short time. The fact that this decrease is seen only in the European Continent is a more hopeful situation in the whole world.

Real-time estimates of carbon (CO_2) dioxide emissions aren't readily available. Because they often come with a 1- or 2-year delay acording to climate and other measurements. In most countries, there has been a lockdown and in 2020 traveling by plane has dropped by about 96 % (Wallace, 2020). With maximum quarantine experienced at the beginning of the pandemic, land transport activities decreased by half, aviation by three quarters and electricity generation by

3 "*Air pollution exposures, including exposure to outdoor PM2.5 and household air pollution, have been linked to increased hospitalizations, disability, and early death from respiratory diseases, heart disease, stroke, lung cancer, and diabetes, as well as communicable diseases like pneumonia* (The State of Global Air, 2020).

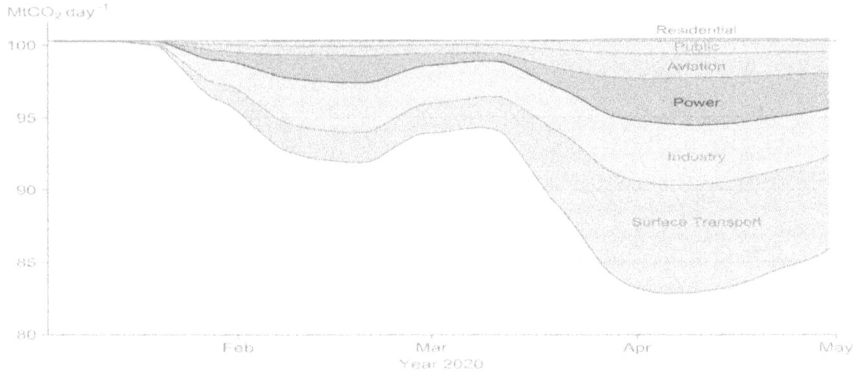

Graphic 2: Global daily fossil (CO_2) emissions. Source: (Global Carbon Project, 2020)

15 %. The reflection of this was manifested in a 17 % decrease in daily carbon (CO_2) emissions (Jackson, 2020).

Positive developments in air pollution and the effect of carbon emission in global warming have decreased recently. Short-term measures are likely to have long-term consequences, as seen in the graph and picture. The measures taken in the fight against Covid-19 have enabled people and states to take the measures they want to take on the environment for many years. With these developments, the decline in the energy markets has actually revealed results that reduce the consumption of fossil fuels. In fact, it is seen that the effect of the pandemic is not unidirectional. There are slightly more positive consequences for the environment. But does the same apply to energy? Because the decrease in energy demand experienced with the pandemic has increased the search for renewable energy in the fossil fuel sector. In this respect, it can be said that the fossil fuel sector has been seriously hit by the effect of the pandemic. Moreover, the decline in oil barrel prices in April 2020 cannot be ignored.

The global oil price became more and more volatile after the crisis in the 1970s. Increasing demand, especially in developing countries, has a significant impact here. The impact of the current COVID-19 pandemic took everyone by surprise, and the benchmark for US crude turned negative for the first time at the end of April. According to the OECD report, low oil prices affected not only buyer countries but also oil-selling countries economically. That's because many oil exporting countries had high debt levels at the start of the COVID-19 pandemic (OECD, 2020).

The long-term adequacy of the energy supply was questioned, with the limited availability of fossil fuels and especially their environmental impact. The costs of carbon dioxide emissions in developing countries can also significantly change the economic outlook of energy resources (Naderipour et al., 2020). In addition to the price drop in the global energy market, the significant impact of the Covid-19 outbreak has been in the renewable energy sector. Because in this period, there are imbalances in supply-demand relations due to the closures. This caused a serious decrease in energy demand due to the epidemic (Eroğlu, 2020). Of course, the decrease in transportation together with the restrictions has created a decrease in consumption since the beginning of 2020.

Electricity demand fell as services under lockdown and industry shut down. In June and July, it was 10 % and 5 % below the same month's 2019 level, respectively, in most countries other than India, with the shutdown and reduced containment. Also in China, electricity demand dropped with confinement measures and it reached – 11 % low in February 2020. The decrease in electricity consumption is important for the reduction in fossil fuel use (IEA, 2021). In addition, the search for renewable energy sources among the countries that turn to alternative energy needs during the lockdown period is remarkable. This is especially a contribution of Covid-19 to the connection of fossil fuels and environmental problems.

At this point, it is seen that especially energy-owning countries are faced with major economic problems in the field of energy. According to the OECD report, countries should diversify away from fossil fuel revenues and carbon-intensive industries in this period. This is essential for long-term recovery (OECD, 2020). Therefore, the energy sector is in search of a compulsory alternative. According to Eroğlu, in Energy sector Covid-19 has caused the sharpest decline of nearly 30 years globally. And it caused new reseach in renewable energy supply. In this period, if the countries are far from their goals in the search for clean energy, it is likely that there will be a serious decrease in clean energy investments and a domino effect (Eroğlu, 2020).

Conclusion

With the Covid-19 pandemic, states have gone into lockdown in the international arena, in a sense, they have indirectly realized this lockdown in many areas of life, in a sense, commercial, cultural, social. Like many epidemics and pandemics in history, the impact of COVID-19 deeply affects world politics. During the pandemic, the methods and patterns followed by the actors in the international system have also begun to change. All around the world people and countries lockedown and it limited freedom. Also Covid-19 causes people to have limited social life although it shows that the environmental problems can be solve. According to the State of Global Air *actions to restrict the spread of COVID-19 offered only a temporary solution, inspiring renewed demands for cleaner air in the longer term* (The State of Global Air, 2020). And also it shows that the air polutions level.

For the energy sector, the Covid-19 pandemic has disrupted the supply-demand balance and created instability. However, this situation creates an advantage regarding environmental problems. Therefore, despite the decrease in air pollution here, the fact of the economic crisis in the energy market is obvious. This situation can support win-win scenarios regarding environmental problems in terms of human history. In this respect, perhaps more environmental problems such as cornucopians can be approached positively. However, the situation in terms of the energy sector, unfortunately, does not have the same positive scenario. The effect of this situation on the environment is thought-provoking. The question we need to ask: While it has been seen that problems such as closures and air pollution can decrease in Covid-19, how much will this be tolerated in the capital world? As a result, do the capital owners want to see the blue sky like us?

References

Banerjee, N., John, H., Cushman, J., Hasemyer, D., & Song, L. (2015). *Exxon: The Road Not Taken.* InsideClimate News.

British Petroleum. (2019). *BP Sustainability Report 2019.* Retrieved from https://www.bp.com/content/dam/bp/business-sites/en/global/corporate/pdfs/sustainability/group-reports/bp-sustainability-report-2019.pdf

Drezner, D. (2020). The Song Remains the Same: International Relations After COVID-19. *International Organization*, 1–18. doi:10.1017/S0020818320000351

Dryzek, J. (2013). *The Politics of the Earth: Environmental Discourses.* Oxford: Oxford University Press.

Eroğlu, H. (2020). Effects of Covid-19 outbreak on environment and renewable energy sector. *Environment, Development and Sustainability*, 1–9. Retrieved from https://www.ncbi.nlm.nih.gov/pmc/articles/PMC7321016/pdf/10668_2020_Article_837.pdf

Flavin, C., & Dunn, S. (1999). A New Energy Paradigm for the 21st Century. *Journal of International Affairs*, *53*(1), 167–190.

Gemazlmaz, M. S. (1987). Bir İnsan Hakkı Olarak Çevre Hakkı Ve Türk Düzenlemesi. *İstanbul Üniversitesi Hukuk Fakültesi Mecmuası, 52*(1–4), 233–278.

Global Carbon Project. (2020). Retrieved from https://www.globalcarbonproject.org/global/images/general/TemporaryReductionInCO2EmissionsDuringCOVID-19_Emissions_timeseries_sectors_stacked.full.png

Gundel, S. (2005). Towards a new typology of crises. *Journal of Contingencies and Crisis Management*, *3*, 106–115.

Haggard, S., & Simmons, B. A. (1987). Theories of regime. *International Organization*, *41*(3), 491–517.

Hays, J. N. (2005). *Epidemics and Pandemics: Their Impacts on Human History.* California: ABC Clio.

Hornborg, A. (2003). Cornucopia or Zero-Sum Game? The Epistemology of Sustainability. *Journal of World-System Reseach*, *9*(2), 205–216.

Huizen, J. (2021, 22 April). *How COVID-19 has changed the face of the natural world.* Retrieved from https://www.medicalnewstoday.com/articles/how-covid-19-has-changed-the-face-of-the-natural-world

IEA. (2020). *Global energy and CO2 emissions in 2020.* https://www.iea.org/reports/global-energy-review-2020/global-energy-and-co2-emissions-in-2020#abstract adresinden alındı

IEA. (2021). *Covid-19 impact on electricity.* Retrieved from https://www.iea.org/reports/covid-19-impact-on-electricity

IEADB Agreement List. (2021). Retrieved from https://iea.uoregon.edu/base-agreement-list?combine=&field_inclusion_value=All&sig_year%5Bmin%5D=1800&sig_year%5Bmax%5D=2021&mitch_id=&field_lineage_value=

Jackson, R. (2020, May 19). *COVID-19 Could Permanently Transform Transportation.* Retrieved from https://blogs.scientificamerican.com/observations/covid-19-could-permanently-transform-transportation/

Johansson, B. (2013). A broadened typology on energy and security. *Energy*, *53*, 199–205.

Krasner, S. D. (1982). Structural causes and regime consequences: Regimes as intervening variables. *International Organization*, *36*(2), 185–205.

Levy, M., Young, O. R., & Zürn, M. (1995). The study of international regimes. European Journal of International Relations. *1*(3), 267–330.

Lindsey, R. (2020, August 14). *Climate Change: Atmospheric Carbon Dioxide.* Retrieved from https://www.climate.gov/news-features/understanding-climate/climate-change-atmospheric-carbon-dioxide

Lister, T., Shukla, S., & Bobille, F. (2020). *Coronavirus sparks a 'war for masks' in desperate global scramble for protection.* Retrieved from https://edition.cnn.com/2020/04/04/europe/coronavirus-masks-war-intl/index.html

Michaels, P. J. (2005). *Meltdown: The Predictable Distortion of Global Warming by Scientists, Politicians, and the Media.* Washington: Cato Institute.

Naderipour, A., Abdul-Malek, Z., Ahmad, N. A., Kamyab, H., Ashokkumar, V., Ngamcharussrivichai, C., & Chelliapan, S. (2020). Effect of COVID-19 virus on reducing GHG emission and increasing energy generated by renewable energy sources: A. *Environmental Technology & Innovation*, *20*, 1–8.

NASA. (2020, March 27). *Coronavirus lockdown leading to drop in pollution across Europe.* Retrieved from https://airquality.gsfc.nasa.gov/news/coronavirus-lockdown-leading-drop-pollution-across-europe

Nunez, C. (2019, April 2). *Fossil fuels, explained.* Retrieved from https://www.nationalgeographic.com/environment/article/fossil-fuels

OECD. (2020). *The impact of coronavirus (COVID-19) and the global oil price shock on the fiscal position of oil-exporting developing countries.* Retrieved from https://www.oecd.org/coronavirus/policy-responses/the-impact-of-coronavirus-covid-19-and-the-global-oil-price-shock-on-the-fiscal-position-of-oil-exporting-developing-countries-8bafbd95/#figure-d1e229

Scott, R. (1974). *Origins and Structure.* Paris: International Energy Agency.

Shiva, V. (2015). *Soil Not Oil: Environmental Justice in an Age of of Climate Crisis.* California: North Atlantic Books.

Sönmezoğlu, F., & Bayır, Ö. E. (2021). Çevre Sorunlarına İlişkin Uluslararası Rejimler. *İ.Ü. Siyasal Bilgiler Fakültesi Dergisi*, *47*, 247–289.

The State of Global Air. (2020a). *A Specıal Report on Global Exposure to Aır Pollutıon and Its Health Impacts.* Retrieved from https://www.stateofglobalair.org/

The State of Global Air. (2020b). *Air Pollution's Impact on Health: A Global Snapshot.* Retrieved from https://www.stateofglobalair.org/

UNEP. (n.d.). *Why Does UN Environment Programme matter?* Retrieved August 1, 2021, from https://www.unep.org/about-un-environment/why-does-un-environment-matter

UNFCCC. (2021). *What is the Kyoto Protocol?* Retrieved August 01, 2021, from https://unfccc.int/kyoto_protocol

UNFCCC. (n.d.). *What is the United Nations Framework Convention on Climate Change?* Retrieved August 01, 2021, from https://unfccc.int/process-and-meetings/the-convention/what-is-the-united-nations-framework-convention-on-climate-change

United Nations. (1992). *United Nations Framework Convention on Climate Change.*

United Nations. (n.d.). *United Nations Conference on the Environment, 5–16 June 1972, Stockholm.* Retrieved August 01, 2021, from https://www.un.org/en/conferences/environment/stockholm1972

Urdal, H. (2005). People vs. Malthus: Population pressure, environmental degradation, and armed conflict revisited. *Journal of Peace Research, 42*(4), 417–434.

Wallace, G. (2020, April 9). *Airlines and TSA report 96% drop in air travel as pandemic continues.* Retrieved from https://edition.cnn.com/2020/04/09/politics/airline-passengers-decline/index.html

Yergin, D. (2011). *The Quest: Energy, Security, and the Remaking of the Modern World.* New York: The Penguin Press.

Kadir Caner Doğan

Ombudsman as an Actor in Environmental Governance: A Conceptual Introduction

1. Governance and Ombudsman

Although the origin of the concept of governance is traced back to the descriptions of good and bad governance in the works of the Italian painter Lorenzetti in the middle of the 14th century, the concept was used for the first time in its current meaning in the report "Sub-Saharan Africa: From Crisis to Sustainable Growth" prepared by the World Bank (WB) in 1989. In the report, it was stated that the main reason for the development problems in Africa is the governance crisis. The report also states that economic prosperity cannot be achieved without a minimum level of law and democracy (Kalkışım, 2019: 20).

The concept of governance is derived from the word "management" in terms of word naming. But, with its philosophy, it is far away from its traditional meaning which is focused on making decisions at the center alone and performing them. Governance refers to a new process of the governing process, the change in rule-making conditions, and a new method of governing society, unlike the classical sense of government. Governance refers to a multi-centered structure, and autonomy of units based on participation in decision-making and application instead of hierarchical relation (Doğan, 2017: 270).

In organizational sense, governance is defined as "the organizational activities in which people empowered for the perfect realization of organizational goals act by putting their common interests before their personal interests, adopt communication and effective information sharing, mutual trust and transparency, make joint decisions, have high emotional intelligence, are empathetic, proactive and act synergistically" (Fidan, 2010/2011: 6–7).

Among the governance principles, the following are generally shown in the literature (Özer, 2006: 79–81):

- Transparency,
- Accountability,
- Participation,
- Responsiveness,
- Rule of law,
- Effectiveness,

- Equality,
- Strategic vision.

Ombudsman is a Swedish word and first appeared in Sweden in history (Doğan and Uğur, 2018: 181) and in Swedish language, it means ambassador, lawyer, deputy, person authorized to act on behalf of a person in the relations between the king and the public. In this context, ombudsman can be expressed as "protector of people and defender of the interests" in Swedish language. Considering the origin of the word, the word ombudsman is a compound word formed by the combination of the words "ombuds" and "man". In this compound word, "ombuds" means spokesperson, representative, delegate; "man" means that it is a person. In this direction, it can be said that the word ombudsman briefly means "the person who is the representative of the people" (Doğan, 2016: 42).

Ombudsman carries out activities for the supervision of the bureaucracy (public administration) and for the protection of the citizens from the damages they have suffered related to the administration. In this context, ombudsman is an institution that examines the complaints and problems of the citizens against the administration and supervises the administration on behalf of the citizen, and in a sense, acts as the lawyer of citizen against the administration. On the other hand, ombudsman activates political and public opinion supervision mechanism to carry out activities within the judicial rules of public administration and criteria of justice. Generally, supervision mechanism of ombudsman institution acts according to legislative department considering aims of execution, and carry outs its functions with the power given by legislative department. However, it absolutely acts independently of legislative department (Doğan, 2015: 147).

In general, the aim of an ombudsman is to lead the state to base citizen satisfaction while providing public services. Therefore, ombudsman is closely related to total quality management and performance evaluation which people have attempted to apply and have been a fashionable concept in recent years. In service delivery, increasing the quality, providing the service from a single source according to its quality, providing service in close relationship with the citizen and in accordance with their views and expectations are among the basic priorities. At this point, transparency, accountability, responsibility and fairness are the first things desired in the quality of public service. Ombudsman institution plays an extremely active and decisive role in the implementation of these principles, which are also called governance principles (Doğan, 2017: 280).

2. Environmental Governance

The environment is the sum of the physical, chemical, biological and social factors that may have an immediate or a later, indirect or direct effect on human activities and living beings (Baykal, 2010: 477). Environment is nature, which includes all living and non-living beings on the earth. It includes the biological, physical, chemical, economic, social and cultural environments that make up the life spaces of all living things, especially humans, animals and plants, and enable them to interact and communicate with each other (Yilmaz Ugur, 2021: 298). At the same time, it is all of the external factors that affect all living and non-living beings. The environment, which provides the conditions for the existence of an organism, is something that has formed natural habitats since the first living creature appeared on earth. Environment and life are two concepts that complement each other and interact at every moment. Any habitat that "is home to" living things such as air, water, soil, oceans, seas, lakes, rivers, streams, mountains, hills, valleys, plains, forests, cities, villages, neighborhoods, houses, parks, fields and wetlands, forms the environment (https://www.makaleler.com/cevre-nedir). However, the mechanism in natural environment is according to the laws of nature. Such a balance has been established in this process that nature can react to interventions made from outside in violation of this law. Problems with climate change, floods, decrease in biodiversity and drought are some of them. This and similar disasters are caused by misuse of nature (https://www.demokrasi.gen.tr/dogal-cevrenin-korunmasi/).

Every area on the earth that we see with our eyes and everything belonging to nature can be defined as "environment". The environment has been seen as a resource by people for years. It has been used unlimitedly, and as a result of this unlimited consumption, environmental problems have started to emerge (Bozkurt, 2014: 62). Continuously developing technologies have also increased the consumption of raw materials. Considering nature as a source of raw materials is among the main reasons for the destruction of the environment. Today, the constantly increasing human population and the consumption of natural resources, which increase in parallel with this issue, have brought a global dimension to environmental problems (Bek, 2019: 37). Today, environmental problems have increased in recent years and national countries have increasingly understood the seriousness of this issue (Yıldız and Yılmaz, 2015: 103). The reason for this is that environmental problems threaten human life everywhere, without borders. In recent years, climate changes in the world, increasing temperatures, melting of glaciers, storms and change in natural vegetation have caused many countries to act together in the international arena, and such situations threatening the environment have been accepted as global problems rather than international problems. With the effect of globalization, environmental problems started to be discussed internationally in the 70s and 80s, and the United Nations environment and human conference was held in Stockholm for the first time, and environmental problems were discussed on a global scale (Baykal and Baykal, 2008: 2; Uğur, 2019: 85–86). As a matter of fact, globalization, as a process, not only offers new opportunities to humanity, but also causes new problems to emerge. Environmental problems come first among these problems. The ecological balance, which is deteriorated as a natural result of environmental problems, threatens the lives of humans and other living things. Humans' use of nature in a measureless way, forcing their inner dynamics and consuming more and more, causes the environment to suffer from these developments. Along with industrialization, growth efforts in the world economy, excessive production and consumption, unconscious consumption of natural resources bring environmental problems and create an imbalance between the economy and the environment (Kaypak, 2013: 18).

In the period we live in, states alone are not enough to solve environmental problems. Any country may not have sufficient economic power and resources to cope with environmental problems, or even if it does, it may need the cooperation of other countries or organizations (Sönmezoğlu and Bayır, 2012: 249). Many environmental problems that require urgent solutions such as global warming, climate change, endangered creatures, water pollution, ozone layer have a global character. The inadequacy of national policies in solving global environmental problems has revealed the concept of "environmental governance" with its global emphasis (Sevük et al., 2020: 96). In the emergence of this concept, it is referred to the concept of governance and the sustainable development approach (Uzel, 2006: 104). Sustainable development approach is one of the most used concepts today, with the environmental problems that emerged gradually in different parts of the world after the 1960s and crossed the borders of countries and gained a global dimension, starting to be discussed in international platforms. This approach has been used not only for economic issues, but also for social and environmental issues, especially since the 1970s. As a matter of fact, since this date, this approach has been defined as a process that ensures the prudent use of all environmental and human resources for both the needs of today's people and the needs of future generations, and covers the entire society on the basis of respecting this (Uğur and Doğan, 2015: 47–48).

Governance, with its social, political and economic dimensions, ensures the participation of individuals at all levels – household, village, district, town, nation, regional or international. In this context, environmental governance is expressed as "the interaction between formal and informal institutions and actors in society that are effective in defining and delineating environmental problems". As a multidimensional concept, governance includes many organizations, communities, policy and decision-making tools, supporting financial mechanisms, regulations, legal rules, governmental and non-governmental organizations and rules in overcoming environmental problems. There are three main determinants in the implementation of environmental governance: The first is the development of processes for the creation of new institutions and norms at the international level. Secondly, non-governmental organizations, business world, academic circles, local governments and other actors are encouraged to participate in the solution of environmental problems. Third and lastly, it is to ensure that the underlying causes of global environmental problems such as population growth, poverty and underdevelopment, technological inadequacies and market failures are addressed more directly (Sipahi, 2010b: 335). In this context, governments, non-governmental organizations, supranational organizations, multinational companies, non-governmental organizations and even individuals can collectively play an active role in the environmental governance platform (Özkan and Sevim, 2018: 448). In this context, environmental governance is defined as a set of rules, practices, institutions and policies that determine the interaction between society and nature. It is a concept emphasizing initiatives developed by actors that have a significant impact on the management of environmental problems, which have been increasing in number on a global, national, regional and local scale, from climate change to ozone depletion (Korkmaz and Ayna, 2018: 415). Since the complex environmental problem consists of interconnected problems that cut across borders and nations, it is more beneficial for states to act with global cooperation and handle the problems from a holistic environmental perspective rather than struggling with these problems separately (Sönmezoğlu and Bayır, 2012: 249).

In this context, environmental governance at national, regional and global level is critical to ensure environmental sustainability. Enhanced environmental governance should be a policy included at all levels to respond quickly and effectively to emerging environmental challenges and to address agreed environmental priorities. The following actions are required for this (as cited in Sipahi, 2010a: 5–6):

- To support coherent international decision-making processes for environmental governance;
- To accelerate international efforts to follow up the implementation of internationally recognized actors,

- To support regional, sub-regional and national environmental governance processes and institutions,
- To promote and support the environmental basis for sustainable development at the national level.

Environmental governance is a concept that emerged as a result of the search for solutions to environmental problems that have a multifaceted effect on individual and social welfare. Davidson and Fricked argue that environmental governance is a concept that has been discussed in social sciences for nearly half a century. Although environmental governance is interpreted in different ways, in its simplest form, it can be expressed as management efforts to alleviate environmental problems (Bal et al., 2015: 181). According to Razzaque, governance is an important concept and good governance should include inclusive decision-making, transparency and accountable policies, taking the views of various interest groups. Therefore, only a transparent, accountable government that ensures public participation can achieve environmental justice (Artuç, 2019: 417). Pellizzoni argues critically that the diminishing legitimacy of political, economic and scientific institutions to which governance responds is vitally associated with a decrease in the effectiveness of policy action. Therefore, there is still a wide policy-implementation gap between the ongoing environmental degradation and the agreed environmental agreements and the harmonization outcomes that can be noted for them (Mazi, 2009: 302).

Environmental ombudsman is one of the global and national actors in eliminating environmental problems and protecting the natural ecological balance. As a matter of fact, this concept, which will be explained in detail below and examples of global applications will be given, can be evaluated as a multi-faceted concept related to different thinking methods such as environmental ethics and environmental governance (Ergün, 2014).

3. Environmental Ombudsman

Environmental Ombudsman is a special branch of ombudsman (Shindo, 2013: 212). Environmental Ombudsman is spreading rapidly and getting new application areas day by day, especially with the rapid consumption of natural resources in recent years, the damage to the environment threatening the future of humanity and the increasing importance of environmental policies in public administration (Erdoğan, 2018: 237). Environmental Ombudsman is a private institution established or a public officer responsible to solve environmental problems caused by bad practices of government and local governments in a particular country or city, to defend the environmental rights of citizens and to make recommendations for the elimination of environmental problems in order to live in a better and healthier society. Although the working methods and forms of environmental ombudsmen differ from country to country, their powers and duties are used independently and impartially within the framework of the authority granted to them. Their decisions are not legally binding. Environmental Ombudsmen make recommendations to the administration in order to eliminate environmental problems caused by the administration's mismanagement, to improve environmental practices and to better environmental legislation in matter coming under their authority (Boyalı and Gündoğdu, 2020: 455).

Perhaps, one of the most important functions of environmental ombudsmen is to be a system that protects the public and the environment against arbitrary and poor management of the administration, which can take strong and unilateral decisions on environmental issues, and guarantees the rights of citizens. Environmental ombudsmen can carry out all kinds of investigations and researches in the relevant administrative units upon complaint applications made to them or by acting ex officio, and at the same time, they perform the audit function by accessing the necessary information and documents (Erdoğan, 2018: 237).

The establishment of an environmental ombudsman in a country can show how much the damage to the environment is, on the other hand, it can be seen as an indicator of environmental awareness for that country (Boyalı and Gündoğdu, 2020: 454–455). In the following part of the study, examples are given related to country and international union ombudsmen who have environmental ombudsman mechanisms in the world.

In New Zealand, Environmental Ombudsman is in the form of an independent parliamentary commissioner and it dates back to the late 1980s (Rose, 2001: 311). Overall, it operates as an independent mechanism with broad mandates, acting to investigate environmental concerns and deal with citizens' environmental complaints and find solutions to them. It provides independent reports and advice on environmental issues. Ombudsman has functions such as investigating an issue, opening an investigation, making recommendations and reporting the results to the parliament (Boyalı and Gündoğdu, 2020: 456).

In Hungary, the "Environmental Protection Ombudsman" was established in 2008, called the "Green Ombudsman", whose main task is to ensure the sustainability of the environment in order to advocate for the natural environment and protect intergenerational justice. The Green Ombudsman has three main tasks. The first of these is to offer legal solutions related to environmental complaints before they are submitted to the courts. Its second task is to express its views on bills in the parliament. The third is to conduct research and present reports that support policy recommendations on environmental issues. The Environmental Ombudsman does not have offices throughout the country, but functions as a parliamentary body advising on constitutional matters. The Ombudsman serves as an advisory body to the parliament on environmental legislation, can sue the Constitutional Court or intervene in court cases on behalf of future generations, making efforts to establish the right to a healthy environment (Boyalı and Gündoğdu, 2020: 456–457).

In Argentina, efforts are made to resolve conflicts related to the management and use of water resources through the national ombudsman. In addition, efforts are made to solve environmental problems in a public way. Ombudsman plays an active role in the creation of environmental policies by acting together with non-governmental organizations sensitive to the environment (Boyalı and Gündoğdu, 2020: 458; Christel and Gutie´rrez, 2017: 336). On the other hand, in Ontario, which is a provincial ombudsman in Canada, the ombudsman has areas of expertise and duties related to energy and environmental issues (https://www.ombudsman.on.ca/what-we-do/topics/energy-environment). In addition, in the European Union, it is expressed in some platforms that the union ombudsman plays an important role in the protection and strengthening of the European Union environmental law. In this context, the Union's effort to create a green policy, especially on issues such as economic, sociological and foreign policy related to the environment, comes to the fore and the ombudsman gains a feature that ensures this aim (https://www.ombudsman.europa.eu/speech/en/10558).

Conclusion and Evaluation

The environment is a natural habitat in which the whole organism comes to life and all the animate and inanimate phenomena take place. When human-induced economic and social interventions are made on nature, which has a delicate balance, important environmental problems can be encountered. In the 20th century, the number of such problems has increased and global efforts have begun to find solutions to them. Now, dealing with increasing and changing environmental problems has crossed national borders.

At this point, the concept of governance, which refers to global cooperation and mutual solidarity, emerges in order to address environmental problems in a global sense and to minimize the problems. With the governance mechanism, an environmental model can be created in which both national and international cooperation and participation channels based on synergy are open. With the environmental governance networks to be established, important solutions and projects can be provided to the environmental problems that endanger the future of humanity.

Environmental ombudsman, which has the opportunity to practice in different countries around the world, is also important in this regard. Ombudsman is an organization that generally attempts to minimize the bad management practices of the public administration and protects human rights. A specialized ombudsman which carries out activities in the field of environment can bring many issues to the fore, first in the national borders and then in the global arena. In terms of environmental governance, the ombudsman tries to solve environmental problems primarily through citizen complaints, and their close connection with the parliament reveals opportunities for participation in politics and democracy. On the other hand, the ombudsman's relations with the private sector, non-governmental organizations and the media in the society also contribute to environmental governance with the principles of co-management, accountability, openness and participation.

In this respect, it can be said that ombudsman, which provides a great opportunity for the realization of governance principles, has the capacity to activate both national and global mechanisms in providing solutions to environmental problems, considering it within environmental aspect. Ombudsman, in essence, has the principles of governance and the related gains can be used in the field of environment. Environmental problems can be solved through multidimensional, synergetic, open and participatory policies and projects.

References

Artuç, Murat (2019). "Kitap İncelemesi – 1: Avrupa ve Asya'da Çevresel Yönetişim: Kurumsal ve Yasal Çerçevelerin Karşılaştırmalı İncelemesi", *İstanbul Gelişim Üniversitesi Sosyal Bilimler Dergisi*, Cilt: 6, Sayı: 2, Ekim, ss. 416–418.

Bal, Harun, Neşe Algan ve Pınar Özdemir (2015). "Yeni Kurumsalcı Perspektifte Çevresel Yönetişim ve Kurumsal Çerçevenin Önemi", *Doğuş Üniversitesi Dergisi*, Cilt: 16, Sayı: 2, ss. 179–191.

Baykal, Hülya ve Tan Baykal (2008). "Küreselleşen Dünya'da Çevre Sorunları", *Mustafa Kemal Üniversitesi Sosyal Bilimler Enstitüsü Dergisi*, Cilt: 5, Sayı: 9, ss. 1–17.

Baykal, Tan (2010). "Türkiye'de Çevre Yönetim Sisteminin Yerel Örgütlenmesi", *Mustafa Kemal Üniversitesi Sosyal Bilimler Enstitüsü Dergisi*, Cilt: 7, Sayı: 13, ss. 476–492.

Bek, Nahit (2019). "Çevresel Performans Endeksi ve Sürdürülebilir Yönetişim Göstergeleri Kapsamında Ülke Karşılaştırması: Türkiye ve İsviçre Örneği", *Uluslararası Sosyal Bilimlerde Yenilikçi Yaklaşımlar Dergisi*, Vol. 3, No. 2, ss. 36–45.

Boyali, Handan ve Serkan Gündoğdu (2020). "Çevre Ombudsmanlığı" (Ed. Oğuzhan Erdoğan), *Ombudsmanlık: Dünyada Uygulanan Özel Amaçlı Ombudsmanlık Türleri ve Uygulamaları*, Nobel Basım Yayım, Ankara, ss. 447–465.

Bozkurt, Yavuz (2014). "Çevreye Duyarlı İşletmecilik" (Eds. İhsan Günaydın, Tufan Özsoy), *Disiplinler Arası Bir Bakış İle Çevre*, Hiperlink, İstanbul, ss. 62–87.

Christel, Lucas G. and . Gutie´rrez, Ricardo A. (2017). "Making Rights Come Alive: Environmental Rights and Modes of Participation in Argentina", *Journal of Environment & Development*, Vol. 26, No. 3, pp. 322–347.

Doğan, Kadir Caner (2015). "Pakistan Ombudsmanı: Yapısal-Kurumsal ve İşlevsel Yönleri", *Gümüşhane Üniversitesi Sosyal Bilimler Elektronik Dergisi*, Cilt: 6, Sayı: 13, ss. 145–157.

Doğan, Kadir Caner (2016). "Türkiye Ombudsmanı: Yapısal Kurumsal ve İşlevsel Yönleri", *Uluslararası Bilimsel Araştırmalar Dergisi*, Cilt: 1, Sayı: 1, ss. 41–49.

Doğan, Kadir Caner (2017). "Yönetişim Kavramı ve Türkiye'de Demokratikleşme Reformları: Kamu Denetçiliği Kurumu (Ombudsman) Örneği", *Akademik Sosyal Araştırmalar Dergisi*, Sayı: 47, Haziran, ss. 267–287.

Doğan, Kadir Caner and, Ugur, Ömer (2019). "The Effectiveness of Ombudsman in Improving Good Administration in the European Union (EU)" (Eds. Marin Rusev, Eric Straus, Cevdet Avcıkurt, Abdullah Soykan, Bekir Parlak), *Social Sciences Researches in the Globalizing World*, ST. Kliment Ohridski University Press, Sofia, pp. 180–192.

Erdoğan, Oğuzhan (2018). "Çevre Ombudsmanlığının Türkiye'de Uygulanabilirliği Üzerine Genel Bir Değerlendirme" (Eds. Burak Hergüner, Erol Kalkan), *Türkiye'de Çevre Politikaları: Sürdürülebilir Kalkınma İçin Eksik Halkayı Tamamlamak*, Nobel Basım Yayım, Ankara, ss. 231–248.

Ergün, Turan (2014). Türkiye'de Çevre Denetimi ve Çevre Etiği Bağlamında Yeniden Yapılandırılması, T.C. Ankara Üniversitesi Sosyal Bilimler Enstitüsü Sosyal Çevre Bilimleri Anabilim Dalı, Doktora Tezi, Ankara.

Fidan, Yahya (2010/2011). "Yönetimden Yönetişime: Kavramsal Bir Bakış", *Yalova Sosyal Bilimler Dergisi*, Sayı: 1/Ekim – Mart, ss. 5–10.

Kalkişim, Hasan Mahmut (2019). "Yönetişim Kavram ve Teorisi Üzerine Bir Değerlendirme" (Eds. Bekir Parlak, Kadir Caner Doğan), *E-Yönetişim: Kavramsal/Kuramsal Çerçeve, Ülke İncelemeleri ve Türkiye'ye Yansımaları*, Beta Basım Yayım, İstanbul, ss. 19–32.

Kaypak, Şafak (2013). "Çevre Sorunlarının Çözümünde Küresel Çevre Politikalarının Önemi", *Muğla Sıtkı Koçman Üniversitesi Sosyal Bilimler Enstitüsü Dergisi*, Sayı 31, Güz, ss. 17–34.

Korkmaz, Yıldırım ve Yunus Emre Ayna (2018). "The Role of Non-Governmental Organizations in Environmental Governance in Turkey", *ADAM Akademi*, Vol. 8, No. 2, pp. 409–431.

Mazi, Fikret (2009). "The Evolution of the Global Environmental Governance: The Transition to Politics of Sustainable Development", *Electronic Journal of Social Sciences*, Spring, Vol. 8, No. 28, pp. 299–317.

Özer, M. Akif (2006). "Yönetişim Üzerine Notlar", *Sayıştay Dergisi*, Sayı: 63, ss. 59–89.

Özkan, Arda ve Uğur Sevim (2018). "Sürdürülebilir Kalkınmayı Sağlamada Küresel Çevresel Yönetişimin Önemi ve Ekonominin Rolü", *The Journal of Academic Social Science Studies*, No: 71, Autumn II, pp. 443–454.

Rose, G. L. (2001). "Environmental Performance Auditing of Government – The Role for an Australian Commissioner for the Environment", June 2001, https://ro.uow.edu.au/cgi/viewcontent.cgi?article=1039&context=lawpapers (02.04.2021).

Sevük, Handan Yokuş, Ezeli Azarkan, Fazıl Hüsnü Erdem ve Neşe Baran Çelik (2020). "Küresel Çevresel Yönetişim Bağlamında Uluslararası İşbirliği ve Çevresel Yönetişim Uygulamasında İsveç Örneği", *Dicle Üniversitesi Sosyal Bilimler Enstitüsü Dergisi*, Ekim, Sayı: 25, ss. 96–120.

Shindo, Mahito (2013). The Environmental Ombudsman and Administrative Decision Making: An Assessment of its Suitability for Japan, Macquarie Law School Macquarie University, Sydney, Australia, This thesis is presented for the degree of Doctor of Philosophy in Law.

Sipahi, Esra Banu (2010a). "Environmental Governance as an Aternative Solution to Global Environmental Problems", BALWOIS 2010 – Ohrid, Republic of Macedonia – 25, 29 May, pp. 1–12.

Sipahi, Esra Banu (2010b). "Küresel Çevre Sorunlarına Kolektif Çözüm Arayışları ve Yönetişim", *Selçuk Üniversitesi Sosyal Bilimler Enstitüsü Dergisi*, Sayı: 24, ss. 331–344.

Sönmezoğlu, Faruk ve Özgün Erler Bayır (2012). "Çevre Sorunlarına İlişkin Uluslararası Rejimler", *İstanbul Üniversitesi Siyasal Bilgiler Fakültesi Dergisi*, No: 47. (Ekim), ss. 247–289.

Ugur, Omer (2019). "Climate Change in Global Politics in the Postmodern Era: A New Challenge and Responses" (Eds. Ömer uğur, Kadir Caner Doğan), *Contemporary Debates on Politics and Public Administration in the Postmodern Era*, Peter Lang, Berlin, ss. 83–99.

Uğur, Ömer ve Doğan, Kadir Caner (2015). "Avrupa Birliği'nin Sürdürülebilir Kalkınma Stratejisi: İklim Değişikliği Çerçevesinde Teoriden Pratiğe", Doğu Karadeniz Bölgesi Sürdürülebilir Turizm Kongresi Bildiriler Kitabı, 14 – 16 Mayıs, Gümüşhane.

Uzel, Esra (2006). Küresel Çevresel Yönetişim (İyi Yönetim), T.C. Ankara Üniversitesi Sosyal Bilimler Enstitüsü Sosyal Çevre Bilimleri Anabilim Dalı, Yüksek Lisans Tezi, Ankara.

Yildiz, B. and Yilmaz, C. (2015). Kirlilik Cennetlerinin Oluşumunda Çevre Vergilerinin Rolü, Gümüşhane Üniversitesi Sosyal Bilimler Elektronik Dergisi, 12, 102–120, (http://sbedergi.ghu.edu.tr/belgeler/sbe-cilt6-sayi12/MakalelerPDF/VI.pdf, 12.12.2015).

Yilmaz Ugur, C. (2021). "Struggling with Covid-19 Outbreak in the Framework of Global Public Goods" (Eds. K. C. Dogan and Ö. Ugur), *Public Administration and Public Finance Research*, Livre de Lyon Publication, Lyon.

https://www.demokrasi.gen.tr/dogal-cevrenin-korunmasi/ (14.06.2021).

https://www.makaleler.com/cevre-nedir (12.05.2021).

https://www.ombudsman.on.ca/what-we-do/topics/energy-environment (13.04.2021).

Sıla Turaç Baykara

Competitive Powers in the Arctic Region and the Effect of the Climate Change

Introduction

The Arctic Region, which has difficulties in finding its place among hot topics of international politics until now, has made a rapid entry into the agenda of international politics as the region where the struggle against climate change significantly increases the power struggle. Nowadays, the effects of global climate change have been observed more clearly in the Arctic. While global warming causes the glaciers to melt, it poses a threat to the lives of local people and other living things and forces them to change their living patterns. With the rise of sea level and the melting of glaciers, local people are forced to relocate. The harmful gases that exist in the thawed frozen soil are also released. Besides all these negative changes, climate change in the Arctic could be observed through various indicators such as air temperature, frozen soil, and carbon cycle, and decrease in snow level, fires. Although the developments that have occurred or are likely to occur in the Arctic because of the climate change create an environmental concern, the main interest of the states is the dominance and economic interest in the region. Today, the Arctic Region is in the top of international agenda through the issues such as the armament of the region, the security of raw materials and energy resources, the protection of the legal rights of indigenous peoples, the competition of the great powers and the emergence of alternative energy routes, especially after the meltdown of the glaciers.

States showing presence in the region are Russia, Canada, the US, Norway, and Denmark, which have borders in the Arctic Ocean and are also called as the Arctic Five; Sweden, Iceland, and Finland, which have territory in the region and China as a rising power in the world. The main power struggle in the region is between two parties: the US and the EU vs. Russia and China. The possibility of conflict between the great powers in the Arctic Region, combined with the meltdown of glaciers caused by climate change and technological developments, has accelerated the efforts to create competition areas such as mining, energy, armament, and settlement in the Arctic Region. The problem here is that certain great powers, trying to take advantage of the situation arising from the meltdown of glaciers and the development of technology, stay indifferent to the environmental disaster that these two developments will create.

This study examines the transformation of international relations in the Arctic Region and the impact of climate change on this transformation. The problem of climate change will welcome to new possibilities in the Arctic Region as well as new challenges. The increasing strategic importance of the region has also a great effect on this struggle. This study consists of three main parts. In the first part, the study aims to make the definition of the Arctic region and mentions the legal framework especially the most important legal body of the Arctic: Arctic Council. Second part underlines whether the climate change in the Arctic results in cooperation or competition between two main parties of the Arctic. Among two parties in the region, this study evaluates China and Russia as power seekers in the Arctic, and the EU and the US as climate supporters. Last part of the study envisages two scenarios for the Arctic: uncurbed and curbed warming scenarios. Finally, this study concludes that the Arctic's potential of a conflict will increase as the climate change melts the ice. Besides, EU could be the leader in the region and should put security of the Arctic at the top of its Arctic agenda which also should cover a compromise between China, Russia, and the US.

1. Definition of Arctic and Legal Framework

The Arctic Council gives the definition of the Arctic by all areas north of the Arctic Circle and the including eight Arctic states namely Canada, Denmark (Greenland), Finland, Iceland, Norway, Russia, the US, and Sweden (SMFA, 30.07.2021). Besides, Russia, the US, Canada, Norway, and Denmark, which are littoral to the Arctic Ocean, are called as the Arctic Five.

There is currently no international agreement determining the legal status of the region. Accordingly, activities in the region are governed by several bilateral agreements, national legislation of the Arctic countries and international agreements that do not affect the legal status of the region. Among several documents constituting the legal framework of the Arctic Region, the most important document is the United Nations Convention on the Law of the Sea (UNCLOS). Besides UNCLOS, the Ilulissat Declaration of 2008 and the International Maritime Organization's (IMO) Polar Code of 2014 are other documents needed to be mentioned regarding the legal framework of the Arctic Region. The Arctic Council, which was established with the Ottawa Declaration in 1996, also publishes declarations to contribute to the legal framework of the region.

In the Arctic, main problem regarding the territorial share between the states is about establishing clear boundaries since natural resources within it. The United Nations Convention on the Law of the Sea (UNCLOS) is the official body responsible from settling the territory disputes. The UNCLOS sets that Arctic states have the right on energy resources in their exclusive economic zones and continental shelves. Moreover, territorial claims on the extent of the continental shelf have been debated under the UNCLOS. The areas beyond the exclusive economic zones and continental shelves of the Arctic states are as an open sea and no state can claim rights over them. This decision is based on the international law since states can have free movement right, fish and make a scientific research in the open sea. The UNCLOS was signed in 1982 and came into force in 1994. According to Article 76 of UNCLOS, the continental shelf of a coastal state is the natural extension of its land within the 200 nautical miles (IBRU, 22.07.2021). Moreover, UNCLOS determines the Exclusive Economic Zone (EEZ) as 'an area beyond and adjacent to the territorial sea' and it 'shall not extend beyond 200 nautical miles from the baselines from which the breadth of the territorial sea is measured'. Beyond this limit, states are not permitted to fish or drill (UN, 31.07.2021). Unfortunately, UNCLOS is only guide for laws of the sea, it does not propose clear solutions for disputed issues. Moreover, decisions taken by UNCLOS could take long time or decisions could not be accepted by states which are not ratifies the UNCLOS yet such as the US.

The Ilulissat Declaration was issued in 2008 by the Arctic Five namely Canada, Denmark, Norway, Russia and the US. The Ilulissat Declaration basically refers to not only the negative consequences of climate change and global warming on the ecosystem, local and indigenous people but also how to share newly found natural resources in the Arctic. Besides, Ilulissat Declaration underlines that the Arctic Five respect for the law of the sea. Regarding international cooperation, the Ilulissat Declaration aims to be the cornerstone in the Arctic's future (Arctic Portal, 17.08.2021).

The International Maritime Organization (IMO) adopted the Polar Code (the International Code for Ships Operating in Polar Waters) as an international regulation in 2014. The Polar Code is interested in shipping rules in the polar regions (The Guardian, 2014). In 2019, the IMO became observer in the Arctic Council. The Arctic Council and its Working Group on the Protection of the Marine Environment (PAME) became responsible for the implementation of the Polar Code (IMO, 10.07.2021).

1.1. Arctic Council

The most important development that can be considered positive in terms of cooperation and stability in the region is the intergovernmental Arctic Council. Permanent membership status in the Council includes the Arctic countries Norway and Russia, as well as Sweden, Finland and Iceland. While no other country is granted permanent membership status, various state and non-state actors also take part in the council as observer members. The Arctic Council accepted 13 non-Arctic countries, 13 intergovernmental and inter-parliamentary organizations and 12 non-governmental organizations as observers. Now, Russia chairs the 2-year presidency of the Arctic Council from 2021 to 2023 (Arctic Council, 11.08.2021).

Krasner defines the regime as 'principles, norms, rules, and decision-making procedures around which actors' expectations converge in a given area of international relations' (Krasner, 1982: 186). Arctic governance is also regime, and the Arctic Council is the center which gets the Arctic regime together. The Arctic Council is a form of a regional cooperation whose members try to solve the problems diplomatically such as border disputes, exclusive economic zones, climate change, environmental protection, and sea-lanes for commercial navigation. Since the Arctic Council was founded with the aim to rule out common economic, environmental, and geopolitical issues relating to the Arctic, the Arctic council basically left security issues out of its agenda. Under the Arctic Council's framework, the Arctic states signed three agreements on fostering the cooperation and underlying the challenges: Agreement on Cooperation on Aeronautical and Maritime Search and Rescue in the Arctic of 2011, Agreement on Cooperation on Marine Oil Pollution Preparedness and Response in the Arctic of 2013 and Agreement on Enhancing International Arctic Scientific Cooperation of 2017. Besides, two cooperation platforms for the good governance in the Arctic were formed respectively in 2014 and 2015: the Arctic Economic Council and the Arctic Coast Guard Forum (Arctic Council, 15.07.2021). The reason why the rapid institutionalization in Arctic issues has been realized by the Arctic Council is that military security issues are exempt from the responsibility of the Arctic Council (Arctic Institute, 16.07.2021). However, former U.S. Secretary of State Mike Pompeo during the Arctic Council Ministerial meeting in Rovaniemi, Finland in May 2019 warned China and Russia to stop aggressiveness in the Arctic and brought the security issues into the Arctic Council's agenda (NY Times, 15.07.2021). Even though Arctic states always repeat to 'maintain peace, stability and constructive cooperation in the Arctic', changing geopolitics is the biggest challenge to the Arctic cooperation (Arctic Council, 15.07.2021).

Although the Arctic Council is significant for the region and its significance comes from its respect for international law, there are other cooperation mechanisms in the region. First of all, the Northern Dimension (ND) between the EU, Russia, Norway and Iceland was created in 1999 and renewed in 2006. ND aims at sustainability and continuous development in the areas such as environment, nuclear safety, health, energy, transportation, logistics, trade and investment, research, education and culture in the Arctic (ND, 20.07.2021). Second, the Barents Euro-Arctic Cooperation was established in 1993 for sustainable development especially for the issues relating to the Barents Sea on two bases, the Barents Euro-Arctic Council at the interstate level and the Barents Regional Council at the interregional level. Under the frame of this cooperation, the members develop policies on issues such as economy, culture, environment, and social welfare. Among those two Councils, the Barents Euro Arctic Council (BEAC), founded in 2005, is an intergovernmental cooperation forum for the Arctic. The BEAC has a practical and project-based structure (BEAC, 20.07.2021). Since changing geopolitics also affected the BEAC, in recent years, it has been very difficult to cooperate in certain issues in the BEAC such as biodiversity and urgent environmental problems due to the lack of participation. Especially Russia does not give necessary interest to those issues.

To sum up, even though there is no international agreement determining the legal status of the Arctic and activities in the Arctic are governed by several bilateral agreements, national legislation of the Arctic countries and international agreements that do not affect the legal status of the region, documents and Arctic Council constituting the legal framework of the Arctic Region always refer to the climate change problems and environmental issues because of two reasons. First, military issues are out of Arctic's agenda even though Russia has certain military actions in the region. Second, the phenomenon of the expansion and deepening of security has put environmental and climate security on the agenda in the Arctic as well as all over the world. However, Conley and Melino (2016) suggests changing the current structure of the Arctic Council and form an organization for the Arctic security and cooperation which would cover economic, human, and security perspectives.

2. Climate Change in the Arctic: Region of Cooperation or Region of Competition?

The disappearance of the bipolar world and the end of ideological polarization in 1990s directed the Arctic states to the cooperation in the region. Yet, the conflicts about the continental shelf continue in the region and this makes the future of the region uncertain. For instance, on one hand, regarding the claims in the North Pole, Russia, Canada, Norway, Denmark via Greenland, and the US via Alaska have had claims to the North Pole (The Observer, 22.06.2021). Another border dispute is between Canada and the US over the Beaufort Sea, which has coast to Yukon of Canada and Alaska of the US due to huge hydrocarbon resources expected to have (BBC, 22.06.2021). On the other hand, certain important boundary problems which was obstacles to cooperation in the region have been resolved. For example, in 1990, an agreement was signed between Russia and the US on the border in the Bering Sea. Besides, in 2010, Russia and Norway have settled a 40-year-long dispute over their maritime borders in the Barents Sea, and equally divided the territory they mutually claimed (The Guardian, 24.06.2021). This way of cooperation in the Arctic could be explained through the term of 'Arctic exceptionalism', which means that Arctic states are willing to cooperate for the sake of their common interests by giving up their geopolitical interests (Smieszek, 2019).

The significance of the Artic comes from the natural resources the regions already has had. According to the US Geological Survey of 2008, there are 47.3 trillion cubic meters of natural gas, 44 billion barrels of liquid natural gas and 90 billion barrels of oil in the region. This amount equals to 25 % of proven natural gas reserves and 6 % of proven oil reserves worldwide. Since 84 % of these resources are located on the ocean bed, discussions about where the boundaries of the continental shelf will pass are an important issue for the Arctic states (USGS, 24.06.2021). Besides being rich in natural resources and minerals, another reason for the ongoing geopolitical rivalry between states in the Arctic is the struggle for access to energy resources. Thereof, the Arctic region has begun to turn into a source of new international tensions. It is also worth to note that the Arctic is defined as a region where big powers are small and small powers are big. For instance, Norway and Canada are Arctic's big powers although those countries are modest as globally. In contrast, the U.S. is a global superpower; however, it acts an Arctic's small power. If great power competition increases in the region, the Arctic could transform into one of the regions in the world's new geopolitics which could make the region competitive instead of cooperative.

Today, the relation between geopolitics and climate change in the Artic is coming from the rapid warming in the Arctic and new sea routes occurring because of melting ice. These routes could provide the possibility to decrease the travel time and increase the profits. For instance, the Northern Sea Route, a gate to the northern Russia, decrease the travel time from Europe to Asia. To put it in numbers, the route through the Suez Canal, which is used to reach East Asia from Western Europe today, is 23,000 kilometers, while the Northern Sea Route through the Arctic region is approximately 14,000 kilometers. Besides, by 2040, there is a high probability that new sea routes will be discovered in the region in addition to the Northern Sea Route through Russia's northern seas (Pflüger, 2020). The Northern Sea Route also becomes more important than before for the East Asia to reach to the Russian Arctic's oil and gas resources. Worldwide known Maersk shipping company is searching for the possibilities to pass through the Northern Sea Route instead of the Suez Canal. It is claimed that this route shortens the route by 40 %. Maersk Shipping Company also collaborate with the company using icebreakers to explore this route (World Economic Forum, 20.06.2021). As another example, the Northwest Passage, which is a gate through the top of Canada, was not accessible before due to thick ice. It is expected that trade flows will increase in this area soon. Canada claims that the sovereignty over the gate belongs to itself. In this picture, Canada's Arctic Policy refers to national security and sovereignty. However, the US and certain European states claim that it is in international waters (Economist, 22.08.2021). Therefore, since new sea routes were opened and new energy sources were found, the Arctic region has turned into a new field of competition between Arctic powers in the region. The states of the region embarked on a struggle to establish dominance over the new sea routes. However, there is a dilemma in terms of the climate change since on one hand, using the shorter route means using less hydrocarbons which helps to decrease carbon emissions. Different sides of the same shield, economic opportunities, and climate change, leave the world in a conflict of interests.

If the picture of the region is drawn from the end of the Cold war till to the remilitarization of Russia in the region, the Arctic region has been designated as a no conflict region and a region of the international cooperation. In addition to the remilitarization of Russia, China has started to invest in region and proceed research, infrastructure, and energy facilities to open sea lines and access to natural resources. The U.S. is also trying to adopt to these new developments in the region. The rising competition between great powers in the Arctic could turn into a conflict in the region due to the limited maneuver of the Arctic Council. The U.S.- Russia challenge in the Arctic is based on conflicting interests not climate change and melting ice since both states are testing their national defense limits in the region. After China entered the game in the Arctic, the matters have become more complicated. Only Northern European states continue their low profile in the Arctic. What the EU did in the Arctic is that like China, the Union asked for observer status in the Arctic Council. The EU applied for being observer in the Arctic Council at the Kiruna Ministerial Meeting in 2013; however, the Arctic Council postponed its final decision. Until the Arctic Council gives its final decision, the EU was welcomed to observe the Council proceedings

(Arctic Council, 24.08.2021). In terms of the climate change, although Russia and the West are cooperating for the environmental transformation and economic opportunities in the Arctic, current military developments in the Arctic still leads to a skepticism.

2.1. China and Russia as Power Seekers in the Arctic

Russia and China are working together to access to geostrategic and economic advantages, such as new fishing area, new sources of oil, gas and minerals, and new waterways which could create new optimum navigation ways, coming from the melt of the sea ice and the thaw of the tundra in the Arctic Ocean and Northern Siberia. Russia is increasing its military developments in northern Siberia from Kola Peninsula to Kamchatka Peninsula (Pflüger, 2020).

Since more than half of the coast of the Arctic Ocean belongs to Russia and most of the energy resources in the Arctic region are in the part of Russia, the Arctic region has vital importance for Russia, unlike other Arctic states. Moreover, Arctic has become very significant for Russia due to the commercial and geopolitical benefits it could bring. Besides, Russia claims that the Northern Sea Route is under its sovereignty and increases the transports via the route. Regarding the commerce, first, Russia aims to use the Northern Sea Route as an alternative trade passage for its cargo ships instead of the Suez Canal. Second, Russia aims to establish a port in the shipping route, the Kola Peninsula and the Kamchatka Peninsula, to make much more trade in the future. Third, Novatek, liquefied natural gas (LNG) producer in Russia, China National Petroleum Corporation and China National Offshore Oil Corporation search for new opportunities in the Arctic in order to export LNG along this route (Pflüger, 2020). Russia also increases its military power and bases in the region and invests in new infrastructure and technology. Regarding geopolitics, Russia wants to increase both its defense and strike capabilities against its rivals in the Arctic and its claim on resourceful and geographically significant Arctic region.

Although it was the year of 2007 when Russia first had a claim in the Arctic, it is the year of 2019, when its interest in the region revives. In 2019, Russia realized a great military exercise in the Arctic and commenced the first combat icebreaker of the world. Furthermore, Russia upgraded the number of its military installations at Nagurskoye, where its northern airbase is located. Nagurskoye Air Base is important for Russia since it has an ability to strike Thule Air Base (Pflüger, 2020). New military positions Russia opened in north of Siberia is threat to the polar bears. Furthermore, the Vostok Project is composed of activities in the Russia's Fat North and now is the largest hydrocarbon project in the world. It is also threat to the Arctic climate. This is also the reason why Russia is against to sign the Paris Climate Agreement of 2015 (Köni and Özdal, 2017).

Despite having no territory or border, China is also interested in the region. China, which aims to increase its influence in the Arctic via investments, wants to increase its maritime presence in the Arctic (Spohr and Hamilton, 2020). Therefore, China has become the partner of Russia in the region to find a way entering into the Arctic. As part of its Belt and Road Initiative (BRI), China invested in Russia's liquefied natural gas (LNG) and founded several facilities in the region (Reuters, 20.07.2021). Sino-Russian collaboration have also been formed for the future of the Northern Sea Route (Dams and van Schaik, 2019). To increase China's economic presence in the Arctic, one of state-owned countries of China invested in rare earth elements (REE) and uranium mining project at Kvanefjeld in southern part of Greenland. Besides, in 2017, another Chinese company wanted to buy former naval station to establish a satellite ground station. Probably, China will continue to invest in the Artic in the near future. China could give major contribution to the economy of Greenland. China also opened the largest embassy of Iceland.

As a non-regional actor, China claims that it exists peacefully in the Arctic. The official discourse of China rests upon having common goals with the Arctic states and building the future of the Arctic together with the rest of the world. After discovering the political, economic, scientific and military potential in the Arctic, China has chosen to insist on being a close neighbor to the Chinese Arctic Circle, and aims to be active in Arctic politics both through its bilateral relations and its observer status in the Arctic Council. While China offers its strength and experience in the fields of economy, diplomacy, technology, science and trade for the Arctic, it does not hide its pursuit of national interests. China announced its official policy on Arctic by announcing the White Paper in 2018. In the White Paper, the basis of China's activities and cooperation in the Arctic is announced to encourage the participation of relevant partners for the governance of the region and to work with the international community to achieve peace, stability and sustainable development in the Arctic. In the White Paper, it also is stated that China is close to the Arctic Circle, and it is particularly interested in climate change, environment, scientific research, trade routes, natural resource exploration and extraction, security and global governance. On one hand, China recognizes the rights of the riparian states according to UNCLOS, expresses its respect for the law, and aims to be the desired country in the region by establishing bilateral relations, as seen in the examples of Norway and Russia. On the other hand, based on UNCLOS, it emphasizes the rights of non-regional states such as scientific research, fishing and exploration in international waters

(Çıtak, 2020). China's engagement efforts to the Arctic region should be deliberated since China should take the sovereign rights of the Arctic states into account and should not damage the stability of the region.

The Polar Silk Road Project is a part of China's Belt and Road Project (BRI), which was announced in 2013. The aim of the Polar Silk Road Project is to connect the Arctic region with the global trade route. Since China aims to shorten the distance and cost of transportation between Asia, Europe and North America, the Polar Silk Road Project is supported by Russia. However, the Polar Silk Road Project is criticized due to environmental concerns and due to the fact that the Project is seen as China's attempt to increase its influence in the Artic. In fact, the idea of a new sea route over ice was put forward by Russia. The idea came from view on the introduction of the Northern Sea Route to maritime trade and the delivery of energy resources in the Arctic region to the growing economies of Southeast Asia. Finally, in November 2017, Chinese President Xi Jinping and Russian Prime Minister Dmitry Medmedev agreed to develop the use of the Northern Sea Route and implement the Polar Silk Road (Çıtak, 2020).

2.2. EU and the US as Climate Supporters

The EU plays a significant role for further Arctic cooperation and supports the region to fight with the challenges it faces. EU engagement in Arctic is not only for the citizens of the EU and the EU Member States, but also for the people of the Arctic. The EU spends efforts for protecting fragile Arctic environment, develops strategies via science, research and innovation for finding solutions climate change problem in the Arctic and the rest of the world (EEAS, 14.07.2021). The EU explains the priority of its Arctic Policy as the protection of environment and sustainable development not searching for new routes in the Arctic maritime routes or exploring natural resources. Besides, cooperation is highlighted in the Policy since concerns about Arctic is needed a joint action both in the region and in the world. Moreover, research, science and innovation are announced as key players. Therefore, in 2016, the EU announced an Integrated European Union policy for the Arctic, which has three aims to achieve: fighting with the climate change and protecting the environment of the Arctic; supporting sustainable development in the Arctic; and enhancing the international cooperation on Arctic (European Commission, 13.06.2021). To sum up, the EU's Arctic Policy consists of environmental and climate change issues in the Arctic, economic development in the Arctic via sustainable use of resources and developing a dialog with Arctic states and local people of the region (EEAS, 14.07.2021). By the EU, the Arctic Council is recognized as the main body for regional cooperation. The EU applied for being observer in the Arctic Council at the Kiruna Ministerial Meeting in 2013; however, the Arctic Council postponed its final decision. Until the Arctic Council gives its final decision, the EU is welcomed to observe the Council proceedings (Arctic Council, 24.08.2021).

In addition to develop a sole Arctic policy and make efforts to gain observer status in the Arctic Council, the EU creates different channels to penetrate to the Arctic region. As result, the EU became a party of the Northern Dimension Policy, which was announced in 1999 and renewed in 2006, with Russia, Norway and Iceland. Main target of the Northern Dimension Policy is to enhance stability, welfare and sustainable development in the Arctic via cooperation. The cooperation model of the Northern Dimension Policy is the partnership model and takes place within four partnerships (The Northern Dimension, 12.06.2021).

The EU's interest in the Arctic could also be understood from its current initiatives. For instance, the EU has made a public consultation on Arctic Policy in 2021 (European Commission, 23.07.2021). This demonstrates that future of the Arctic is so important for the Union since the Arctic is endangering the world since it is warming twice as fast as the rest of the world and resulting in a rapid territorial change. The EU's Arctic policy includes the climate change actions in polar regions based on both new possibilities and new threats for the international environment (Łuszczuk, 2011). Therefore, the EU's Arctic policy is twofold. First, the Arctic is important for the EU to diversify its energy supply and energy routes; however, extractive ventures in the Arctic are criticized to result in a damage the Arctic biome's environmental integrity. Second, melting in the Arctic region results in the reallocation of the territories and interests in the region by Russia, China, and the US. This rivalry will increase the environmental risks in the region since it is not certain whether these three states give an importance to the environment. In this framework, the EU's main target should be both the protection of the Arctic biome's environmental integrity and taking the geopolitical, geo-economic and geostrategic concerns into its consideration. Therefore, the EU's Arctic policy should have multiple. On one hand, the EU should cooperate with indigenous society in the region, protect their legal rights and support them to protect their environment. On the other hand, the EU should cooperate with the U.S. to proceed the international law in the region.

Regarding the US, the Arctic point of view of the US could be extracted from former US Secretary of State Mike Pompeo's speech at the Arctic Council Summit in 2019 since he underlined that the climate change is an economic opportunity not a threat. He also added that the Arctic is not a science and cooperation area but the power and competition (Dams and van Schaik, 2019). Another example comes from the era US President was Donald Trump. He had an idea to buy Denmark's Greenland. Although this idea was negatively reacted, the reason behind this idea is important. Since Greenland is between Russia and North America, it has militarily strategic importance. In 1940, the US controlled the island to prevent North America from an invasion. During the Cold War, the Greenland was again important for the US since the island's strategic location which allowed the US to follow Soviet submarines and missiles and install early warning systems at the Thule Air Base of the US in the island. Today, Greenland is still important both for the US and NATO since Russia is increasing its military capabilities and China aims to increase its economic presence in the Arctic (Pflüger, 2020). Although the US does not ignore the militarization of the region, current U.S. President Joe Biden gives an importance to fight with climate change. Moreover, his climate policies are close to the ones of the EU. Therefore, Europe could initiate significant projects for the environmental transformation and economic opportunities of the Arctic.

3. Climate Change in the Arctic: Two Scenarios

Climate change has had a significant effect on the changing security of the Arctic geopolitics. Besides, climate change has affected the environment, economy and communities in the region. Since climate change has brought ice-covered areas, shipping routes and natural resources into use, sovereignty and international law issues also have come up for the discussion. Spohr and Hamilton (2020: 33) defines the climate change as a slower-moving pandemic having worse effects such as natural and disasters, weather changes, and death of wildlife and habitats, climate refugees and mass migrations (Spohr and Hamilton, 2020: 33). As a result of global warming and melting sea ice, both new reserves of oil, gas, uranium, gold, fish and rare earth minerals, and new shipping routes are expected to occur. It means that Arctic is entering into a new stage that could bring both new interests and new threats to the Arctic.

The Center for Climate and Security (CCS), an institute of the Council on Strategic Risks (CSR), and The Norwegian Institute of International Affairs (NUPI) issued a report in the beginning of 2021. Based on the report, two warming scenarios were envisaged for the future of the Arctic region: Uncurbed Warming Scenario and Curbed Warming Scenario. In the Uncurbed Warming Scenario, the region's stability could be in danger due to significant challenges such as a rise in commercial, civilian, and military activities, new threats to the population of the region, and inclusion of new institutions and new states in the Arctic geopolitics. Besides, according to uncurbed warming scenario, climate change will negatively affect the international cooperation on trade, arms control, and cyber operations. According to the report, the early years of this decade will have very significant consequences regarding security and stability in the Arctic. The U.S. President Joe Biden is expected to follow an aggressive foreign policy in the climate change to reach to targeted global emission cuts. Besides, the COVID-19 and current economic depression coronavirus pandemic created could direct the countries to take significant actions for reaching carbon neutrality by 2050. These developments could support to realize a Curbed Warming Scenario. The U.S. is planning to settle in the Artic with significant diplomatic power. Similarly, NATO aims to integrate climate change to its strategic planning for the year of 2030. The EU is very important player in coordinating climate change issues in the region. Finally, the Report envisages that the current decade will be very significant for the future security of the Arctic regarding cooperation, clean energy transition, institutional strengthening, and military activity (Femia and Sikorsky, 2021). The two possible scenarios could also determine two competing parties namely Russia and China, and the EU and the US, how they pursue their own interests and create connections at local, national, regional and international levels. In other words, responses of both parties to climatic changes in the Arctic could be a problem both regional and global politics (Depledge, 2016).

Conclusion

Nowadays, the effects of global climate change have been observed more clearly in the Arctic. Although the developments that have occurred in the Arctic because of the climate change create an environmental concern, the main interest of the states is the dominance and economic interest in the region. Therefore, the Arctic Region is in the top of international agenda The main power struggle in the region is between two parties: the US and the EU vs. Russia and China. The possibility of conflict between the great powers in the Arctic Region, combined with the meltdown of glaciers caused by climate change and technological developments, has accelerated the efforts to create competition areas such as mining, energy, armament, and settlement in the Arctic Region. The problem here is that certain great powers, trying to take advantage of the situation arising from the meltdown of glaciers and the development of technology, stay indifferent to the environmental disaster that these two developments will create.

This study concludes that the Arctic's potential of a conflict could increase as the climate change melts the ice. Therefore, the early years of this decade could have very significant consequences regarding security and stability in the Arctic. The EU could be the leader in the region and should put security of the Arctic at the top of its Arctic agenda which also should cover a compromise between China, Russia, and the US. The U.S. President Joe Biden is expected to follow an aggressive foreign policy in the climate change to reach to targeted global emission cuts. Besides, the COVID-19 and current economic depression coronavirus pandemic created could direct the countries to take significant actions for reaching carbon neutrality by 2050.

In conclusion, the Arctic's potential of a conflict will increase as the climate change melts the ice. Although climate change negatively affects the nature of the Arctic and melting the ice, positively affects economic utility of the melting ice and accessibility to natural resources in the Arctic. Therefore, it is obvious that diplomatic channels should work harder for the security of the Arctic. Although the Arctic Council spends efforts for the protection of the Arctic environment, the Council could not take adequate actions in fighting with climate change which affects not only the regional politics but also the security of the Arctic states. In anyway, a mutual trust is needed in the Arctic. Military existence in the Arctic, the civilian safety, credible borders policing and illegal migration flows are the most crucial issues to be debated in the Arctic Region.

References

Arctic Council (2015). https://www.thearcticinstitute.org/arctic-coast-guard-forum-big-tasks/ (Accessed at 11.08.2021).

Arctic Council (2019). https://oaarchive.arctic-council.org/bitstream/handle/11374/2418/Rovaniemi_Ministerial_Statements.pdf?sequence=1&isAllowed=y (Accessed at 15.07.2021).

Arctic Council (2021a). https://arctic-council.org/en/about/ (Accessed at 15.07.2021).

Arctic Council (2021b). https://www.arcticcouncil.org/en/about/observers/ (Accessed at 24.07.2021).

Arctic Institute (2019). https://www.thearcticinstitute.org/why-military-security-should-be-kept-out-of-the-arctic-council/ (Accessed at 16.07.2021).

Arctic Portal (2008). https://arcticportal.org/images/stories/pdf/Ilulissat-declaration.pdf (Accessed at 15.05.2021).

BBC (2019). https://www.bbc.co.uk/news/world-europe-30481309 (Accessed at 22.06.2021).

BEAC (Barents Euro Arctic Council) (2021). https://www.barentscooperation.org/en/Barents-Euro-Arctic-Council (Accessed at 20.07.2021).

Çıtak, Emre. (2020). "Arktik Bölgesi Siyaseti: Ottava Deklarasyonu'ndan Bugüne Aktör Politikaları ve Çin'in Kutup İpek Yolu Projesi". *OPUS*, 10(15), pp. 5440–5473.

Conley, Heather A. and Melino, Matthew (2016). "An Arctic Redesign - Recommendations to Rejuvenate the Arctic Council", https://espas.secure.europarl.europa.eu/orbis/sites/default/files/generated/document/en/ArcticRedesign_Web.pdf (Accessed at 14.07.2021).

Dams, Ties and Van Schaik, Louise (2019). "The Arctic Elephant. Why Europe must address the geopolitics of the high north", https://www.clingendael.org/sites/default/files/2019-11/Poliy_Brief_The_Arctic_Elephant_November_2019.pdf (Accessed at 22.06.2021).

Depledge, Duncan (2016). "Climate Change, Geopolitics, and Arctic Futures". E- International Relations, https://www.e-ir.info/2016/05/16/climate-change-geopolitics-and-arctic-futures/ (Accessed at 25.05.2021).

EEAS (European Union External Action) (2017). https://eeas.europa.eu/headquarters/headquarters-homepage/20955/climate-change-and-arctic-environment_en (Accessed at 14.07.2021).

European Commission (2016). "An integrated European Union policy for the Arctic", https://eur-lex.europa.eu/legal-content/EN/TXT/?uri=CELEX%3A52016JC0021 (Accessed at 13.06.2021).

European Commission (2021). https://ec.europa.eu/oceans-and-fisheries/news/summary-public-consultation-way-forward-european-unions-arctic-policy-2021-01-26_en (Accessed at 23.07.2021).

Femia, Francesco and Sikorsky, Erin (2021). "Climate Change and Security in the Arctic." https://climateandsecurity.org/wp-content/uploads/2021/01/Climate-Change-and-Security-in-the-Arctic_CCS_NUPI_January-2021-1.pdf (Accessed at 30.06.2021).

IBRU (Centre for Borders Research) (2015). https://www.dur.ac.uk/resources/ibru/resources/Arcticmap04-08-15.pdf (Accessed at 22.07.2021).

IMO (International Maritime Organization) (2021). https://www.imo.org/en/OurWork/Safety/Pages/polar-code.aspx (Accessed at 10.07.2021).

Köni, Hasan and Özdal, Barış (2017). *İklim Değişikliği Göç ve Politika*, TESAM, Bursa.

Krasner, Stephen D. (1982). "Structural Causes and Regime consequences: Regimes as Intervening Variables". *International Organization*, 36(2), pp. 185–205.

Łuszczuk, Michał (2011). "Climate Change in the Arctic and It's Geopolitical Consequence: the Analysis of the European Union Perspective". *Papers on Global Change IGBP*, 18(1), pp. 93–100.

ND (Northern Dimension) (2016). https://eeas.europa.eu/diplomatic-network/northern-dimension/347/northern-dimension_en (Accessed at 20.07.2021).

ND (Northern Dimension) (2021). https://www.northerndimension.info/northern-dimension (Accessed at 12.06.2021).

NY Times (2019). https://www.nytimes.com/2019/05/06/climate/pompeo-arctic-china-russia.html (Accessed at 15.07.2021).

Pflüger, Friedbert (2020). "A new security challenge: The geopolitical implications of climate change". https://www.atlanticcouncil.org/blogs/energysource/a-new-security-challenge-the-geopolitical-implications-of-climate-change/ (Accessed at 25.06.2021).

Reuters (2018). https://uk.reuters.com/article/uk-china-arctic/china-unveils-vision-for-polar-silk-road-across-arctic-idUKKBN1FF0JC (Accessed at 20.07.2021).

SMFA (Sweden Ministry for Foreign Affairs) (2020). https://www.government.se/4ab869/contentassets/c197945c0be646a482733275d8b702cd/swedens-strategy-for-the-arctic-region-2020.pdf (Accessed at 30.07.2021).

Smieszek, Malgorzata (2019). "Informal International Regimes. A Case Study of the Arctic Council", Academic Dissertation, *University of Lapland*, Finland.

Spohr, Kristina and Hamilton, Daniel S. (2020). "The Arctic and World Order", https://transatlanticrelations.org/wp-content/uploads/2020/12/The-Arctic-and-World-Order.pdf (Accessed at 15.06.2021).

The Economist (2019). https://www.economist.com/the-economist-explains/2019/05/22/who-owns-the-northwest-passage (Accessed at 22.08.2021).

The Guardian (2010). https://www.theguardian.com/world/2010/sep/15/russia-norway-arctic-border-dispute (Accessed at 24.06.2021).

The Guardian (2014). https://www.theguardian.com/environment/2014/nov/21/polar-code-agreed-to-prevent-arctic-environmental-disasters (Accessed at 24.06.2021).

The Observer (2020). https://theobserver-qiaa.org/territorial-claims-in-the-arctic-circle-an-explainer (Accessed at 21.04.2021).

UN (United Nations) (1982). https://www.un.org/depts/los/convention_agreements/texts/unclos/unclos_e.pdf (Accessed at 31.07.2021).

USGS (World Energy Assessment Team) (2008). https://www.usgs.gov/centers/cersc/science/world-oil-and-gas-resource-assessments?qt-science_center_objects=0#qt-science_center_objects (Accessed at 24.06.2021).

World Economic Forum (2019). https://www.weforum.org/agenda/2019/09/4-ways-climate-change-is-opening-the-arctic-up-to-business/ (Accessed at 20.06.2021).

Hatice Çelik

The Environmental Politics in East Asia: Issues and Discussions through Covid-19 Pandemic

Introduction

With the first confirmed cases of Covid-19 in Wuhan, China in December 2019, the world met with this century's first and shocking pandemic. At the beginning, many countries and societies were expecting that disease would be stay only in China and not spread to other geographies. However, the situation steadily got out of the control although the Chinese government applied a strict and quick way of control mainly in Wuhan. Not surprisingly, the first countries who faced with the pandemic became the Asian neighbors of China namely South Korea, Japan, and Taiwan. North Korea, a neighbor of China and one of the close allies of Chinese state, had expressed several times that they didn't have Covid-19 cases. Due to this reason, North Korea will not be included in this study since also there is not any confirmed data about the possible Covid-19 cases. Starting with the quarantine measures of China, people stayed at homes for days, weeks and even months and gradually it became a kind of norm in most of the countries, too. During these official lockdowns and in some cases people's unofficial participation in quarantine measures led to a questioning of the consumption traditions and habits. It also became common that many people decreased their shopping expenditures and in the first months of the pandemic, it was mostly the food consumption that people continued to focus. By going through such an experience, the consumption behaviors and the damage that have been given to the environment was started to be questioned. The environmental sensitivity became more visible and environmental policies gained significance within the societies. From this perspective, this study aims to shed light on the environmental politics and discussions in the East Asian countries starting with the emergence of the pandemic. To do this, each country will be examined under a separate title. Taking into account that Japan, South Korea and Taiwan are the industrialized countries and China has been following high rates of growth for almost three decades, sustainable development and environmental issues are linked with each other and have a place in those governments' agendas. For this aim, this paper tries to answer the question that how the East Asian countries tackle with the environmental challenges which intensified through the Covid-19 pandemic and what the possible opportunities are for the governments to assess.

Environmental Politics: A Basic Introduction

The Earth has been in a constant change and it has enormous impact on the people's living conditions. Although different geographies have been under different environmental changes, the recent decades have shown that each community is under risk due to the global climate change. The industrialized and mostly Western states have been promoting themselves in their attempts to tackle with the environmental problems. In addition to that, they are criticizing the developing countries since they have been staying at relatively high levels of growth rates than developed countries and giving more damage to the environment in general. However, the counter argument of the developing states mostly is that the current developed states had already damaged to the environment for centuries and since they are now able to cover the cost of their damage, it is the developed states' responsibility to compensate that damage. The discussion about the responsibility sharing in addition to the environment's harsh responses like floods, forest fires, and many natural disasters contributed to the foundation of a compressive literature on environmental politics. As a relatively new subject in the international politics, environmental politics is a dynamic field and attracting more interest due to the global warming. In this part, a brief literature on the fundamental discussions of the environmental politics is tried to be presented.

To begin with, it is seen that the research on international environmental politics started to arise in the late 1960s and early 1970s. Similar to the most of the social sciences phenomena, the definition, the boundaries and the limitations of the issue is not clearly defined. As Dauvergne mentions there are a variety of group of scholars whose works take different parameters "as the core of the discipline such as the states and global governance; the ecological impact of the global political economy, the politics of growth, trade, corporations, financing and consumption; environmental security, ethics, civil societies and private global governance" (Dauvergne, 2005: 8). Besides this grouping, there is also another grouping that says to mentor remarkable amount of analysis of international environmental politics which are "international anarchy, knowledge processes, pluralism, structural inequalities, capital accumulation, and sustainability" (Paterson, 2014: 55). In the international environmental politics literature, there is also a discussion on the methodology. When the researchers have been debating and conducting their research on what to include and from which theoretical framework, it is also being discussed that how the researchers should do that. In other words, which method should be used or chosen in the study of the international environmental politics. It is said that "much of the existing literature on methods in IEP focuses on the question of whether qualitative or quantitative studies are more appropriate for its research questions" (Hochstetler and Laituri, 2014: 83). Hochstetler and Laituri also adds that "the predominant mode of analysis of IEP so far has been largely qualitative, with most researchers selecting a small number of case studies for close study" (2014: 83).

This widespread parameters are giving the environmental politics an interdisciplinary character in the academic sense. The research has also showed itself in the increasing number of interdisciplinary works. As Dauvergne points out the works of Michael Zürn (1998), Ronald Mitchell (2002) and Matthew Paterson (2014) are some examples (Dauvergne, 2005: 9). Moreover some other examples of the literature also includes the works of Harris (2004a), Betsill, Hochstetler and Stevis (2006), Chasek, Downie, and Welsh Brown (2010), Dauvergne (2012), and Brenton (2019). The ongoing interdisciplinary approach shows its impact on the role of the state and sovereignty perceptions. For a long period of time, states have been perceived as the only responsible unit and actor to deal with the environmental issues. Although this seems to be still the case, the interdisciplinary character of the international environmental problems are standing as a challenge to that perception. This challenge is possible to be seen in the real life, too. The environmental issues are increasing their impact on everyday lives of millions of people and pushing the governments and non-governmental organizations to produce solutions. Although the international political system is still fundamentally relying on the nation-states, the international community has been endeavoring to contribute to the environmental challenges greatly. Within this regard, the credit should be given to the international community's efforts to cope with the environmental challenges. The 1970s saw the first international gathering addressing this particular issue. The United Nations Conference on the Human Environment (also known as the Stockholm Conference) was an international conference held in Stockholm, Sweden from June 5–16, 1972. It was the UN's first major conference on international environmental issues, and marked a turning point in the development of international environmental politics (UN SDGS, 20.05.2021). At the end of the Conference, The Stockholm Declaration and Action Plan for the Human Environment was adopted. The Action Plan contained three main categories: "(a) Global Environmental Assessment Program (watch plan); (b) Environmental management activities; (c) International measures to support assessment and management activities carried out at the national and international levels" (UN Conferences: Environment and Sustainable Development, 20.05.2021). In addition to that comprehensive plan, another significant output of the Stockholm Conference was the foundation of the UN Environment Program (UNEP). The UNEP, at the time of its foundation, might have increased the expectations of the people waiting for a more established manner in finding solutions to the environmental problems, but there occurred some difficulty regarding the bureaucratic structures and mechanisms, too. Biermann explains this as following:

> "When UNEP was set up in 1972, it was a comparatively independent player with a clearly defined work area. Since then, however, the increase in international environmental regimes has led to a considerable fragmentation of the system. Norms and standards in each issue area of environmental policy are set up by distinct legislative bodies-the conferences of the parties to the environmental treaties-without much respect for repercussions and linkages with other policy fields. This situation is made worse by the organizational fragmentation of the various convention secretariats that have evolved into distinct medium-sized bureaucracies with strong centrifugal tendencies" (Biermann, 2000: 24).

Although the institutionalization and bureaucratic mechanisms for the environmental issues have not been progressed easily, there is a continuing endeavor of the international community. The first and foremost attempt was the signing of the United Nations (UN) Framework Convention on Climate Change (FCCC) at the 1992 UN Conference on Environment and Development (the Earth Summit) (Harris, 2004b: 3). After 2 years of preparation and negotiation, 154 states signed the FCCC at the UN Earth Conference on Environment and Development in June 1992; while within one and a half years, the requisite 50 states had ratified, and the convention entered into force in March 1994 (Von Stein, 2008: 245). This concrete step of the international community can be accepted as a clear intention of the nation states to unite for the sake of the environment. However, at this moment, another parameter comes into the picture. It is the nature of the governments worldwide. In other words, the regime and administration type of the governments have certain impacts on the management of the environmental problems and issues. The relation between regime character and environmental public policies have been an important sub field of environmental politics literature. Scholars have produced a large amount of literature on the democratic and authoritarian governments' attitude and management towards environmental issues. Gilley (2012) says that authoritarian environmentalism was enunciated first by Heilbroner. Gilley mentions it as following:

> "........Heilbroner (1974, p. 38) who believed that 'an absence of inhibitions with respect to the exercise of power' and limits on the freedom of speech would be needed to control population growth" (Gilley, 2012: 288).

A more recent explanation comes from Mark Beeson. He mentions that,

> "One possible consequence of environmental degradation is the development or consolidation of authoritarian rule as political elites come to privilege regime maintenance and internal stability over political liberalization" (Beeson, 2010: 276).

According to Beeson, the problems in the environmental sphere has a potential to damage the liberalization of the states in political perspective. He also adds that this situation may also lead to a worsening of individual liberties since the administrations try to find solutions to environmental problems created by people (Beeson, 2010: 276). Not surprisingly, as an opposite alternative to the authoritarian environmentalism, there is also another concept called as democratic environmentalism in the literature. Gilley says that (2012, 288–289):

> "By implication, then, we can define democratic environmentalism as a public policy model that spreads authority across several levels and agencies of government, including representative legislatures, and that encourages direct public participation from a wide cross-section of society (Holden 2002, Humphrey 2007)".

At this point, East Asia is a suitable geography to look from the environmental perspective. Firstly East Asia region has a mixture of both authoritarian and democratic states. These states have experienced different development and growth paths resulting in different environmental policies and attitudes. Although Covid-19 pandemic seems not to be a direct environmental problem, the beginning of the story is actually quite linked with the people-environment relation. Since it is widely agreed that the Covid-19 pandemic started through a wildlife market in Wuhan, China, the eating habits or behaviors of the people started to be questioned and criticized. Living aside the meaningful discussion of cultural and sociological ground of the societies' different habits, the wildlife markets became a sudden issue for the world to watch. This automatically brought the issue to the wildlife trade of China, too. Starting with wildlife trade, the Covid-19 pandemic carried many other related issues to the discussion of relation between environment and people. Moreover, the response and management of this situation, which is a crisis that states will face almost once in a century, has become a controversial issue from many distinct perspectives. The production mechanisms, the consumption behaviors, the public health, the environmental degradation (excessive use of water for cleaning purposes and disposable plastics in the first periods of pandemic), its impact on the already scaring climate change are among those phenomena. Within this regard, the Covid-19 pandemic's impact on East Asian states' environmental policies will be examined in next part of the paper. It will be done country by country since pandemic created several divergent issues in every country. The only exemption here is North Korea. North Korea is not included in this paper because from the very beginning of the pandemic, North Korean administration has been saying that they are implementing PCR tests but they don't have any Covid-19 cases in the country (DW, 15.06.2021).

China

China has been able to preserve its development and growth steady for almost three decade long. However, it was shaken by the Covid-19 pandemic like many other states. The production has decreased all over the world in many industries due to the demand decrease worldwide and related to that the air pollution showed some progress though limited. As being the first country that faced the Covid-19 cases, China has been always at the forefront of the pandemic management. The source of the pandemic, commonly thought to begin as related to a coronavirus in a wildlife market (Huanan Seafood Wholesale Market) in Wuhan in the last month of 2019. In a very short time period, the issue turned out to be a global health crisis. Although there are some arguments that the Covid-19 was produced/prepared and spread intentionally, none of those has been proved. Since the coronavirus is said to spread from a wild animal (bat) to humans, the wildlife trade again became one of the controversial issues both worldwide and in China. After the reactions, China annunciated that there will be a ban on the country's wild animal trade until the country has got rid of the Covid-19 (Denyer and Li, 2020). According to the new restrictions, the transport and sale of wild animals, specifically barring markets, supermarkets, restaurants and e-commerce platforms from trading in any form were banned (Denyer and Li, 2020). However, this was not seen as a total solution to the problem. Because during the SARS (severe acute respiratory syndrome) outbreak, there was also a ban on the wild life trade. As clearly understood, it was not a permanent ban but rather a temporary one. Therefore, "Christian Walzer, chief global veterinarian at the Wildlife Conservation Society, defined the measure an "important first step" but said the ban needs to be permanent" (Denyer and Li, 2020). However, it is almost impossible to argue that eating wild animals' meat is so common in whole China. In a study for which structured questionnaire and face-to-face interviews were conducted in Beijing, Shanghai, Guangzhou, Kunming and Nanning of China, it is argued that "the rates of wildlife consumed as food and as ingredients for traditional medicines in Guangzhou and Nanning ranked in the top" (Zhang and Yin, 2014: 2371). It is clear that the apart from eating there is also an incentive to use wild life animals for traditional medicines. However, the Chinese government also applied different methods to transform the society's perspective for the wild life animals. The government come to such a position mainly considering the initiative of WildAid and its partners, the China Wildlife Conservation Association and the Pangolin Crisis Fund. These organizations started a new series of outdoor advertisements to put attention to the pangolins. The message that was being delivered is that pangolins should be protected and that consumption of their meat and products is illegal (WildAid, 2020). Within this regard, the related organizations have put effort to contribute to the management of the wild life animals' protection in China. In addition to this, posters promoting the protection of wildlife animals were placed at billboards in China (Sandford, 2020). By trying to influence the eating habits of the people and also the usage of the wild life animals in traditional medicine, the Chinese government showed its effort to put an end to the wild life animals' trade in China. Those efforts were mostly the discussions and precautions related to the source of the pandemic.

Yet, pandemic created a huge pressure on the lives of people. The Chinese government was successful enough to take control of the virus spread thanks to its strict measures mainly in Hubei province. In addition to the first stage measures, China has been among the first countries to produce Covid-19 vaccine. However, until the vaccination starts and people movement turned to its ordinary level, the people's relatively limited movements had an impact on the nature, too. One of these impacts was certainly on air pollution. According to a research, examining the lockdown period in Wuhan, the result is worthy. The study shows that:

> "After the lockdown, the average monthly air quality index (AQI) in Wuhan was 59.7, which is 33.9% lower than that before the lockdown (January 23, 2020) and 47.5% lower than that during the corresponding period (113.6) from 2015 to 2019" (Lian et.al., 2020: 1).

Another study focusing on a larger geography shows that:

> "Recent data released by NASA (National Aeronautics and Space Administration) and ESA (European Space Agency) indicates that pollution in some of the epicenters of Covid-19 such as Wuhan, Italy, Spain and USA etc. has reduced up to 30%" (Muhammad et. al., 2020: 1).

The authors also conclude with a more optimistic perspective. They say that although the pandemic is a serious threat to public health, it can be a "blessing in disguise" since it is also letting the pollution decrease and nature to recover

(Muhammad et al., 2020: 5). In other words, it is also possible to see the pandemic as an opportunity for all people to reconsider our relations with the nature and environment.

Japan

Japan was among the first countries that saw Covid-19 cases mostly due to its intense exchange of people, goods and services with China. However, different than China, Japan did not take harsh measures to prevent the spread of the cases. To the contrary, Japan has followed a rather loose method to combat with the pandemic. Nevertheless, this did not prevent pandemic to have an impact on the environment, either. Firstly Ministry of Environment announced that there would be an online meeting on the 3rd of September 2020, "share experiences and views on climate actions and environmental protection measures as part of the recovery from the coronavirus pandemic" (Ministry of the Environment, 2020). It is added that the website "Platform for Redesign 2020" would also be prepared. After the online meeting was held, the ministry published a summary of the meeting's agenda. In the summary, it was emphasized that while working to go back to the pre-pandemic conditions, the states also should think of a more sustainable version. It is stated also that:

> "While our recovery from the pandemic will be accompanied with a rise in global energy demand, we cannot fall back to the same rebound in emissions that followed economic stimulus packages from the 2008 financial crisis. Therefore it is critical to address the issues of decarbonization of both energy sectors through the development of renewable energies and the social implementation of hydrogen, as well as decarbonization in the process of energy use in industrial sectors and households" (Online Platform Ministerial Meeting, 2020).

Within this context, Japanese government showed its eagerness to get prepared for a better design of the world economy and environment regarding the post-pandemic future. Moreover, The Bank of Japan expressed that "Under the new climate-related program, the BOJ will offer 1-year, zero-interest funds to financial institutions for their loans and investments in such products as green bonds to tackle climate change" (Suzuki, 2021). With this step, Japan's central bank contributed to the overall aim of the Japanese government to tackle with the shocking impact of the pandemic. However, the environment activists in Japan are looking a little skeptical to the developments. According to Jesse Chase-Lubitz's news, the activists are facing a challenge for their gatherings due to Covid-19; however, through online gathering they are working to spread their messages (Chase-Lubitz, 2020). Yet, the activists that the reporter had interviewed emphasized the point that altogh at the beginning of the pandemic there occurred some progress like the fall of air pollution etc. but the necessary environmental changes may get slowed in the long run (Chase-Lubitz, 2020).

South Korea

South Korea, like Japan, was among the first countries to face with the Covid-19 cases. But the country's effective measures, especially in the first waves of the pandemic, showed and admirable result that can be seen both in the number of losses and cases.[1] However, the pandemic offered a chance to realize the transformation of the economy and put forward a more green economy for the next generations. On July 14, 2020, South Korean President Moon Jae-in unveiled an initiative which is called "Korean New Deal". In his speech, The Green New Deal was proposed as part of the agenda and the President indicated that climate change responses were also imperative for preventing infectious diseases on which there is a consensus among advanced European countries so that Korea should also catch this agenda (Cheong Wa Dae, 2020a). Just after three days, the President visited Jeollabuk-do province and pointed out that the Green New Deal was an initiative to move from a carbon-dependent economy to a low-carbon one and green energy would have an enormous impact on achieving great socioeconomic transition (Cheong Wa Dae, 2020b). The effort of the Korean government is also appreciated by the World Bank. Hoon Sahib Soh, the Special Representative, World Bank Group Korea Office says that

> "The World Bank is committed to supporting Korea in its efforts to further sustainable development, including through the World Bank's Korea Green Growth Trust Fund (KGGTF) and the World Bank Group Korea office's dedicated green growth innovation" (Soh, 2020).

In addition to the government's initiative, it is also important to listen to the non-governmental organizations like the Korea Federation for Environmental Movements (KFEM).[2] Jieon Lee, Climate and Energy Coordinator at KFEM, gave an interview to Minjee Kum (a Seoul-based freelance journalist, and this

---

1 When looked at the data of more than 200 countries, Korea, with its loss of 2202 people, is ranked the 82nd, https://www.worldometers.info/coronavirus/#countries. In addition, Korea has the 3rd lowest number of deaths among the G-20 countries, https://tradingeconomics.com/country-list/coronavirus-deaths?continent=g20 (Access Date: 21.08.2021).

2 The Korean Federation for Environmental Movements is Korea's oldest and Asia's biggest environmental organization which was created in 1993.

interview was translated by Eric Rosencrantz) and shed light on Korea's new initiative. Mr. Lee said that "in 2020, ultra-fine particulate matter pollution has fallen by as much as 27 per cent compared to last year" (Goethe-Institut Korea).[3] However, Lee also adds that according to a study that KFEM conducted COVID-19 had increased the amount of waste because of disposable products in addition to the fact that food delivery services and online shopping introduce a great deal of packaging waste (Goethe-Institut Korea). He concludes that to achieve a goal of more sustainable society, green infrastructure and carbon neutrality should be the things to focus on in the long run (Goethe-Institut Korea).

Taiwan

Taiwan, like South Korea, has been praised thanks to its successful management of the pandemic.[4] In addition to its triumphant management of the pandemic, Taiwan is also differentiating itself from many other developed countries based on its economic data. It is argued that Taiwan's GDP jumped 7.43 % year-on-year in the quarter ending June of 2021 (Trading Economics, 22.08.2021) which is not bad at all. However, the climate change is there as a reality. It is mentioned that the droughts and blackouts are creating some questions marks in the minds of producers in Taiwan like whether to move out their factories or not (Pang, 2021). Yet another issue is the waste management during the pandemic. Lin Yu-huei, head of recycling at Taipei's Department of Environmental Protection, expressed that the amount of discarded takeaway containers in the capital Taipei between January and May rise by 85 % compared with the same period last year (The Strait Times, 10.08.2021). Like many other countries, Taiwan has also faced a growing amount of waste during the pandemic.

Conclusion

East Asian countries have been performed a much better management ability regarding the Covid-19 pandemic as compared to many developed countries such as the USA, the UK, Italy. There are many factors that helped this picture to be realized but the aim of this paper is not to discuss these factors. Rather,

3 The date of the interview isn't available at the web page, but the full version of the interview can be accessed via https://www.goethe.de/prj/eco/en/pol/21917565.html.

4 According to the data of more than 200 countries, Taiwan, with its loss of 10 people, is ranked the 148th, https://www.worldometers.info/coronavirus/#countries (Access Date: 21.08.2021).

it is aimed to concentrate on a shared issue of interest which is environment and the fact that the global nature of the world is certainly effecting the global environment by creating problems for all people. Within this regard, the issues, problems, and discussion that East Asian states have faced during the ongoing pandemic are tried to examine. As a general outlook, it is seen that all East Asian states have realized the urgency of the need to deal with the environmental issues in a better manner. Although each of them has concentrated on different parts of the crisis, they have been working to reduce the impact of the pandemic over environment. For this specific aim, states are using the necessary mechanisms like China immediately banned the wildlife animals' trade. In Korea case, it was witnessed that the Korean government announced a New Deal program which also includes a Green Deal perspective which is a source of hope to demonstrate that there is a common will to modify the environmental policies. Japan has another prominent example initiating an online platform for the countries to share their experiences and data for the sake of the environment. Nevertheless, the actions of the individual states are not enough to revert the already terrible situation and issues of the nature and environment. However, it is still promising that East Asian countries are standing as a robust example to cope with the environmental problems.

References

Beeson, Mark (2010). "The coming of environmental authoritarianism", *Environmental Politics*, Volume: 19, Issue: 2, pp. 276–294.

Betsill, Michele Merrill, Hochstetler, Kathryn, and Stevis, Dimitris (ed.). (2006) *Palgrave advances in international environmental politics*. Hampshire: Palgrave Macmillan.

Biermann, Frank (2000). "The case for a world environment organization", *Environment: Science and Policy for Sustainable Development*, Volume: 42, Issue: 9, pp. 22–31.

Brenton, Tony (2019). *The greening of Machiavelli: the evolution of international environmental politics*. London: Routledge.

Chasek, Pamela, Downie, David Leonard, and Welsh Brown, Janet (2010). *Global environmental politics* (5th Edition), Boulder: Westview Press.

Chase-Lubitz, Jesse (2020). "COVID-19 a threat and opportunity for Japan's environmental activists", https://www.japantimes.co.jp/news/2020/04/16/national/covid-19-environmental-activists/ (Access Date: 17.04.2021).

Cheong Wa Dae (2020a). "Keynote Address by President Moon Jae-in at Presentation of Korean New Deal Initiative", http://english1.president.go.kr/BriefingSpeeches/Speeches/852 (Access Date: 17.05.2021).

Cheong Wa Dae (2020b). "Remarks by President Moon Jae-in while Visiting Korean New Deal and Green Energy Site", http://english1.president.go.kr/BriefingSpeeches/Speeches/853 (Access Date: 17.05.2021).

Dauvergne, Peter (2005). "Research in global environmental politics: history and trends" (Ed. Peter Dauvergne), *Handbook of global environmental politics*, Cheltenham: Edward Elgar Publishing, pp. 8–32.

Dauvergne, Peter (2012) *Handbook of global environmental politics* (2nd Edition), Cheltenham: Edward Elgar Publishing.

Denver, Simon and Li, Lyric (2020). "China bans wild animal trade until coronavirus epidemic is eliminated", https://www.washingtonpost.com/world/asia_pacific/china-bans-wild-animal-trade-until-coronavirus-epidemic-eliminated/2020/01/26/0e05a964-4017-11ea-971f-4ce4f94494b4_story.html (Access Date: 15.06.2021).

Deutsche, Welle. (2021), "Coronavirus digest: North Korea tells WHO it has no COVID cases", https://www.dw.com/en/coronavirus-digest-north-korea-tells-who-it-has-no-covid-cases/a-57989002 (Access Date: 15.06.2021).

Gilley, Bruce (2012). "Authoritarian environmentalism and China's response to climate change", *Environmental Politics*, Volume: 21, Issue: 2, pp. 287–307.

Goethe-Institut Korea, (2020). Interview of Minjee Kum with Jieon Lee (translated by Eric Rosencrantz), "Covid-19 Must Be Used For a Green Change", https://www.goethe.de/prj/eco/en/pol/21917565.html (Access Date: 16.08.2021).

Harris, Paul G. (2004b). "Introduction: the politics and foreign policy of global warming in East Asia" (Ed. Paul G. Harris), *Global Warming and East Asia*, London:Routledge, pp. 20–35.

Harris, Paul G. (ed.). (2004a) *Global warming and East Asia: the domestic and international politics of climate change*. London: Routledge.

Heilbroner, Robert L. (1974). *An inquiry into the human prospect*, Norton, New York.

Hochstetler, Kathryn, and Laituri, Melinda (2014). "Methods in international environmental politics" (Ed. Michele M. Betsill, Kathryn Hochstetler and Dimitris Stevis), *Advances in International Environmental Politics*, Hampshire: Palgrave Macmillan, pp. 78–104.

Holden, Barry (2002). *Democracy and global warming*. Continuum, London.

Humphrey, Mathew (2007). *Ecological politics and democratic theory: the challenge to the deliberative ideal*. Routledge, London.

Lian, Xinbo, et al. (2020). "Impact of city lockdown on the air quality of COVID-19-hit of Wuhan city", *Science of the Total Environment*, Volume: 742, pp. 140556.

Ministry of Environment of Japan. (2020)."Ministerial meeting of the "Online Platform" on a Sustainable and Resilient Recovery from COVID-19 and the website "Platform for Redesign 2020"", http://www.env.go.jp/en/headline/2465.html (Access Date: 15.06.2021).

Mitchell, Ronald B. (2002). "International environment" (Eds. Thomas Risse, Beth Simmons and Walter Carlsnaes), *Handbook of International Relations*, Sage Publications, London.

Muhammad, Sulaman, Long, Xingle, Salman, Muhammad (2020). "COVID-19 pandemic and environmental pollution: A blessing in disguise?", *Science of the Total Environment*, Volume: 728, pp. 138820.

Online Platform Ministerial Meeting. (2020). Chair's summary: Redesign and Three Transitions, http://www.env.go.jp/press/files/jp/114727.pdf (Access Date: 16.04.2021).

Pang, Iris (2021). "Covid hasn't hurt Taiwan's trade but climate change will", https://think.ing.com/snaps/taiwans-covid-hasnt-hurt-trade-but-climate-change-will/.

Paterson, Matthew (2014). "Theoretical perspectives on international environmental politics" (Eds. Michele M. Betsill, Kathryn Hochstetler and Dimitris Stevis), *Advances in International Environmental Politics*, London: Palgrave Macmillan, pp. 45–77.

Sandford, Steve (2020). "Conservation Groups Fear Wildlife Trade Will Resume as China Lifts Restrictions", https://www.voanews.com/science-health/coronavirus-outbreak/conservation-groups-fear-wildlife-trade-will-resume-china-lifts (Access Date: 22.06.2021).

Soh, Hoon Sahib (2020). "S. Korea can make COVID-19 recovery greener", *The Korea Herald*, http://www01.koreaherald.com/view.php?ud=20200628000200 (Access Date: 15.08.2021).

Suzuki, Noriyuki (2021). "BOJ to offer zero-interest funds to lenders serious about climate change", https://english.kyodonews.net/news/2021/07/eed460418cf4-urgent-boj-keeps-ultraeasy-monetary-policy-trims-gdp-outlook-amid-pandemic.html (Access Date: 16.04.2021).

The Strait Times. (2021). "Taiwan's Covid-19 curbs drive spike in food packaging waste", https://www.straitstimes.com/asia/east-asia/taiwans-covid-19-curbs-drive-spike-in-food-packaging-waste (Access Date: 10.08.2021).

Trading Economics. (2021). "Taiwan GDP Annual Growth Rate", https://tradingeconomics.com/taiwan/gdp-growth-annual (Access Date: 15.08.2021).

UN (Conferences: Environment and Sustainable Development) (2021). https://www.un.org/en/conferences/environment/stockholm1972 (Access Date: 20.05.2021).

UN (United Nations Sustainable Development Goals Knowledge Platform) (2021). https://sustainabledevelopment.un.org/milestones/humanenvironment (Access Date: 20.05.2021).

Von Stein, Jana (2008). "The international law and politics of climate change: ratification of the United Nations Framework Convention and the Kyoto Protocol", *Journal of Conflict Resolution*, Volume: 52, Issue: 2, pp. 243–268.

Wildaid. (2020). "Comic-style campaign highlights increased protection for pangolins in China", https://wildaid.org/comic-style-campaign-highlights-increased-protection-for-pangolins-in-china/ (Access Date: 20.06.2021).

Worldometer. https://www.worldometers.info/coronavirus/#countries (Access Date: 21.08.2021).

Zhang, Li and Yin, Feng (2014). "Wildlife consumption and conservation awareness in China: a long way to go", *Biodiversity and Conservation*, Volume: 23, Issue: 9, pp. 2371–2381.

Zurn, Michael (1998). "The rise of international environmental politics: a review of current research", *World Politics*, Volume: 50, Issue: 4, pp. 617–649.

Pelin Pınar Giritlioğlu

Invasive Urbanization and It's Environmental Impacts: Istanbul Case

Today, neoliberal urbanization transforms cities in an invasive manner at many regions around the world. During this process, any and all components forming and shaping the cities get destroyed under the destructive and oppressive dominance of this urbanization, or exposed to unrecoverable damage. Economic crisis in the world, climate change, disasters and lastly the pandemic process showed, in respect to our country, that dissociation of production from local scale, ongoing pressure on natural sites and destructive planning decisions, commercialization of vital ecological sites in the cities to global/mega projects and investment groups, external dependent economic/agriculture policies, health and education policies which have already moved away from a perspective favoring the public, tourism and security policies serving the neoliberal world, weaken the urban resilience. Sensitive ecological sites such as forests, agricultural sites, pastures, water basins, coastal sites hereby get systematically exhausted.

İstanbul has been changing and losing its identity, character and its essential environmental assets rapidly since neo-liberal urbanization policies started to be implemented from the start of 1980's. 1980's were the beginning of the erratic migration caused by the urbanization policies and back-to-back implementations of zoning amnesties that attacked and allowed tourism policies and invasive urbanization to start in expense of water basins, northern forests and coasts. Especially back-to-back mega projects like Avrasya Tunnel, Third Bridge, Kuzey Marmara Highway, Third Airport have been causing depredation since the beginning of the 2000's. Channel Istanbul, which has been debated on since 2012 has also been added to the mega project continuum.

Within the scope of this study, the invasive urbanization process of Istanbul will be explained by focusing mainly on the 2000's, and the environmental effects that emerged in this process, which are an intervention to nature and life values, will be revealed with numerical data.

Theoretical Overview

Each year the world population keeps piling up in cities. According to World Bank (2020) 55 % of the global population is living in cities. In 1982 this was 40 % (Fig. 1).

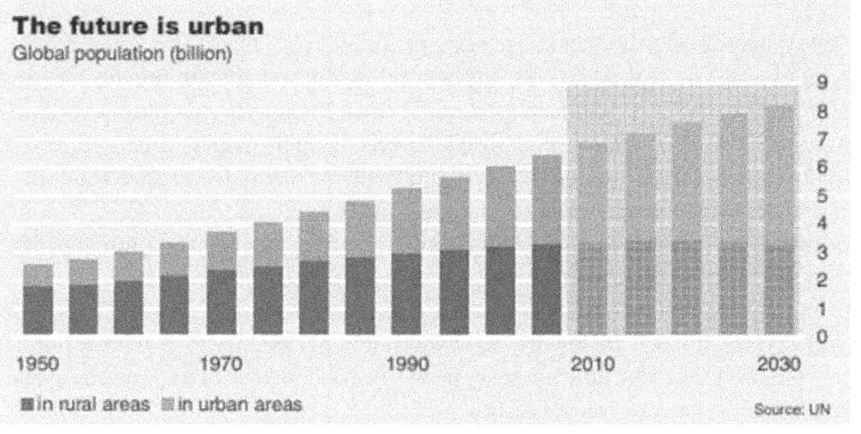

Fig. 1: Future of Urban Population. Source: Deutcche Bank Research, 2008, file:///C:/Users/Dell/Downloads/Megacities_Boundless_growth_.pdf (Access date: 15 December 2020)

Thus, the world becomes one mega city. While the global population is increasing 65 million each year (Urban world: Mapping the Economic Power of Cities Report, McKinsey Global Institute, 2011), half of the population is living in cities that create 80 % of global GDP. In parallel to this, 60 % of the Global GDP is produced by 15 % of the world population which inhabits in 600 urban centers (McKinsey Global Institute, 2011). From 10 mega cities in 1990, the number increased to 28 in 2014 and 33 in 2018 (UNDP, https://www.undp.org/content/undp/en/home/sustainable-development-goals/goal-11-sustainable-cities-and-communities.html). This data indicates the process of invasive urbanization and its accretion.

From the second half of the 20th century, cities have grown and got condensed. Today, cities only cover 3 % of the world but consume 60–80 % of the resources and cause minimum 70 % of the carbon emissions (UNDP, https://www.undp.org/content/undp/en/home/sustainable-development-goals/goal-11-sustainable-cities-and-communities.html). As cities grow larger and the

Image 1: An Example to the City Growth Today. (Source: Anonymous)

traffic creates more pressure on them, the green areas, open spaces and natural habitats are being lost (Photo 1).

Uncontrolled urbanization process today forced the world to encounter environmental (climate change, carbon emissions, resource consumption, natural disasters and pandemics), socio-economical (injustice, inequality, concord, employment and health), spatial (uncontrolled structuring, condensed settlement, inefficient infrastructure, accessibility, earth and water loss) corporate (governance and geographical inequality, water and food safety) problems. In this perspective, the five main hardships that await future cities are environmental threats, sustainability of resources (or constraints), increase in income inequality, technology (inequality related to the accessibility of smart technologies, environment related technologies, smart planning etc.).

Each of these titles remind us that the world is at the hands of uncertainties and risks, and thus force us to soon discuss how the threatening ecological, socio-economical, spatial and political decisions and urban policies in effect would impact the cities and rural areas environmentally in the near future, as well as the measures to be taken against such risk. The problem is prioritized internationally. The 8th Environmental Action Program, which aims for the year 2030, puts an emphasis on how healthy ecosystems are related to human welfare. To this extent, in order to increase the endurance towards climate change, adopt a renovative, protect biodiversity, protect natural capital and decrease pressure on production and consumption (energy, industrial progress, buildings and infrastructure, mobility and food systems etc.) are the main goals of the program.

In today's world, cities are not just localized spaces created by broader global or national projects of neoliberal restructuring, on the contrary, they have become more and more central to the reproduction, transformation and reconstruction of neoliberalism itself since the 1980's (Turut, Özgür, 2005).

Harvey bases the growth history of modern cities on capitalism's production of the built environment by fixing capital in the newly settled area. However, in his work titled The New Imperialism dated 2003, Harvey reveals the functioning of capitalist imperialism in a comprehensive and meaningful whole, from the control of energy resources to capital movements, from neoliberal aggression to accumulation through dispossession, from the export of domestic political crises through war to the capital-state relationship. Until recently, neoliberalism has been treated with reference to national regulatory trends and supranational institutional reorganizations (such as the role of the World Bank and IMF in giving directions for structural adjustment programs in developing countries), whereas since the late 1990s the background political economy dynamics and its geographies extending from the global to the local, with a critical perspective (Brenner and Theodore, 2005). Peck, Theodore, and Brenner (2009) emphasize that to understand contemporary neo liberalization processes, it is not sufficient to analyze only the political-ideological foundations, for this it is necessary to systematically question the multifaceted institutional forms, development trends, socio-political effects and contradictions. An approach from this perspective is needed to explain the neoliberal policies prevailing in cities today.

At the point that we are at, cities change the production site identity completely and become consumption sites, by the instruction of the global city policies such as informatics, media, finance etc. reshape cities with new identities. Industry moves from center cities to the surrounding cities, create sectoral divisions within countries and cause division of labor. "Manufacturing footprint" surpasses the biological capacity (Turkey's Ecological Footprint Report, WWF, 2012) and countries that have ecological gap are becoming dependent on fresh waters, forest and agricultural fields of other areas (Fig. 2).

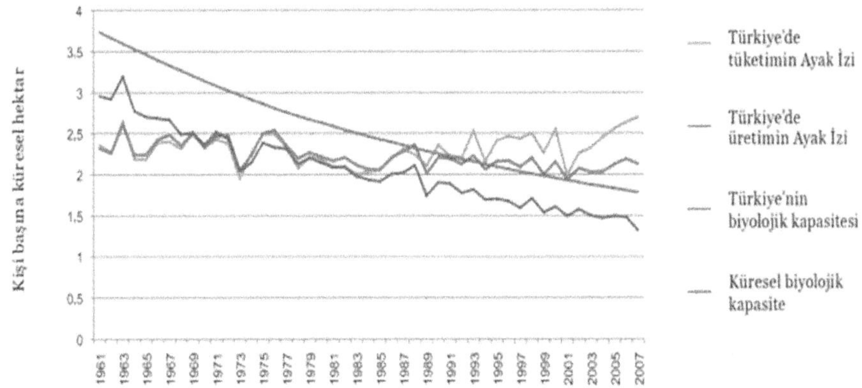

Fig. 2: Turkey's Biological Capacity and Ecological Footprint, 1961–2007.
Source: Turkey's Ecological Footprint Report, WWF, 2012

Globally, increasing consumption of energy and resources as result of mega projects, uncontrolled growth, populist urbanization, privatization practices, etc., on top of the impacts of climate change, impact the cities, starting from the poorest and most vulnerable parts. Urban, social, economic and ecological costs increasingly escalate as a result of this invasive urbanization.

Climate change, which threatens the entire world today, currently evolves into a climate crisis with the impact of destructive and invasive urbanization policies. As the nature gets commoditized rapidly and continuously, cities get more and more fragile, and capitalist urbanization policies condemn the world to climate crisis and an uncertainty as to food and water. The systematical domination and invasion carried out with the collaboration of government and capital groups on cities, rural areas, and sensitive ecosystems increase gradually. Nature loses its value in this global system, which transforms anything into capital for the sake of economic growth, and many large projects originate a major eco-destruction.

In the cities under the impact of these invasive urbanization policies in Turkey, and especially in metropolitan cities such as Istanbul, mega projects which result in major ecological destructions are often constructed. This construction process has got intensified since the 2010s.

Purpose

The purpose of this study is to set forth the unrecoverable damage and the exponential increase of the impacts of invasive urbanization processes, which commonly demonstrate their impacts all around the country, with the help of of mega projects.

Research Methodology

The study principally relies on literature research and analysis. The first section of the study aims to evaluate the invasive urbanization process in Turkey. In this regard, the concept of invasive urbanization and its impact on the cities will be analyzed by way of literature view. The second section will discuss the mega projects, which are produced one by one in recent years in Istanbul where invasive urbanization demonstrates its impacts in the largest sense. Furthermore, the invasion of these projects on urban and rural sites will be set forth by regarding the data concerning these projects in Environmental Impact Assessment and Plan Reports.

Concept

At the very beginning of the study, the concept of invasive urbanization must be defined. In this study, the concept of invasive urbanization is defined, without considering any urban and environmental value, the purpose of which is commodification that is, aiming to convert every value into money, acting in line with the orders and demands of big capital, instead of principles such as urban ethics, public interest, common benefit and social reconciliation. It is used in the sense of urbanization policy that reconstructs urban space by shaping its sovereignty in line with the instructions and goals of international financial institutions and organizations, without distinguishing between urban and rural spaces.

1. An Overview of the Construction Phase of Invasive Urbanization Policies in Turkey

Urbanization policies in Turkey can be defined under five periods in the most general sense (Figure 1).

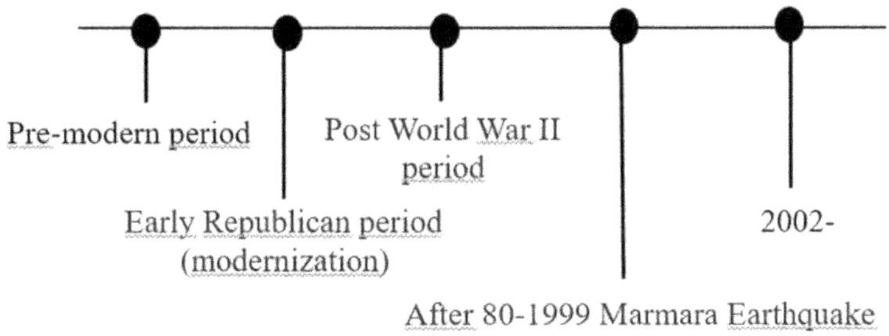

Fig. 3: Planning Process in Turkey from Past to Present. Source: created by author

Pre-modern period is the unplanned period when fire insurance maps in the scale 1/25,000 were issued. In this early era when early industrialization took place and articulation to the world capital system emerged, the mega projects at the time (e.g. mosques, medreses, caravanserais, imarets, etc.) were built. The rescript of Gulhane (1839), the Edict of Reform (1859), and the Land Law (1858) can be named as the fundamental legal provisions forming the land order at this era.

During the modernization period where the modernity project was applicable to urban sites, factories built by the government, public buildings and railway projects, as well as nationalization of the formerly built railways could be named as one of the most significant projects of the time. Due to the lack of planners and architects in the country, the growth of the cities was aimed with the zoning plans prepared by foreign architects and planners (Tekeli, 2000). Zoning plans were used as a tool to generate a Westernizing modern society in parallel to the aims of the new Turkish Republic at the time, and public areas such as squares, stations, parks were built. Especially the capital city, Ankara, was developed as a symbol where the Republic generated its aims. Amendments to the Law on Building and Roads in 1925 and the Municipality Law issued in 1930 are among the fundamental legal tools of the time.

Industry Plans made for the European continent after the 2nd World War and especially in 1954, and for the entire Istanbul in 1955 paved the way of migration to Istanbul, and the government which failed to be a relief to the emerging demand for housing could not play an active role in the housing sector. The limited number of public housing projects was not near enough to resolve the problems. Many districts on both sides of Istanbul were filled with slums and their number has been increasing ever since. The same problem has also been affecting big cities like İzmir and Ankara. The number of slums has increased from 30.000 in 1948, to 50.000 in 1950, to 240.000 in 1960 and 430.000 in 1965 (Çakır, 2007). The amnesties that were granted in Ankara in 1948 and in the whole country in 1949 did not help solve the problem. To the opposite, they made the situation more chronical. In the same period, the development projects that were made possible through expropriation changed the traditional texture of the cities and cities were separated with big avenues.

1980's were the years that neoliberal policies started to be implemented in city life. As Peker (2005) puts it, "The Özal period and onwards gave birth to new cities with the focus on socio- economical changes and global progress for the sake of "stepping up to the next age" at the end of 21st century". After the military coup in 1980 in Turkey, the neo liberal economic policies that were being applied were rapidly put to operation. These applications in accordance with the fall of welfare state were able to find large areas to operate. The policies that encourage free market drawn both local and foreign investments and started the period of big projects in collaboration with privatization and public owned companies. Thus, the World Bank Report published in 1994 says that "Public enterprise reforms, including privatization, are also important for the long-run reduction of public sector deficits and improved efficiency in Turkey" (The World Bank Annual Report, 1994) and can be seen encouraging the policies. The base of this period was made possible by city laws that were a part of neo liberal policies. 1980's were also the years that cities were submitted to illegal growth. The illegal slums that were built in 1950's was turned into illegal apartments in 1980's. In 1990's spatial effects of globalization had started to show signs in big cities. Skyscrapers, high tech office buildings, shopping malls had taken their place in cities. Now the illegal structures that were made legal by amnesties had been replaced by globalizing cities.

The Marmara Earthquake that occurred in 1999 was the end of one period in the countries and a step to a new period of urban transformation. Immediately Justice and Development Party (Adalet ve Kalkınma Partisi) held on the urban transformation policies and passed laws that allowed the process of urban transformation back-to-back and adopted them. Although at the beginning of this period local administrations were authorized, in time their powers were weakened and with the foundation of Environment and Urbanization Ministry in 2011 the authority was taken almost entirely by the centralized government. TOKİ, which has become a strong central actor of urban transformation with the law numbered 5162, which entered into force in 2004, was affiliated to the Ministry of Environment and Urbanization with the Decree Law No. 703 dated 09.07.2018. After military coup attempt in 2016, presidency system was adopted. During this process urban transformation policies reshaped, especially

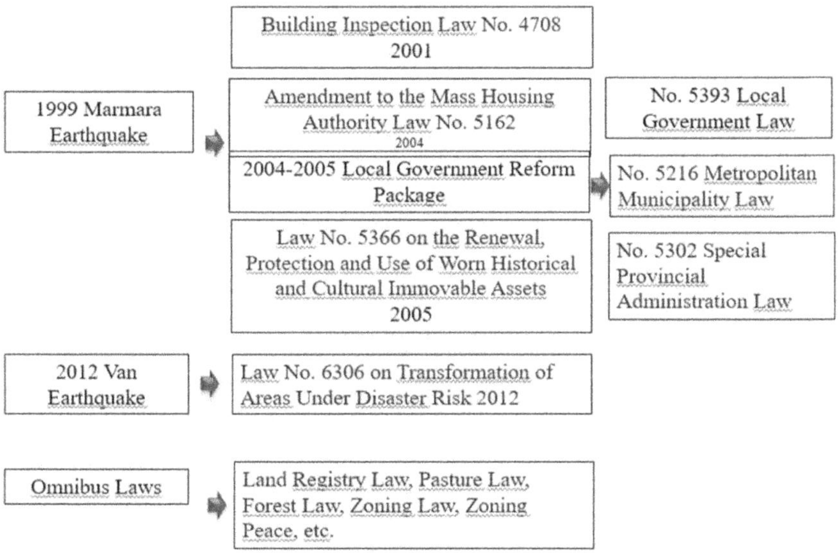

Fig. 4: A Look at Turkeys Urban Settlement in Chrological Order

in big cities became insistent and binding (Özden, 2016). After 2002, the laws of the city were rewritten, articles added to the old laws, frequent changes in the Public Procurement Law, soil protection, forest and pasture laws, Decree-Laws, Omnibus Laws, predominantly Middle East-based agreements, etc. The infrastructure of an invasive urban restructuring process was established without slowing down (Fig. 4).

Thus, as a result of this great invasion the life sources of the cities such as forests, coasts, agricultural lands and water sources have been damaged beyond repair. Within 17 years 3.7 billion square public land has been privatized. According to the information compiled by Sözcü Newspaper in 2020 from the data of the General Directorate of National Real Estate affiliated to the Ministry of Environment and Urbanization, 2.1 billion square meters of deforested land belonging to the Treasury, 971 million square meters of land and 586 million square meters of agricultural land between 2003 and 2019. In total, 3 billion 724 million square meters of land, agricultural land and areas that have lost their forest quality have been disposed of. Moreover, the practices initiated in 2002 on the axis of the "moderate Islam" model changed the scope and scope of the rising conservatism in cities. The reflections of this situation firstly appeared in Ankara and Istanbul in the form of a "settlement with the Republic". The architecture of the Republican period was destroyed by local and central representatives of the power, by imposition, stubbornly, turning a blind eye to social demands and posing victory on the rubble, and projects bearing the signature of the power were built in their place (Image 2).

Image 2: The Victory Pose of the Ankara Metropolitan Municipality Mayor of the Period Over the Demolition of the Iller Bank Building, Which is a Republican Period Structure. (Source: https://odatv4.com/siyaset/bu-nasil-bir-ruh-halidir-2006171200-118085)

Peker (2015) describes this situation with the words "We are faced with a 'new conquest' movement manifested by the attempt to re-conquer the city, which is thought to have been 'Westernized' by the conservative subject". At this point, the actors of this invasive urbanization, which is defined as a kind of "new conquest", in the 1950s are more than one. The process worked with a model in which real estate speculators, land mafias and citizens acted together, which emerged due to the fact that the right to housing and housing, which is the duty of the state, cannot be provided in the cities, and that sufficient employment cannot be created in rural and urban areas. In the post-1980 period, when liberalization,

liberalization and attempts to integrate into the global world increased, this structure did not change much and continued under the influence of illegality and populism. This understanding, which also rejects the concept of planning outside of the early Republican period, evolved with the 2000s. This invasive process, which is mainly indexed to developments and policies within the borders of the country, has taken a completely centralized form, which gradually pushes the citizen and even the nationalist structure outward, getting closer to the global capital with each passing day. He created it "by the hands of plans".

2. Reconstruction of Istanbul in the Post-2002 Period

Throughout the 2000s, Istanbul has been the leading actor of this unabated restructuring process. After the Marmara earthquake in 1999, the urban restructuring approach in Istanbul followed a path parallel to the urbanization policy of the government. Istanbul has been experiencing this invasive urbanization process, which started in the 1950s, intensely in the 2000s by changing its actors. In the last 15 years, these projects, which were carried out at different scales such as illegal construction, high construction, forest and water basin constructions in the past, have been;

- Mega projects with irreparable environmental impacts,
- The areas built in the areas that lost the forest quality and water basins that were legalized with the zoning peace, the areas that were built with privileged zoning rights, etc.
- Projects realized through the privatization of public lands
- Extensive urban transformation projects have been added.

2.1 Mega Projects

In the 2000s, Istanbul Metropolitan Municipality and related ministries changed the zoning plans for 76 mega projects in the city and granted privileged zoning rights. Not content with this, the companies have risen many times over their privileged zoning rights. As of 2018, an additional 12 million 400 thousand square meters of construction has been made throughout the city (https://kuzeyormanlari.org/2018/10/29/emsalsiz-ihanet-ulke-tarihinin-en-buyuk-rant-oyunlarinin-boyutunu-acikuzun/).

One of the most important of these projects is the Third Bosphorus Crossing and Northern Marmara Motorway Project. Third Bosphorus Crossing 59 m. width, 2164 m. length and 322 m. has height. Together with the Northern Marmara Highway, it cost 4.5 billion TL. The project, which was built with the build-operate-transfer model, was built between Garipçe and Poyrazköy in Istanbul, within the scope of the "1/25000 scale Istanbul Northern Marmara Highway master zoning plan amendment" approved on 27.03.2014. Along the route, there are some conservation forests, seed gardens and recreation areas such as urban forest and picnic area; These are as follows: Belgrade Protection Forest: The route passes through the northern border of the forest located on the European side of Istanbul. Elmalı Bendi Protection Forest: Part of the route passes over this forest located on the Asian side. Northern Bosphorus (Upper Bosphorus) KBA (including Belgrad Forest) Other areas: A Seed Garden located between Reşadiye and Alemdağ Nişantepe, an urban forest and various picnic areas in Ümraniye near the existing Istanbul highway (E-80). Most of the route (approximately 35 km) passes over the Bosphorus Important Natural Area (KBA), which runs along the Bosphorus from the European side to the Asian side. The KBA consists of numerous habitats such as dunes, rocks, maquis communities, pastures, forests and lakes along the coastline. There is also an Important Plant Area (IPA) in forest areas on the western and eastern sides of the Bosphorus. While there are a number of sensitive habitats supporting rare plant species within this KBA, some of these areas are designated as Important Plant Areas (IPAs). Another KBA includes the West Istanbul Pastures Important Nature Area on the European side. The KBA has a total area of 9,612 hectares between Bağcılar in the south and Pirinççi in the north. Approximately 11.4 km of the project route passes through this KBA (Environmental and Social Impact Assessment Report for the Northern Marmara Motorway (including the 3rd Bosphorus Bridge Project, 2013). According to the report, in terms of habitats, the main impact will be seen in forest areas with broad-leaved trees. Approximately 345 hectares of oak dense forest area within the 60.5 m construction corridor of the project will be lost. In addition, approximately 284 hectares of coniferous/coniferous trees will be destroyed. As stated in the report, the project caused the loss of 628.6 ha of agricultural land, 345 hectares of oak dense forest area and 284 hectares of conifer/coniferous trees and a total of 628.6 ha of agricultural land permanently along the entire Highway.

The 1/100.000 scaled Istanbul Environmental Plan, which entered into force in 2009 and was accepted as the City Constitution of Istanbul, aims to "develop polycentric (jumping) development in a linear structure along the East-West axis of Istanbul and along the Marmara Sea and in line with the principles of environmental sustainability, and to ensure the development towards the north. under control". At the same time, the plan aims to avoid the pressure of construction on the northern forests and to protect the water basins. The project, on the other hand, was later incorporated into the 2009 approved plan and completely reversed the objectives of the plan, putting great pressure on the boreal forests and watersheds.

According to the Environmental and Social Impact Assessment Report for the Northern Marmara Motorway (including the 3rd Bosphorus Bridge) Project dated 2013, the project will allow for the creation of new forest areas and increased employment, economic activity and national connectivity related to new infrastructure and access in the northern parts of Istanbul.

In addition to this, major projects that were added to the upper-scale plan, such as the Third Airport Project, which was opened on October 29, 2018, and the Eurasian Crossing Project, also had devastating effects on the city's environmental and cultural values. On page 61 of the EIA Report of the Third Airport Project, 81 % of which is forested and 8.6 % is composed of lakes and ponds (KOS Report, 2015), it is stated that "The units planned to be built within the scope of the project (runway, apron, upper structures, etc.), the natural ecosystem (forest areas, large and small puddles containing 70 living things, flowing and dry streams, agricultural areas, pasture areas) will be removed with excavation works in the area where it will be built. Thus, with the construction of the units, the natural vegetation and natural characteristics of these areas will be removed." The last project added to the Mega Projects process is the Kanal Istanbul project, which will be the largest eco-cite project in the history of the city and the region. The last remaining virgin lands of Istanbul will also be removed by this project, and the ecological sustainability of the city and the region will be put at risk.

2.2 Areas Legalized by Zoning Peace and Privileged Building Areas

In the last 20 years, the invasion on cities has continued to increase with legal regulations. Earthquake regulations were put into effect in 1999 but have been in effect since 2007. For this reason, most of the pre-2007 buildings in the city continue to be risky structures. After the Van earthquake, Law No. 6306 was changed 9 times, and the 2019 urban transformation regulation was amended 3 times. In other words, the process is essentially shaped by the application.

Since 2012, the sales of areas that have lost their forest character have increased, and in 2018, 1 million 747 thousand 447 independent units were legalized with the zoning amnesty called "Peace for Reconstruction", which was expressed as an election promise before the June 24 general elections. In other words, approximately one third of the 7 million 450 thousand 578 independent units benefiting from the zoning amnesty in Turkey are in Istanbul. According to the data of the Ministry of Environment and Urbanization, 1.5 million of the 5.9 million residences in Istanbul are risky and 300 thousand are structures that need to be transformed urgently. The districts with the highest number of building registration certificates in Istanbul were determined as Sarıyer, Ümraniye, Pendik, Küçükçekmece and Sultanbeyli. According to the data of the Ministry of Environment and Urbanization, 126 thousand 989 buildings in Sarıyer, 76 thousand 950 in Ümraniye, 76 thousand 129 in Pendik, 70 thousand 891 in Küçükçekmece, 65 thousand 662 buildings in Sultanbeyli were legalized by taking advantage of the zoning peace.

Privatization of Public Lands

The invasive urbanization process in Istanbul also shows its effect on public spaces. Many projects, especially shopping malls and housing projects, have been built on public spaces in recent years.

The 384,398 m^2 Ali Sami Yen Stadium in Istanbul Mecidiyeköy is one of the striking examples of this. After the Ali Sami Yen Stadium was moved from the area, a plan change was prepared by the Mass Housing Administration for the vacant parcel. On 28.08.2006, a protocol was signed between the General Directorate of Youth and Sports, the Ministry of Finance, the Istanbul Metropolitan Municipality and the Mass Housing Administration. With this protocol, 120,000 m^2 of the said real estate was transferred to the Housing Development Administration free of charge. The building permit for the project to be built on the land was approved in 2012. In 2013, a company purchased the area from TOKİ. In the plans made in 2003, the area allocated as "Urban and Regional Large Sports Areas" and partially as "General Parking Lot" was converted into a Partly Tourism + Trade Area, Partly Recreation Area + Partly Underground Parking Lot in the plans made in 2010, provided that the height is freed (Image 3).

According to the plans, there is a construction right of 87 thousand 500 square meters in the project, while 342 thousand square meters have been built.

Another recent example of privatization on public lands is the Housing Complex project, which was built on the land of the Maltepe Küçükyalı General Directorate of Highways. General Directorate of Highways, 1st Regional Directorate Küçükyalı Campus of 118,849 square meters of land was included in the scope of privatization and transferred to TOKİ in 2014. TOKİ revised the zoning plans of the land, which is the earthquake gathering area and park area of the people of the region, in 2016 and turned it into a residential and commercial area. The land purchased by Emlak Konut GYO was put out to tender, and construction began on the land purchased by a construction company. Despite the lawsuits filed by professional chambers, the constructions were completed in 2020 (Image 4).

Image 3: Former Ali Sami Yen Stadium

Image 4: Fikirtepe Urban Transformation Project

Another example is from the European side of Istanbul. 60 new buildings were built on public lands on the Zeytinburnu – Ataköy coastline, which were sold by the government through tender. Buildings with a length of 70 meters have greatly changed the silhouette of the historical city. One of these projects has been implemented on a land of 72 thousand 864 square meters with tourism development under the assurance of TOKİ, with a private-private sector partnership. There are 512 apartments and 78 commercial units in the project, which consists of 7 blocks and has a construction area of 215 thousand square meters. In the development process of another project area, TOKİ put the 124 thousand 980 square meters of tourism-zoned land on the Ataköy coast up for sale in 2008, with the announcement of "precious land". 80 % of the Tourism Real Estate company that won the tender belongs to a company that is an investment of the Qatari state. There are 1401 residences and a hotel in 9 blocks developed on the land. The third project in the region was realized on a land of 62 thousand 373 square meters in Bakırköy, where Sümerbank, a former public factory, is located. The zoning plans of the land purchased by a mining company in 2004 were revised, so a project consisting of 10 blocks with 22 floors each was developed on the changed land. Another project in the same region was the Istanbul Tourism Center, which was developed on an area of approximately 500 thousand square meters on the Ataköy coast. The company, which bought the land from the National Real Estate through a tender and holds the right of use until 2038, is constructing 9 new residence buildings outside the currently operating hotel block. Another project, which was built on a land that was transferred from the Meat and Fish Institution to Emlak Konut Real Estate Investment Trust, which is also a public land, and then purchased by the Union

Image 5: Projects Developed on Public Lands in Zeytinburnu Ataköy Coast

of Chambers and Commodity Exchanges of Turkey (TOBB) in 2007, consists of 6 blocks with 17 floors. There are 848 residences in the project, which rises on a land of 63 thousand 500 square meters (Image 5).

Another example of the privatization of public lands is a housing project built in the military area in Maslak. The area remains in the Military Security Zone in the 1/100,000 scale Istanbul Environmental Plan. In 2003, a 1/5000 scale zoning plan was prepared for the area. However, the plan was canceled due to the high population density and the substandard equipment areas. Then, a new plan was made, and in the new plan, 700 thousand square meters of construction area was foreseen to be built on the 250 thousand square meters remaining in the military area. In various lawsuits filed by the Chamber of Architects and the Chamber of City Planners, the plans that supported the project were renewed and canceled several times in 2010, 2011 and 2012, and their execution was stayed. In the new plans made in 2016, this time the 1/100 000 scale plans were also changed, and the problem was eliminated radically. The project was completed on the axis of these unlawful processes (Image 6).

Image 6: Residence complex built on a military area in Maslak

2.3. *Comprehensive Urban Transformation Projects*

Istanbul has become the application area of wide-ranging urban transformation projects within the scope of the Urban Renewal Law No. 5366 since 2005 and the Urban Transformation Law No. 6306 since 2012. First of all, in 2005, the Tarlabaşı region was declared as a renewal area within the scope of Law No. 5366, and then the Romani population, who had been living in Sulukule for 500 years, was displaced and deported to Taşoluk, the periphery of the city. Today, the Sulukule project has been completely passed into the hands of another class, and the Tarlabaşı project, which is still in progress, has been subject to extensive handovers. Urban transformation projects, which have been continuing in line with the Urban Transformation Law No. 6306 since 2012, are produced as rent projects, far from being soft, integrative and supporting on-site transformation projects.

One of these projects, Fikirtepe project, has an area of 1.310.000 m^2. In 2005, the 1/5000 scale Kadıköy Center E-5(D-100) Highway Buffer Zone was declared a "Special Project Area" in the Master Zoning Plan. In 2007, the expression, which was mentioned as a special project area in the master development plan, was translated into the expression "Urban Transformation Area", and in 2013 it was declared a "Risky Area" with the law numbered 6306 and included in the scope of the Law on Areas Under Disaster Risk. The project area is located in the 1st degree earthquake zone.

The project started to be implemented within the scope of "1/1000 scaled implementation development plan prepared for Kadıköy district, Fikirtepe and its surroundings" approved on 02.08.2013. In November 2015, the Ministry of Environment and Urbanization suspended the "Risky Area 1/5000 Scale Master Development Plan Amendment" regarding Fikirtepe and its surroundings. Fikirtepe Urban Transformation Area consists of Fikirtepe, Dumlupınar, Eğitim and Merdivenköy Districts of Kadıköy District of Istanbul. The area consisting of 4 neighborhoods is bordered by the E5 highway in the north, Kurbağalıdere in the west, Göztepe junction in the east, Mandıra Caddesi and Göztepe Research and Training Hospital in the south (Image 7).

Image 7: Fikirtepe Urban Transformation Project

The project still could not be completed due to various problems, and it was announced by the Minister of Environment and Urbanization in March 2021 that Emlak Katılım Bankası would be the guarantor of the urban transformation contracts in order to prevent unjust treatment in urban transformation areas.

Instead of the Conclusion

It has been almost 40 years since we stopped producing cities, which were shaped under the guidance of capitalism and on the axis of liberal thought, with long-term public strategies. In this process, the actors of the reproduction of cities have been selectively strengthened capital and the central "power" in direct relation with this capital, its subjects have been supply-oriented neoliberal urban policies and strategies and urban transformation. The mission of the capitalist central "power" in the process and its regulatory mechanisms have continued on their way by oscillating on the slippery ground between the managerial paradigm and the class-centered paradigm, by observing and constructing different balances.

After the 2000s, the power, which adopted Islamic liberalism in power sharing over space in Turkey, continued on its way by drawing the liberal policies of the post-80s period to a conservative-liberal line. In this path, which we can define as the conservative and hegemonic re-emergence of urban transformation, the right of central administrations to have a say in the urban space has increased with the new institutionalization practices, and the space has become a kind of competition area for national/international capital by becoming more and more marketed. The turning point of the process we call invasive urbanization is the post-2002 period.

The situation, which is described in the study by giving examples of the ongoing invasive urbanization processes in Istanbul, has created threats on the sustainability of the city in terms of both ecological, cultural and resilience of the city. It is possible to read all the contradictions, grievances and inequalities created by capitalism, which acquires all its savings by commodifying cities, through Istanbul in this invasive urbanization process. In addition to the northern forests, water basins, agricultural areas and pasture areas in the periphery of the city, the public lands within the city have also received their share from this invasive urbanization process. Thus, with the ecological destruction of the city, its resilience has also weakened, and the city has become more fragile in terms of disasters, climate change and cultural values.

It is clear that this situation is not sustainable. The continuation of these destructive policies threatens the sustainability of not only Istanbul but also other cities in many aspects. What we need today is to increase the resilience of cities with policies that are not invasive and destructive, restorative, not weakening, but empowering, and to make sustainability meaningful by reconstructing the relationship between nature and human through cities. In this framework, it is necessary to rethink the ways in which cities can be made more self-sufficient in terms of their needs and possibilities economically, politically and ecologically, preventing them from consuming central and peripheral resources and becoming less dependent on the outside world.

References

Brenner, N., Theodore, N. 2005. Neoliberalism and urban condition. City, Vol. 9, Issue: 1, 101–107.

Çakır, S. 1991."Elazığ'da Kentleşme ve Gecekondu Sorununa Genel Bir Bakış", Fırat Havzasının Sosyal, Kültürel ve Ekonomik Kalkınması Sempozyumu(7–9 Nisan 1988), s. 504, Elazığ

Peck, J., Theodore, N., Brenner N. 2009. Neoliberal Urbanism: Models, Moments, Mutations, The SAIS Review of International Affairs, Vol. 29, No. 1, Cities (Winter-Spring 2009), 49–66.

Peker, A. U. 2015. AKP Döneminde Rövanşist Mimari, Mimarlık Dergisi, Kasım - Aralık 2015, Sa: 386, 13–19.

Tekeli, İ. 2000. Modernite Aşılırken Kent Planlaması, İmge Kitabevi, Ankara.

Reports:

Kuzey Marmara Otoyolu (3. Boğaz Köprüsü dâhil) Projesi için Çevresel ve Sosyal Etki Değerlendirmesi, 2013

The World Bank Annual Report, August, 1994

Internet Resources:

https://www.haberturk.com/iste-imar-barisi-nin-bilancosu-2489947-ekonomi

https://kuzeyormanlari.org/2018/10/29/emsalsiz-ihanet-ulke-tarihinin-en-buyuk-rant-oyunlarinin-boyutunu-acikliyoruz

Elif Acuner

Tourism and Environment: Environmental Impacts, Ecological Footprint, Transport Capacity of Tourism, and Its Relation with Global Warming

Introduction

People have traveled for various reasons since ancient times. Although the first trips were had to survive and performed locally because of the problems with safety and not having any vehicles or roads, it would not be difficult to guess that the person who was curious about nature had various experiences in nature to satisfy his/her sense of curiosity and adventure. Travels, which are considered to have started with the history of humanity, have been shaped and developed with motivations such as trade, religion, health, sports activities, festivals, holidays, and education as the ages of history change (Karamustafa ve Örnek, 2019; Kozak et al., 2013, Sarı Çallı, 2015; Yıldız, 2011). In other words, nature has always been a travel motivation for reasons such as curiosity, health, or sometimes adventure since the early ages. When the basic dynamics of the pre-modern tourism paradigm are examined, it is seen that tourism as an individual movement takes place within the framework of classical tourism types. However, in the tourism paradigm defined as the modern period, tourism has become a more widespread activity with industrial revolutions and regulations in working life and has evolved towards mass travel through holiday tourism (Kozak et al., 2013: 12–19; Karamustafa and Örnek, 2019: 262–264). These developments have made it inevitable that the transport capacities were strained because of the tourism movements concentrated in certain regions. In the post-modern tourism paradigm, tourism has begun to evolve towards special interests and gain an individual feature again. Although changing holiday habits and the fact that tourism gains individuality are seen as an alternative to the destructive effects of mass tourism, unsustainable systems reveal the destructive effect of the sector on the environment. As shown in Fig. 1 below, while tourism is an alternative to quality leisure activities, it has also been stated it has significant benefits in economic (such as creating new employment opportunities, encouraging entrepreneurship) and social aspects (such as improving public services, improving local people's quality of life). However, it has been revealed that besides these benefits,

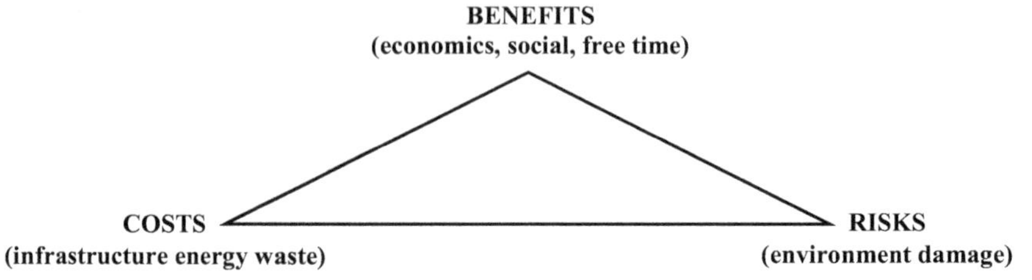

Fig. 1: Relations Between Benefits, Costs and Risks of Tourism. Resource: Šimková, Eva, 2007: 59

tourism includes cost items such as infrastructure, superstructure, and energy and important environmental risks. It is also stated that tourism is an industry that should be evaluated as a whole by making benefit-risk and cost analyzes.

Environmental effects of tourism vary depending on the local characteristics, such as dependence on local resources, the type of tourism activities carried out, the shape of the touristic infrastructure, and the planning practices (Chang et al., 2018: 2). Therefore, the environmental characteristics of tourism activities should be evaluated for each destination separately.

Tourism can have positive or negative effects on the environment. In this study, there have been some evaluations about the positive effects of tourism on the environment, conservation of important natural areas, protection of archaeological, historical sites and architectural characters, awareness, alternative employment, income and environmental management, and planning. The negative effects of tourism are considered water, air, soil, noise, visual and aesthetic pollution, ecological deterioration, damage to wildlife, destruction of archaeological and historical sites, land-use problems, and transport pollution. In addition, the mutual effects of tourism and global warming, the ecological footprint of tourism and the environmental carrying capacity in tourism are also discussed. The relationship between tourism and the natural environment is tried to be presented in a holistic structure. The research subject has been determined according to these titles. Therefore, it was aimed to express the relationship of tourism with the environment and the effects of tourism on the environment in the research. This study, which deals with the relationship of tourism with the environment and its environmental effects and up-to-date evaluations, is important as it explains the issues that need to be considered to ensure the sustainability of the tourism sector, which is important for the national economies. The systematic literature review technique, one of the qualitative research methods, was used in the study. A description is made in this study with the information obtained as a result of the literature review.

1. The Environmental Effects of Tourism

It should be taken into account that the positive or negative effects of tourism on the environment start at the local level and eventually extend to a global scale. With its positive effects at the local level, tourism provides support for the protection and development of the environment. On a global scale, it will be important for the positive effects to be an example to other destinations, and to ensure cooperation with information-project transfer between destinations or countries. The situation is a little more sensitive for the negative effects of tourism. It is because the impact arising from the damage to the environment at the local level turns into a cost that must be borne globally. Therefore, in the world defined as a global village, it is important to protect the environment, and to increase cooperation and solidarity on the purpose of increasing the positive effects and controlling the negative effects in order to ensure the sustainability of tourism, which is among the fastest developing and expanding industries. The negative and positive effects of tourism are explained in more detail below.

1.1. Positive Environmental Impacts of Tourism

Considering the positive effects of tourism, the prominent dynamics are that it creates an alternative to meet the needs of the environment and to provide high awareness of the environment. In addition, tourism is an important incentive for the protection of the natural environment and resources in regions that develop with sustainable systems. It is because the existing natural potential turns into income generating touristic products for the region thanks to tourism. In this way, the value put on and the awareness of the natural environment and resources, which have become raw materials in the industry, increases, and income is provided for the protection and development of these resources. Increasing awareness of the environment on a global scale in recent years and the development of environmentally friendly initiatives in terms of quality and quantity ensure the recognition of the importance of environmental management and its reflection in the activities carried out in the destination, especially in destinations where stakeholder coordination is ensured. It can be said that the environmental positive effects of tourism are quite high and the main effects can be listed as follows: the protection of important natural areas, archaeological sites, historical sites and architectural characters, and the development of the issues such as financial contribution/creating fund for environmental protection, awareness, alternative employment and income, environmental management and planning.

The protection of important natural areas, Although the first protected area status in the world under the protected area system was given to "Yellowstone" (Kalamandeen and Gillson, 2007: 167), which was declared a national park in 1872, there were areas with special protection status in different parts of the world. In other words, although the relationship between conservation and tourism is not new, the sensitivity of the issue is understood much better with many initiatives on a global scale, and significant developments are being achieved in this regard every passing day (Bushell and Bricker, 2016: 6). Protected area statuses are very important to protect biological diversity, maintain ecological processes, and prevent the extinction of endemic species under threat (IUCN, 2008: 2). Tourism is considered as an incentive for the protection of sensitive natural areas. On the other hand, public policies are developed to ensure the sustainability of sensitive areas, which are very popular with visitors due to tourism activities, and the local people tend to own and protect these areas more (IUCN, 2018: 4–5). This development or developments are accepted as one or some of the positive environmental effects of tourism.

The protection of archaeological sites, historical sites and architectural characters, The preservation of archaeological sites, historical sites and architectural characters, archaeological sites and historical sites that significantly increase the attractiveness of the destination appeal to an ever-evolving market segment that combines nostalgia and passion for the past with feelings of adventure and discovery (Srivastuva, 2015: 34). While archaeological and historical areas allow the development of the image of the region and the increase in touristic attractiveness, it also creates increased income and alternative job opportunities for the destination. In addition, tourism providers can position archaeological and historical sites, which are not known or do not attract much attention, as an attraction factor, through their creative skills and constructive approaches to cultural heritage interpretation (Ross et al., 2017: 37). Thus, while achieving the conservation status of archaeological and historical sites and ensuring their sustainability, on the other hand, the people of the region can gain economic and social benefits from the mobilized tourism activities.

Financial contribution/fundraising for environmental protection, Revenues from tourism, such as financial contribution/resource creation for environmental protection, and the fee charged from visitors at the entrance of national parks in a destination can be considered as an important financial resource in the protection of tourism-related natural resources used as raw materials in that destination.

Awareness, It is known that the level of awareness on a global scale has increased through awareness, national and international organizations' informing studies on environmental pollution and extinction, and environmental problems that have now reached a visible level. There is a similar awareness situation among the stakeholders within the tourism industry. Therefore, it is possible to say that the tourism industry directly increases the level of awareness of environmental resources. For example, visitors find the opportunity to spend time in nature and thus they come into closer contact with natural resources thanks to tourism. This interaction increases the awareness of the visitors about the value of natural resources, while increasing environmentally friendly behaviors and activities aimed at protecting the environment (Faraji rad and Aghajani, 2010: 40). It is because the fact that the demanding stakeholders value this situation can create a reinforcing situation for other stakeholders.

Alternative employment and income, Alternative employment and income provides touristic consumption tourism with direct, indirect, and induced employment opportunities (Witt et al., 2004: 167). In addition, tourism, which is a service-oriented industry, has some unique dynamics. One of these dynamics is the reverse operation of distribution systems. In other words, in tourism, the visitor comes to the destination where the touristic product is produced and thus goes out of his/her usual environment. The visitor, who goes out of his/her usual environment, has many different needs that must be met. Thus, the development of tourism in the visited destination directly and indirectly provides added value to many sub-sectors, thus creating income sources and alternative employment opportunities for the people of the region. On the other hand, being an industry in which women, those with a second job, students or retirees are employed part-time or seasonally, tourism can provide additional income opportunities to households (Şit, 2016: 105).

The development of the issues environmental management and planning, Development in Environmental Management and Planning is one of the key factors in supporting the developing tourism in a destination with management plans decided by the organization or commissions where all the stakeholders are represented, and in keeping the environmental impacts of tourism activities in that destination under control. The most important effect of the tourism industry on the protection of environmental resources is that it adds a planning and managerial dimension to the measures related to this issue (Doğan, 2010: 167). In addition, tourism encourages measures to be taken to protect the environment, natural resources, wildlife or natural scenery (Mason, 2003: 55). Thus, the stakeholders who participate in all the decisions taken will have a more rigorous approach in the implementation of these decisions. In addition, a planned environmental management will ensure the balance of protection and use of the resources in the destination.

1.2. Negative Environmental Impacts of Tourism

There are some basic principles of activities that take place in the natural environment. The first of these principles is that the use of natural resources has an impact even in the most planned and professional systems, and these effects are multidimensional. The second principle is that indirect effects are much more insidious and destructive (such as the deterioration of wildlife habitat), while direct effects are the immediate results of visitor behavior (such as leaving garbage in the field). Another principle is that activity types are as critical as the number of users in terms of the use effects of time (Ewert, 1999: 1–2). In order to keep the environmental impacts of tourism under control, the listed principles must be considered. Environmental resources are resources that naturally have the capacity to renew themselves. In other words, it is essential to benefit from environmental resources without exceeding their self-renewal rate. However, the negative effects of tourism on the environment arise in cases where the usage levels of the visitors exceed the environmental carrying capacity (Cooper, as cited in 2005; Faraji rad and Aghajani, 2010: 39). One of the significant negative effects of tourism on the environment is the pollution on various sources. The main pollution situations that have a negative effect on the destination can be listed as follows: water pollution, air pollution, soil pollution, visual and aesthetic pollution, noise pollution, waste problem, ecological degradation, damage to wildlife, destruction of archaeological sites and historical sites, land use problems, transport pollution.

Pollution, Natural resources are the most basic raw material of touristic products. Especially the mass touristic activities seriously threaten natural resources such as water, soil and air. Therefore, tourism activities with their negative effects threaten the environment.The most important negative result of tourism to the environment is pollution. Pollution can be listed separately under many headings. Water, soil and air pollution is the most frequently discussed and evaluated pollution type. Apart from these, environmental problems such as visual and aesthetic pollution, noise pollution, and transport pollution,which create negative effects, are also included in the pollution classifications.The polluting formations are explained under the headings below.

Water pollution, In many countries or regions around the world, consumption of fresh water originating from agricultural, industrial, domestic and other needs is becoming one of the most critical environmental problems. Intensive water consumption in service sectors such as the tourism sector increases the pressure on fresh water resources (United Nations, 2003: 5).Tourists naturally have to consume water to continue their daily lives. Although it is difficult to compare the pressure created by tourism activities on water with the pressure arising from daily water needs, there is evidence that tourism increases water consumption (Gössling and Peeters, 2015: 644). For example, tourism accounts for 17 % of domestic water consumption. In accommodation sector, daily water use including room usage, pool and garden water needs is 350 liters per person on average.On the other hand, the most intense water consumption is in golf tourismamong all tourism activities.In addition, an average of 6000 liters of water is used per day for touristic food production on a global scale (Giulietti et al., 2018: 51). These findings show that tourism increases water consumption. As it is known, consumed water also turns into waste water and waste water causes water pollution.

Cases arising from tourism and causing water pollution can be listed under two headings as direct and indirect. Among the direct effects of the tourism industry on water pollution, there are activities such as tourism services, the construction and maintenance of infrastructure needs, recreational boat tours and cruise tourism, in which the water generated by tourism and consumed water turns into wastewater (Rabbany et al., 2013: 120). In addition, marinas cause changes in undercurrents and coastlines, and disruption of land-sea connections resulting in erosion of habitats (Giulietti et al., 2018: 50).Among the indirect causes of water pollution originating from the tourism industry, there are oil spills, industrial wastes pumped into the sea, and chemicals used in agriculture (Faraji rad and Aghajani, 2010: 39).

Air pollution, The use of fossil fuels to meet the energy needs in the tourism industry is high, and these fossil fuels directly or indirectly cause various greenhouse gas emissions including carbon dioxide (CO2), methane (CH4), nitrous oxide (N2O), hydrofluorocarbons (HFCs), perfluorocarbons (PFCs), and sulphur hexafluoride (SF6) (Gössling and Peeters, 2015: 642). Among the activities in the tourism industry, the one that has the highest impact on air pollution is touristic transportation. It is estimated that CO2 emissions arising from tourism-related transport will increase by 25 % between 2016 and 2030. Emissions arising from tourism-related transport accounted for 5 % of total human emissions in 2016, and this rate is estimated to be 5.3 % in 2030. The ratio of tourism-based transport in total transport emissions is 22 %, and it is predicted that this ratio will continue to be similar in 2030 (21 %) (UNWTO, 2019). Air pollution should be considered as one of the important factors that will cause a destination to lose its attractiveness. Although the World Health Organization (WHO air quality guidelines) carries out studies to raise awareness that air pollution has many negative effects including psychological effects on human health, many visitors are not fully aware of these effects, but visitors' becoming conscious of this issue may affect their behavior choices related to tourism (Zhang et al., 2019: 2).

Soil pollution, The main pollutants of soil are biological pollutants and anthropogenic pollutants. Regardless of whether biological or human-induced, the three main activities that cause soil pollution are agricultural activities, industrial activities and urban activities (Mishra et al., 2016: 5). In this context, tourism has the potential to produce pollution from all three activities. Visitors who participate in tourism activities such as mountaineering, trekking, hiking and bird watching in mountainous or forested areas can leave their solid waste and garbage in these sensitive areas. If there is no organized system for the collection of garbage, especially in areas far from settlements and not under protection, this situation can reach dimensions that will cause serious problems. On the other hand, sports activities, especially in sensitive or protected areas, can cause serious soil erosion problems (Belsoy et al., 2012: 71). On the other hand, other pollutants originating from tourism include the melting of liquid wastes mixed with chemicals, the use of chemicals that pollute the soil in green areas and gardens or tourism-oriented agricultural activities, the deterioration of vegetation and ecological balance and the loss of the top layer of soil by converting agricultural areas, forest areas or other natural areas into touristic areas, or the occurrence of soil erosion due to excessive compaction.

Visual and aesthetic pollution, The clearest indicators of visual pollution are city silhouettes filled with incompatible, disrespectful and unidentified buildings (Yılmaz and Sağsöz, 2010: 98). This issue should be considered as a very important issue in terms of the tourism industry as it will cause loss of image and therefore economic damage due to loss of visitors. It is because the visual and aesthetic features of a destination affect the visitors' perception of the destination. In this context, a negative visual or aesthetic perception at any moment of the tourism experience is reflected on all the services which are benefited from in that destination and consequently on the whole perception of the destination (Wang et al., 2008: 205). In many destinations, tourism structures do not integrate with the natural features and original architecture of the destination, and especially large structures in different designs can create image confusion (Sunlu, 2003: 265). In other words, the development of infrastructure or superstructure in the destination, and the fact that the materials and structures used in the buildings are not compatible with the local characteristics in terms of architecture cause visual pollution.

Noise Pollution, The factors that cause noise pollution in the tourism industry can be listed as noise caused by the increasing number of visitors, noise of the transportation vehicles, traffic noise, noise of the recreational vehicles,and noise of the entertainment venues. Especially with the development of mass tourism, crowded visits to popular destinations can cause noise pollution that seriously disturbs the local community (Ay and Günay Aktaş, 2019: 71). Noise pollution, which is generally considered to be an important problem for the local people in urban areas, is also an important problem for wildlife in rural areas. Noise pollution caused by recreational vehicles such as transportation vehicles, snowmobiles or jet skis can cause distress and discomfort for both local people and wildlife (Giulietti et al., 2018: 50). In addition, the human population leading to a high population density in popular destinations or rural areas can be considered as an uncomfortable situation not only for the local people and wildlife, but also for the visitors who come to the destination for reasons such as resting, relaxing or having fun.

Waste Problem, Although the waste problem is seen as a complex problem mostly for urban areas, when it comes to the tourism industry, it poses an important seasonal problem, especially in regions where there is no urban life and where there is less population (Mutlu, 2006: 27). When it comes to waste generation and management, the most important issue is the existence and implementation efficiency of sustainable waste management systems rather than waste generation (Shamshiry et al., 2011: 2). Sustainable waste management includes reducing the amount of waste produced, reducing the impact of the hazardous content of wasteon the environment by controlling it, and encouraging recycling (Zorpas et al., 2014: 2). The last point reached in eliminating the waste problem is the "zero waste" approach. The zero waste approach, which has started to emerge since the 1990s and aims to eliminate waste instead of managing it, adopts the principles of efficiency, economics and ethics (3Es) instead of recycling, reducing and reusing (3Rs) (Dileep, 2007: 379). The zero waste approach, which has started to be implemented in some countries and companies in the world, is evaluated under four headings as industrial waste, e-waste, food waste and packaging waste (Song et al., 2015: 200–203). Although all four waste areas are important in the tourism industry, it can be said that industrial waste and food waste should be handled a little more critically.

Ecological Degradation, Interest in flora-based tourism activities is increasing thanks to the diversification of alternative tourism types in line with post-modern tourism dynamics. Increasing interest in flora-based activities also encourages many tourism planners to offer it as a product. Travel businesses planning tours for sensitive natural areas should have in-depth knowledge of

Tab. 1: The Impacts of Tourism Activities on Vegetation of Land

Tourism activity	Vegetation impact
Motorized vehicles use	Vegetation clearing/damage, reduced cover, change in litter, reduction in height, and reduced sapling and seedling species
Horse riding	Root damage, vegetation clearing/damage, reduction in height, reduced cover, change in litter, and changes in species
Hiking	Root damage, vegetation clearing/damage, reduction in height, reduced cover, change in litter, changes in species, reduced sapling and seedling species, biomass changes, plant density, plant size and reproductive performance, and plant richnessand cover
Camping	Vegetation clearing/damage, reduction in height, reduced cover, change in litter, damage to seedlings, changes in species, and damage to wildflowers and epiphytes
Biking	Introduction of invasive plants and vegetation clearing/damage
Mountain and rock climbing	Vegetation clearing/damage, biomass changes, reduced cover, changes in species, and reduced sapling and seedling species

Resource: Jahani et al., 2020: 2

the ecological processes that make their existence sustainable, such as the flora and fauna of those areas, and should decide every detail of their activities in line with this information (Salam et al., 2000: 60). Otherwise, these activities can have very destructive effects. In this context, there are risks such as extinction of endemic species and other plant populations. Another risk is plant trafficking. Tab. 1 below shows the effects of various tourism activities on vegetation. As can be seen from Tab. 1, activities carried out without sustainable management plans may cause significant adverse effects on the flora.

Damage to Wildlife, Wildlife tourism, which will take place without adequate protection measures, may cause overcrowding and extreme disturbances in the relevant areas. For example, in tourist-wildlife interaction, it may cause effects such as behavioral changes in some wild species, and this may even reflect on all species communities in the area in the long run (IUCN, 2018: 23). In the interaction of tourists with wildlife, feeding them unnaturally, even with good intentions, both disturbs the animals and harms their natural life (Demir, 2002: 95). Similarly, sportive and recreational activities carried out in sensitive or protected areas may cause adverse effects on wildlife (Belsoy et al., 2012: 71). The effects that may arise in this context can be gathered in four groups. The first group includes *the change of the habitat* for reasons such as the destruction of animals' nests, the changes in the behavior of the wildlife caused by the changes in the natural environment, the overcrowding of the game paths, the change of the water/soil chemistry, and the destruction of the shelters. The second group includes *the disturbance of the habitat* for reasons such as feeding, taking photographs, protection/housing, investigation of nests, effects arising from automobiles, effects of snowmobile/bicycle use, and the presence of humans and animals. The third group includes *pollution* caused by plastic, oil/petroleum products and various foreign materials. The last group includes *harvest* that occurs due to reasons such as collecting, hunting, trapping and the existence of a fish market (Cited from Evert 1999 by Demir, 2002: 96).

Destruction of archaeological and historical sites, Although cultural tourism has been an important travel motivation since the first days in which tourism emerged, destination stakeholders are becoming more eager to present these values as products due to the increasing interest in archaeological and historical sites. This emerging situation reinforces the potentially dangerous cooperation among tourism – economy – archeology (Hueber, 1991: 38). For the protection of archaeological and historical heritage, there is a need for legally, scientifically, artistically, technically and managerially multidimensional and holistic systems (Ahunbay, 2010: 104). If effective planning and management systems are not established for the protection of these areas while presenting the archaeological and historical heritage as a product in tourism, these values may be lost irreversibly (Comer and Willems, 2011: 506). Archaeological and historical values, which are naturally worn out by the climate and time lapse, can be seriously damaged by the infrastructure, superstructure and landscaping works in their immediate surroundings, insufficient and inappropriate maintenance, physical damage caused by some visitors' activities such as touching, sitting, climbing, drawing or writing in cases where there is no barrier, as well as the visitor pressure, especially in high seasons, the materials and other elements used in some special events held in these areas, the damage caused by photographing and video shooting, taking a piece as a souvenir or throwing away garbage (Comer and Willems, 2011: 507; Mustafa, 2019: 586). Stakeholder coordination is important in the management plans realized for the protection of the archaeological and cultural heritage, and its involvement in tourism with a sustainable system. Tourists are one of the critical stakeholders that should be considered. On the other hand, the demand structure for cultural tourism has a heterogeneous structure and therefore the administrative decisions to be made are quite complex (Alazaizeh et. al,, 2016: 149–150). Since this situation may cause some conflicts between the parties, it is considered as another problem related to the subject.

Land use problems, To some extent, the tourist attraction of any destination depends on the environment. While a harmonious superstructure development in an attractive natural environment increases the attractiveness of the region, on the contrary, the attractiveness of the destination decreases and at the same time the environment is damaged. As the number of visitors to the destination increases, the need for services such as accommodation, food and beverage, and entertainment also increases, and for this reason, natural and rural areas are used for transportation, accommodation, souvenir shops, parking areas and other activities (Güneş, 2011: 47). In such a case, when land use planning is not done in the relevant region, land prices rise and construction pressure on agricultural lands increases due to increased competition for land resources (United Nations, 2003: 5). In addition, activities such as clearing forest areas for ski resorts or emptying and filling coastal wetlands for tourism facilities and infrastructure can cause deterioration and erosion in ecosystems (Giulietti et al., 2018: 50).

Transport pollution, The construction of transportation infrastructure to ensure accessibility to destinations especially with sensitive environmental areas or to make them more comfortable can cause very serious environmental impacts. Also, providing transportation infrastructure to a destination or increasing the comfort of this infrastructure may cause uncontrolled human circulation to that region. Comfortable transportation to sensitive areas with all kinds of vehicles may cause easy transportation of not only people but also all kinds of building materials and therefore may lead to concretization in that sensitive nature or construction that is not suitable for the identity of the region. On the other hand, one of the means of transportation that cause pollution is air transportation. Today, touristic travels are mostly made by air transportation. Tourism constitutes 50 % of air transport traffic on a global scale (Giulietti et al., 2018: 49–50). Therefore, tourism causes pollution on the environment with carbon dioxide emissions originating from all transportation vehicles, especially from air transportation. Moreover, transportation is one of the most important pollutants of the tourism industry. It is because the carbon dioxide emission originating from tourism is caused by transportation, which constitutes 75 % of the energy demand (Gössling and Peeters, 2015: 642).

1.3. Tourism and Global Warming

The excessive fossil fuel consumption that started with the industrial revolution and the greenhouse gas emissions that emerged in parallel with this situation can be stated as the leading causes of global warming. Parallel to this situation, the concept of global warming has managed to be high on the world agenda since the very first moment it emerged. Global warming is a phenomenon that is affected by many factors as well as affecting many factors in the world. In this context, energy use, industrialization, deforestation, and agricultural activities are indicated as factors which increase global warming (Gülbahar, 2008: 166). In addition to the pressure created by the use of fossil fuels on the atmosphere, especially due to energy generation, transportation, heating and industrial activities, deforestation and unplanned land use lead to a decrease in greenhouse gas absorption areas (Sevim and Ünlüönen, 2010: 44). Tourism is one of the industries which have an impact on the emergence of the factors listed above, with its volume and growth momentum. Tourism industry is affected by global warming while it acts as a catalyst for global warming (Sunlu, 2003: 262–267).

Climate is an important determinant in tourism industry because there is a seasonal period to which almost every different type of tourism is related. The increase in global warming causes climate change, warming of the world, and an increase in sea water level. This situation directly affects the climate and environmental variables that constitute the basic raw material of tourism industry and thus affects, changes, or transforms the types of tourism in parallel. The table below shows the effects of the major climate change on tourism activities. As can be understood from the table, climate change can have significant effects on many tourism products such as water and nature sports, especially coastal and sea tourism, winter tourism, and nature-based tourism. Climate change also leads to different costs such as increased insurance costs, and poses serious threats such as an increasing risk of disease. In addition, climate change affects the direction of demand. Accordingly, destinations can lose their popularity or new destinations can become popular. It is because there are four important factors affecting the visitors' choice of destination as climate, natural environment, travel costs and personal safety, and climate change is expected to affect tourism in the context of these four factors at the regional level (Scott et al., 2012: 215; UNWTO, 2008: 31). In addition to these, new tourism activities such as "disappearing destinations", "last chance tourism", "climate change voyeurism" and "climate disaster tourism" are emerging with the motivation to visit the regions exposed to climate-related environmental changes before they disappear (Scott et al., 2012: 221–222). Moreover, it may not be only the direction of the demand that is affected. Visitor perception is another factor affected by climate change. For example, if any region has a compelling climate for the target market that is expected to demand the type of tourism that is planned to be developed, an unsuitable climate perception will be created by potential visitors and tourism demand will be adversely affected (Freitas, 2001: 4). This negative perception may cause tourism investors not to choose the destination, or tourism experts such as tour operators and travel agencies not to prefer selling the relevant region.

Tab. 2: Major Climate Change Impacts and Implications for Tourism Destinations

Impact	Implications for tourism
Warmer temperatures	Altered seasonality, heat stress for tourists, coolingcosts, changes in plant-wildlife-insect populations and distribution, infectious disease ranges
Decreasing snow cover and shrinking glaciers	Lack of snow in winter sport destinations, increased snow-making costs, shorter winter sports seasons, aesthetics of landscape reduced
Increasing frequency and intensity of extreme storms	Risk for tourism facilities, increased insurance costs/loss of insurability, business interruption costs
Reduced precipitation and increased evaporation in some regions	Water shortages, competition over water between tourism and other sectors, desertification, increased wildfires threatening infrastructure and affecting demand
Increased frequency of heavy precipitation in some regions	Flooding damage to historic architectural and cultural assets, damage to tourism infrastructure, altered seasonality
Sea level rise	Coastal erosion, loss of beach area, higher costs to protect and maintain waterfronts
Sea surface temperatures rise	Increased coral bleaching and marine resource and aesthetics degradation in dive and snorkel destinations
Changes in terrestrial and marine biodiversity	Loss of natural attractions and species from destinations, higher risk of diseases in tropical-subtropical countries
More frequent and larger forest fires	Loss of natural attractions; increase of flooding risk; damage to tourism infrastructure
Soil changes (e.g., moisture levels, erosion and acidity)	Loss of archaeological assets and other natural resources, with impacts on destination attractions

Resource: UNWTO, 2008: 61.

As can be seen from the effects indicated in the Tab. 2, changes in climate and the environment have consequences on tourism industry that can be evaluated as positive or negative. For example, the increase in temperature as a result of global warming causes an extension of the summer season. This situation extends the duration of touristic activities and therefore contributes positively to tourism industry. However, this situation, which seems positive for tourism industry, creates a negative result in terms of global warming. It is because tourism activities include human activities, and these activities especially based on energy increase greenhouse gas emissions in the atmosphere. This situation also has ecological effects (Scott, 2003: 2). In this framework, the extension of the summer season is shown as a negative situation caused by tourism industry on global warming (Sevim and Zeydan, 2014: 23). As mentioned before, the most important negative impact of tourism industry on global warming is tourism-related travel, especially air travel (Shani and Arad, 2014: 83). In addition, as mentioned before, the impact of infrastructure systems, accommodation businesses, and other recreational activities on anthropogenic climate change caused by energy consumption is gradually increasing (Dubois and Ceron, 2006: 405–413; Scott et al., 2012: 213).

1.4. Tourism and Ecological Footprint

The concept of ecological footprint, first introduced by Mathis Wackernagel and William Rees (Akıllı et al., 2008: 3), is a measure of the burden imposed on nature by a particular population (Wackernagel and Rees, 1997: 5), and is a tool that measures the level of sustainability (Şimşek, 2020: 140). In other words, ecological footprint is "*a tool that measures the biological field used by humans to meet all their needs*" (Turkis and Çil, 2017: 175). Ecological footprint is an important criterion for environmental sustainability in terms of being able to evaluate sustainability in different aspects (ref. Erden Özsoy and Dinç, 2016: 42; Keleş, 2010).

As stated before, activities within the scope of the tourism industry can cause serious pressure on natural resources. Even ecotourism activities carried out with a responsible attitude and principles towards nature can be sustainable at the local level (Karwacki and Boyd, 1995: 225), but they cannot be globally sustainable in most cases (Gössling et al., 2002: 200). Ecological footprint is a useful method for evaluating the sustainability of tourism activities (Castellani and Sala, 2012: 136). Ecological footprint in the tourism industry can be considered as the footprint of consumption and production. To reduce the ecological footprint of consumption in the tourism industry, choosing small-scale activities and businesses, preferring local and regional food and beverages and consuming less animal food, preferring transportation vehicles and systems using clean and renewable energy systems instead of carbon-intensive transportation systems, and catching the original rhythm of nature and choosing carbon-zero activities by adopting the slow philosophy can be encouraged (DestiMED, 2019: 60). The calculation of the production footprint in tourism emerges as a blurry concept. It is because the infrastructure and superstructures required for tourism are used not only by the visitors but also by the people of the region (Hunter, 2002: 13). However, it is important to prefer low-carbon systems in infrastructure systems in reducing the ecological footprint in tourism and in meeting infrastructure systems, superstructure systems, and energy needs, and to provide incentives for awareness and use of these systems. In other words, the conscious action of the stakeholders with a holistic perspective in the tourism industry may lead to a decrease in the ecological footprint and this decrease may lead to an increase in the sustainability of touristic destinations (Temizkan and Ceyhanlı, 2020: 204).

1.5. Tourism and Carrying Capacity

The concept of carrying capacity is considered as an important data field in defining environmental problems and determining management strategies by tourism planners and scientists (McCool and Lime, 2001: 372). Carrying capacity is defined as "*the maximum use of any site without causing negative effects on the resources, reducing visitor satisfaction, or exerting adverse impact upon the society, economy and culture of the area*" (ref. Lindberg et al., 1996: 462; McIntyre, 1993). Carrying capacity is beneficial in terms of contributing to sustainability in the long term by keeping the tourism development capacity in a destination at an optimum level (Saveriades, 2000: 151). It is because as the tourism activities in the destinations increase, many regions experience difficulties in balancing their touristic carrying capacities with supply (Seçilmiş and Kılıç, 2018: 507). However, taking advantage of resources in line with the determined carrying capacities will limit the impact of tourism activities on resources. It is because the determination of carrying capacities will cause the development of tourism in a destination and the number of tourists who will visit there to be limited. What is important here is to balance the conservation and use of resources, and the welfare of local people in the destination. Destination and local people in the destination are more important than tourists in tourism carrying capacity (O'Reilly, 1986: 254). Tourism carrying capacity types are classified as social carrying capacity, environmental (ecological) carrying capacity, economic carrying capacity, physical carrying capacity and perceptual carrying capacity, with the view that visitor mobility in a destination puts pressure on the destination's carrying capacities from various aspects (Ünlüönen and Tokmak, 2009: 17). The listed carrying capacity types are interrelated. In addition, it should be necessarily remembered that the carrying capacity limits of each destination are formed within the framework of their own dynamics. Ensuring the sustainability of tourism in a destination can only be possible by providing tourism development without exceeding the limits of that destination. For this reason, it is important to manage the destinations with the plans made in line with the determined carrying capacities in order to avoid the negative effects of tourism, which are very difficult to compensate.

Result and Suggestions

Tourism is an industry that can create many opportunities for the environment, but can also pose many threats. Planned management approach based on professional perspective and sustainable systems will position tourism as an industry that creates opportunities for all stakeholders. However, a tourism development that is not based on knowledge, data, education, experience and strategies may cause problems for stakeholders in the long term and pose high risks for the environment.

In this context, the positive environmental impacts of tourism can be listed as the protection of important natural areas, archaeological sites, historical sites and architecture, financial contribution for the environment, contribution to the awareness level of stakeholders, creating alternative employment opportunities and improving environmental management and planning. In the protection of important natural areas, the protection status of the area is of great importance. In this context, it would be beneficial to encourage local, regional or national level destination managers to develop these systems. Standards can be provided for the protection of these areas, which can be considered as world heritage, through the collaborations at the global level. In addition, cooperation at the global level will facilitate the transfer of knowledge, experience, technology and projects, and the efficiency of the processes will increase. Archaeological and historical sites and architectural works are heritage assets that reflect the cultural accumulation of the society they belong to, primarily for the relevant society but for humanity at the macro level. Curiosity about getting to know other cultures is an important travel motivation in the tourism industry. Opening archaeological, historical sites and architectural works, which have become more attractive with this motivation, to the visitor experience enables administrative and financial support to be provided for the protection of these works. In addition, every element that creates tourist attraction offers social, economic and environmental benefits to the destination it belongs to and therefore to the destination stakeholders through the tourism industry. Thus, awareness of the protection and development of these attractions, which are deemed valuable by stakeholders, is increased. Management plans are created to ensure the sustainability of the relevant resources thanks to the increasing awareness. Thanks to tourism, natural and cultural resources that cannot be exported physically are presented to visitors as a touristic product. In the industry where an integrated service is provided, visitors come to destinations with very different motivations and therefore they have very different needs. Especially with evolving of post-modern tourism into original products, the width and depth of the product variety in tourism increases. This creates alternative employment and income opportunities especially for the local people of the destination. In this context, by regarding the increase in the tendency towards nature-based tourism activities as an opportunity, natural resources will be presented to the visitors as alternative touristic products through sustainable systems, thereby ensuring their protection and improvement.

On the other hand, the negative effects of tourism can be listed as water, air, soil, noise, visual and aesthetic pollution, waste problem, ecological degradation, disturbance of wildlife, land use problems, and transportation problems. The use of chemicals causes the accumulation of permanent pollutants in the air, water and soil and naturally leads to pollution in these sources. By raising awareness about the harmful effects of chemical substances for both human health and the environment, it can be encouraged to take measures to reduce chemical pressure in the industry and thus risks. In order to reduce the pressure of the tourism sector, it is important to prefer clean and efficient energy systems, to spread the use of sustainable agricultural techniques, and to consider the recommendations of the relevant institutions in terms of hygiene and sanitation. Solid and liquid waste disposal is another important issue. It will be beneficial to complete the necessary infrastructure for the collection, storage and disposal of tourism-related waste and to arrange waste management in tourism destinations according to the tourism season. The issue of waste management is also closely related to the reduction of waste sources and recycling. Thanks to awareness-raising activities for recycling wastes originating from tourism, waste control will be ensured and resource efficiency will be enabled. In addition, the zero waste approach, which has been implemented in some cities around the world, may be important in terms of conserving resources for many destinations and attracting the demand for qualified tourism to the destination. Especially by taking a step forward in sustainability, which is one of the basic dynamics of post-modern tourism trends, it will be possible to gain an advantage over competitors. Flora and fauna diversity is one of the important resources for the tourist attraction of a destination. Presenting these resources to visitors as a touristic product through sustainable systems may ensure their protection, and also contribute to the local community by providing economic benefits. It is important to protect the areas where flora and fauna tourism is carried out through appropriate status, and to carry out inventory and labeling studies on flora and fauna species in order to protect the species. On the other hand, it is very important that the tracks are established prominently in these areas and that the businesses that organize tours to these areas and especially the guides are educated and knowledgeable. One of the most important environmental factors arising from tourism is transportation. In this context, it is important to prefer and encourage systems with less polluting effects in transportation. For example, rail and sea transportation has less negative effects than transportation by air and private vehicles. As predicted especially by post-modern tourism dynamics, negative consequences can be reduced to certain levels by supporting alternative and boutique activities such as bicycle tourism. In addition, the process of transformation of transportation vehicles into the designs that consume clean energy resources can be accelerated by investments and incentives. Although the transport sector conducts various studies to prevent air pollution in general, stakeholders in the tourism industry should encourage decarbonization by carrying out more effective studies on developing prevention and action plans to reduce greenhouse gas emissions. In addition, as it is known, air pollution causes a number of physical and psychological disorders on human health. Visitors can be made more aware of these effects. In this way, destinations where air pollution is heavily felt will lose their attractiveness and as a result, regions, countries and ultimately the industry will be able to tend to take more rapid measures against the elements that cause pollution thanks to a holistic perspective. Apart from these negative effects, tourism can cause other negative effects such as overcrowding, cost of living, slums, immigration, problems in accessing local opportunities like education, health, and periodic unemployment.

Climate change and tourism interact with each other. The tourism industry should develop a holistic perspective to prefer and encourage sustainable production and consumption systems to reduce the effects that cause climate change. Also, climate change has an intense effect on three main types of tourism in the industry: holiday tourism, winter tourism, and nature-based tourism. Climate change also changes the dynamics in the industry in terms of geography, time and product diversity, especially at the regional scale. Therefore, it is very important to make plans to adapt to these effects and changes.

The ecological footprint of the tourism industry is a highly functional concept for determining the impact of a destination's visitors on the destination's ecological system. In order to reduce the ecological footprint of tourism, information can be provided for visitors to raise their awareness about the environment through environmental education on a global scale. For example, they will be able to carry out social responsibility activities such as preferring more boutique activities and businesses instead of mass movements, or showing environmentally responsible behaviors like preferring the existence of sustainable systems in the production of goods and services and the use of clean and renewable energy, and even participating in environmentally friendly activities at a later stage.

One of the key factors in ensuring the sustainability of environmental resources is the determination of transport capacities. It is because determining the carrying capacities provides the key data in answering the question of at what point the sources exceed the threshold limit and begin to deteriorate and therefore disappear in the future. Nature has the capacity to renew itself in its natural rhythm. Therefore, what needs to be done should be to keep up with this natural rhythm. In particular, an industry such as tourism whose basic raw material is nature should act more precisely and be a pioneer in this issue, serving as a model.

References

Ahunbay, Zeynep (2010). "Arkeolojik Alanlarda Koruma Sorunları Kuramsal ve Yasal Açılardan Değerlendirme", *TÜBA-KED*, Vol: 8, pp. 103–118.

Akıllı, Hüsniye, Kemahli, Funda, Okudan, Kadriye, and Polat, Ferihan (2008). "Ekolojik Ayak İzinin Kavramsal İçeriği ve Akdeniz Üniversitesi İktisadi ve İdari Bilimler Fakültesi'nde Bireysel Ekolojik Ayak İzi Hesaplaması", *Akdeniz İ.İ.B.F. Dergisi*, Vol: 8, No: 15, pp. 1–15.

Alazaizeh, Mohammad M., Hallo, Jeffrey C., Backman, Sheila J., Norman, William C., and Vogel, Melissa A. (2016). "Value Orientations and Heritage Tourism Management at Petra Archaeological Park, Jordan", *Tourism Management*, Vol: 57, pp. 149–158.

Ay, Eşref and Günay Aktaş, Semra (2019). Sound Pollution and Tourism in the Urban Area, Part 6: Environmental Issues/Sustainability & Green Tourism, Co-Editors: Cihan Çobanoğlu, Muhittin Çavuşoğlu and Abdulkadir Çorbaci, *Advances in Global Busıness and Economıcs*, Vol: 2., pp. 66–75.

Belsoy, Josphat, Korir, Jacqueline and Yego, Jacob (2012). "Environmental Impacts of Tourism in Protected Areas", *Journal of Environment and Earth Science*, Vol: 2, No: 10, pp. 64–73.

Bshell, Robyn and Bricker, Kelly (2016). "Tourism in Protected Areas: Developing Meaningful Standards", *Tourism and Hospitality Research*, Vol: 17, No: 1, pp. 1–15.

Castellani, Valentina and Sala, Serenella (2012). "Ecological Footprint and Life Cycle Assessment in the Sustainability Assessment of Tourism Activities", *Ecological Indicators*, Vol: 16, pp. 135–147.

Chang, Kaowen Grace, Chien, Hungju, Cheng, Hungyao and Chen, Hsin-i (2018). "The Impacts of Tourism Development in Rural Indigenous Destinations: An Investigation of the Local Residents' Perception Using Choice Modeling", *Sustainability*, Vol: 10, pp. 1–15.

Comer, Douglas C. and Willems, Williem J. H. (2011). "Tourism and Archaeological Heritage Driver to Development or Destruction?", *ICOMOS*, Vol: 3, No: 1, pp. 506–518.

Demir, Cengiz (2002). "Turizm ve Rekreasyon Faaliyetlerinin Olumsuz Çevresel Etkileri: Türkiye'deki Milli Parklara Yönelik Bir Uygulama", *D.E.Ü.İ.İ.B.F. Dergisi*, Vol: 17, No: 2, pp. 93–117.

DestiMED (2019). A Guide to plan and promote ecotourism activities and measure their impacts in Mediterranean Protected Areas following the MEET approach, Meet Network.

Dileep, M. R. (2007). "Tourism and Waste Management: A Review of Implementation of "Zero Waste" at Kovalam", *Asia Pacific Journal of Tourism Research*, Vol: 12, No: 4, pp. 377–392.

Doğan, Mesut (2010). Turizm ve Çevre, İstanbul Üniversitesi Açık ve Uzaktan Eğitim Fakültesi, İstanbul.

Dubois, Ghislain and Ceron, Jean-Paul (2006). "Tourism and Climate Change: Proposals for a Research Agenda", *Journal of Sustainable Tourism*, Vol: 14, No: 4, pp. 39–415.

Erden Özsoy, Ceyda and Dinç, Ahmet (2016). "Sürdürülebilir Kalkınma ve Ekolojik Ayak İzi", *Finans Politik & Ekonomik Yorumlar*, Vol: 53, No: 619, pp. 35–55.

Ewert, Alan W. (1999). "Outdoor Recreation and Natural Resource Management: An Uneasy Alliance", *Parks and Recreation*, Vol: 39, No: 2, pp. 1–9.

Faraji Rad, Abdoreza and Aghajani, Somayyeh (2010). "The Relationship Between Tourism and Environment", *Iranian Journal of Tourism & Hospitality*, Vol: 1, No: 1, pp. 37–49.

Giulietti, Silvia, Romagosa, Francesc, Esteve, Jaume Fons and Schröder Christoph (2018). Tourism and the environment Towards a reporting mechanism in Europe, *European Topic Centre on Urban Land and Soil Systems, ETC/ULS Report.*

Gössling, Stefan, Hansson, Carina Borgstrom, Hörstmeier, Oliver and Saggel, Stefan (2002). "Ecological Footprint Analysis as a Tool to Assess Tourism Sustainability", *Ecological Economics*, Vol: 43, No: 2–3, pp. 199–211.

Gössling, Stefan and Peeters, Paul (2015) "Assessing Tourism's Global Environmental Impact 1900–2050", *Journal of Sustainable Tourism*, Vol: 23, No: 5, pp. 639–659.

Gülbahar, Onur (2008). "Küresel Isınma, Turizme Olası Etkileri ve Türkiye", *KMU İİBF Dergisi*, Vol: 10, No: 15, pp. 160–198.

Güneş, Gül (2011). "Konaklama Sektöründe Çevre Dostu Yönetimin Önemi", KMÜ Sosyal ve Ekonomik Araştırmalar Dergisi, Vol: 13, No: 20, pp. 45–51.

Hunter, Colin (2002). "Sustainable Tourism and the Touristic Ecological Footprint", *Environment, Development and Sustainability*, Vol: 4, pp. 7–20.

IUCN, International Union for Conservation of Nature and Natural Resources (2008). Guidelines for Applying Protected Area Management Categories, Edited by Nigel Dudley, Gland, Switzerland.

IUCN, International Union for Conservation of Nature and Natural Resources (2018). Tourism and Visitor Management in Protected Areas, Guidelines for Sustainability, Gland, Switzerland.

Jahani, Ali, Goshtasb, Hamid and Saffariha, Maryam (2020). "Tourism Impact Assessment Modeling of Vegetation Density for Protected Areas Using Data Mining Techniques", *Land Degradation and Development*, pp. 1–18. https://doi.org/10.1002/ldr.3549.

Kalamandeen, Michelle and Gillson, Lindsey (2007). "Demything "Wilderness": Implications for Protected Area Designation and Management", *Biodiversity and Conservation*, Vol: 16, pp. 165–182.

Karamustfa, Kurtuluş and Örnek, Nazlı (2019). "Modernite ve Postmodernite Etrafında Şekillenen Turizm Olgusu ve Gelişimi", *Tüketici ve Tüketim Araştırmaları Dergisi*, Vol: 11, No: 2, pp. 259–290.

Karwacki, Judy and Boyd, Colin (1995). "Ethics and Tourism", *European Review*, Vol: 4, No: 4, pp. 225–232.

Kozak Akoğlan, Meryem, Evren, Savaş ve Çakır, Onur (2013). "Tarihsel Süreç İçinde Turizm Paradigması", *Anatolia: Turizm Araştırmaları Dergisi*, Vol: 24, No: 1, pp. 7–22.

Lindberg, Kreg, Mccool, Stephen and Stankey, George (1996). "Rethinking Carrying Capacity", *Research Notes and Reports*, Vol:24, No: 2 pp. 461–465.

Mason, Peter (2003). Tourism Impacts, Planning and Management, Butterworth-Heinemann an imprint of Elsevier, Oxford.

Mccool, Stephen F. and Lime, David W. (2001). "Tourism Carrying Capacity: Tempting Fantasy or Useful Reality", *Journal of Sustainable Tourism*, Vol: 9, No: 5, pp. 372–388.

Mishra, Rajesh Kumar, Mohammad, Naseer and Roychoudhury, Nilanjan (2016). "Soil Pollution: Causes, Effects and Control", *Van Sangyan*, Vol: 3, No: 1, pp. 1–14.

Mustafa, Mairna Hussein (2019). "Tour Guides and the Protection of Archaeological Sites: A Case from Jordan", *Anatolia*, Vol: 30, No: 4, pp. 586–600.

Mutlu, Ahmet (2006). "Turizm Bölgelerinde Katı Atık Sorunu ve Belediyeler", *Yerel Yönetim Ve Denetim*, Vol: 11, No: 9, ss. 23–28.

O'reilly, A. M. (1986). "Tourism Carrying Capacity Concept and Issues", *Tourism Manegement*, Vol:7, No:4, pp. 254–258.

Rabbany, Md. Ghulam, Afrin, Sharmin, Rahman, Airin, Islam, Faijul and Hoque, Fazlul (2013). "Environmental Effects of Tourism", *American Journal of Environment, Energy and Power Research*, Vol: 1, No: 7, pp. 117–130.

Ross, David, Saxena, Gunjan, Correia, Fernando and Deutz, Pauline (2017). "Archaeological Tourism: A Creative Approach", *Annals of Tourism Research*, Vol: 67, pp. 37–47.

Salam, M. Abdus, Lindsay, G. Ross and Beveridg, Malcolm C. M. (2000). "Eco-Tourism to Protect the Reserve Mangrove Forest the Sundarbans and its Flora and Fauna", *Anatolia: An International Journal of Tourism and Hospitality Research,* Vol: 11, No: 1, pp. 56–66.

Sari Çalli, Didar (2015). "Uluslararası Seyahatlerin Tarihi Gelişimi Ve Son Seyahat Trendleri Doğrultusunda Türkiye'nin Konumu", *Turizm ve Araştırma Dergisi*, Vol: 4, No: 1, pp. 4–28.

Scott, Daniel (2003). "Climate Change and Tourism in the Mountain Regions of North America", In *1st International Conference on Climate Change and Tourism*, pp. 9–11.

Scott, Daniel, Gössling, Stefan and Hall C. Michael (2012). "International Tourism and ClimateChange", *WIREs Climate Change*, Vol: 3, pp. 213–232.

Seçilmiş, Cihan and Kılıç, İlker (2018). "Turistik Destinasyonlarda Yerel Halk ve Turist Gözünden Taşıma Kapasitesinin Değerlendirilmesi: Eskişehir Örneği", *Seyahat ve Otel İşletmeciliği Dergisi*, Vol: 15, No: 3, pp. 506–522.

Sevim, Burhan and Ünlüönen, Kurban (2010). "İklim Değişikliğinin Turizme Etkileri: Konaklama İşletmelerinde Bir Uygulama", *Sosyal Bilimler Enstitüsü Dergisi*, Vol:28, No: 1, pp. 43–66.

Sevim, Burhan and Zeydan, Özgür (2007). "İklim Değişikliğinin Türkiye Turizmine Etkileri", *Çeşme Ulusal Turizm Sempozyumu*, pp. 159–174.

Shamshiry, Elmira, Nadi, Behzad, Mokhtar, Mazlin Bin, Komoo, Ibrahim, Hashim Halimaton Saadiah, and Yahaya, Nadzri (2011). "Integrated Models for Solid Waste Management in Tourism Regions: Langkawi Island, Malaysia", *Journal of Environmental and Public Health*, Vol:2011, No: 9, pp. 1–6.

Shani, Amir and Arad, Boaz (2014). "Climate Change and Tourism: Time for Environmental Skepticism", *Tourism Management*, Vol: 44, pp. 82–85.

Šimková, Eva (2007). "The Potential of Rural Tourism and the Sustainable Development of Rural Areas", *E + M*, Vol: 10, No: 4, pp. 57–62.

Şit, Mustafa (2016). "Türkiye'de Turizm Sektörünün İstihdama Katkısı", *Akademik Yaklaşımlar Dergisi*, Vol: 7, No: 1, pp. 101–117.

Song, Qingbin, Li, Jinhui and Zeng, Xianlai (2015). "Minimizing the Increasing Solid Waste Through Zero Waste Strategy", *Journal of Cleaner Production*, Vol: 104, pp. 199–210.

Srivastava, Surabhi (2015). "Archaeotourism: An Approach to Heritage Conservation and Area Development". *Global Journal of Engineering, Science & Social Science Studies*, Vol: 1, No: 2, pp. 31–42.

Sunlu, Uğur (2003). "Environmental Impacts of Tourism", pp. 263–270. In: Camarda, D. and Grassini, L. (eds.), *Local resources and global trades: Environments and agriculture in the Mediterranean region. Bari: CIHEAM, (Options Méditerranéennes: Série A. Séminaires Méditerranéens; n. 57).*

Temizkan, Rahman and Ceyhanlıi, Kaan (2020). "Turizm Lisans Öğrencilerinin Ekolojik Ayak İzi Farkındalıkları", *Turizm Akademik Dergisi*, Vol: 7, No: 2, pp. 203–223.

Turkis, Sevda and Çil, Elif (2017). "Çevre Eğitimi Dersinin Öğretmen Adaylarının Ekolojik Ayak İzi Boyutuna Etkisi", *Kesit Akademi Dergisi*, Vol: 3, No: 12, pp. 174–179.

United Nations by Frederico Neto (2003). A New Approach to Sustainable Tourism Development: Moving Beyond Environmental Protection, *DESA Discussion Paper*, No. 29.

Ünlüönen, Kurban and Tokmak, Cüneyt (2009). "Topkapı Sarayı'nda Çalışanlar ve Ziyaretçilerin Sosyal Taşıma Kapasitesine Yönelik Değerlendirmeleri", *İşletme Araştırmaları Dergisi*, Vol: 1, No: 1, pp. 17–30.

UNWTO (2008). Climate Change and Tourism – Responding to Global Challenges, *World Tourism Organization and United Nations Environment Programme.*

UNWTO (2019). Transport Relatede CO2 Emissions of the Tourism Sector. Retrived from https://www.unwto.org/news/tourisms-carbon-emissions-measured-in-landmark-report-launched-at-cop25 (Date of access: 24.03.2021).

Wackernagel, Mathis and Rees, William (1997). "Our Ecological Footprint: Reducing Human Impact on the Earth", *UCLA Electronic Green Journal*, Vol: 1, No: 7, pp. 1–3.

Wang, Yı, Xia, Zancaı and Chen, Weı (2008). "Aesthetic Values in Sustainable Tourism Development: A Case Study in Zhangjiajie National Park of Wuling Yuan, China", *Journal of China Tourism Research*, Vol: 4, pp. 205–218.

Witt, Stephen F., Song, Haiyan and Wanhill, Stephen (2004). "Forecasting Tourism-Generated Employment: The Case of Denmark", *TourismEconomics*, Vol: 10, No: 2, pp. 167–176.

Yildiz, Zafer (2011). "Turizmin Sektörünün Gelişimi Ve İstihdam Üzerindeki Etkisi", *Süleyman Demirel Üniversitesi Vizyoner Dergisi*, Vol: 3, No: 5. pp. 54–71.

Yilmaz, Demet and Sağsöz, Ayşe (2010). "In the Context of Visual Pollution: Effects to Trabzon City Center Silhoutte", *Asian Social Science*, Vol: 7, No: 5, pp. 98–109.

Zhang, Ke, Hou, Yuansi, Li, Gang and Huang, Yunhui (2019). Tourists and Air Pollution: "How and Why Air Pollution Magnifies Tourists' Suspicion of Service Providers", *Journal of Travel Research*, Vol: 59, No:4, pp. 1–13.

Zorpas, Antonis A., Voukkalib, Irene and Loizia, Pantelitsa (2014). "The Impact of Tourist Sector in the Waste Management Plans", *Desalination and Water Treatment*, Vol: 52, No: 1, pp. 1–9.

Pelin Pinar Giritlioglu

From Mega-Projects and Environmental Sustainability Perspective an Artificial Waterway Project Overview: Canal Istanbul Project

Introduction

Istanbul has been changing more and more every day under the pressure of mega-projects since the early 2000s; and it loses its identity and character. In recent years, it has been brought to the agenda one after the other, although it is not included in the upper-scale plans, it has been implemented by being included in the plans, mega projects such as the Eurasia Tunnel, the Third Bridge, and the Third Airport, whose legal infrastructures were later prepared and legitimized. These projects have caused and continueto destroy natural, cultural, socio-economic structure and therefore the sustainable development of the city. Canal Istanbul discussions, which have been on the agenda since 2012, have also been added to this mega-projects process.

The Canal Istanbul project, which was first introduced to the public in 2011, has a distinctive feature that distinguishes it from the others. Canal Istanbul is not just a real estate project or a transportation project. This project is also an ecocide project that will have large-scale effects on Istanbul, Thrace, the Sea of Marmara and the Black Sea. Although the construction has not been implemented yet, the legal infrastructure of the project has been designed, the tenders for the initial stages and the expropriation processes have been started, In the near future, together with other mega projects, it is expected to affect Istanbul, its surroundings and the countries that have a coast to the Black Sea . In this sense, it poses a great threat to the sustainable development of the city and the region in which it is located.

Aim

In this study, first of all, the concept of mega-project is discussed, The effects of mega projects on sustainable development will be mentioned, then the canal Istanbul project, It will be discussed with its effects on the sustainable development of Istanbul metropolis. The study is based on the claim that mega-projects create permanent and irreversible effects and traumas on cities. The main fundamental research problem of the study, as a mega-project, Cannel Istanbul Project, It aims to find answers to the effects of Istanbul on the sustainability of the city as a whole and its environment.

The most important output expected from this discussion, effects beyond the borders of Istanbul and its region, For the canal Istanbul project, which is inevitable to be based on international borders, to raise awareness on an international scale and to take the first step towards a global environmental struggle.

Research Methodology

The study is mainly based on literature review and analysis. In the first part of the study, it is aimed to carry out a conceptual discussion on mega projects. In this context, The concept of mega projects and the effects of mega projects on the sustainability of cities will be examined with the current literature review.

In the second part, the mega projects that have been produced one after the other in Istanbul in recent years will be discussed. Of these, information will be given about the Third Bridge and Third Airport projects, which are directly related to the canal Istanbul Project, and their effects on the whole city of Istanbul. Information on this subject, will be mostly based on the numerical data included in the reports of the projects in question (Environmental Impact Assessment). In this chapter, The effects of Istanbul on mega projects will be analyzed by taking into account the technical reports, expert opinions and Environmental Impact Assessment Reports prepared for the projects. Although many mega-projects have been implemented in Istanbul in recent years, In this study, the 3rd Bridge and 3rd Airport projects, which are parts of a whole with Canal Istanbul, were selected. These three projects, which are large-scale, together form a mega-project. In this sense, they affect the city, the Thrace region and the countries bordering the Black Sea together. As a result of the examination of the reports of both projects (Environmental Impact Assessment), some potential impacts (Environmental Impact Assessment) are not mentioned in the reports, it was seen that some of them were developed without much emphasis. Neglected effects were also investigated through literature reviews. What can be said for both projects is that the projects – especially for the newly active Third Airport, have both environmental consequences, and, accordingly, academic research is more recent and limited. Therefore, both these projects, as well as the canal Istanbul project discussed in the last section, mainly (Environmental impact assessment) Reports, lawsuit petitions of professional chambers and non-governmental organizations, evaluated through technical reports prepared by professional organizations.

In the last section, based on these evaluations, The urban, regional and international effects of canal Istanbul will be discussed in the context of sustainability. In this context, The costs of the canal Istanbul project, which is expected to last 100 years, will be discussed in terms of sustainability. The results of the study, technical reports for the project, expert opinions and Environmental Impact Assessment Report data, universal economic, It will be reached by evaluating it in the context of social and environmental sustainability criteria. These criteria will be designed according to the project to be realized in a rural area by examining the universal criteria. Regarding canal Istanbul, Recently, the workshops and panels organized by the Istanbul Metropolitan Municipality, related professional organizations and some (Non-Governmental Organizations) were also examined, It has been discussed within the scope of the study by including both.

1. Mega Projects and Their Impact on Sustainable Development

Mega projects are handled in many different dimensions. According to Grun (2004), who considers mega projects as multi-organized enterprises, the characteristics of these projects are as follows: (i) singularity, (ii) complexity, (iii) goal-directedness (technical, financial, time), and (iv) nature and number of project owners. Many large-scale projects are carried out in the world today, but mega-projects have a different content from other large-scale projects. They could be distinguished from other urban projects by their extent and magnificence of scale, cost, time and impact (Sarkhely et al., , 2017).

Mega projects contain more than one purpose. Therefore, Flyvbjerg et al. (2003) reports that such projects have a large number of It emphasizes that it requires the management of simultaneous and complex activities.

Sturup and Low (2019) highlight the positive aspects of megaprojects, while also pointing out that these projects automate their lifestyles, impose local and global costs on society, and thus ignore their environmental consequences. According to them, these projects are generally, have wide-ranging effects on the economy of regions and nations, and even on the global economy, They are very large-scale construction activities involving various stakeholders or businesses and with a price tag in excess of US$ 1 billion. Mega-projects, often supported by governments, There are possibilities for generating employment and profits and creating social and economic opportunities in certain sectors. Socially and environmentally undesirable lifestyle habits are made "sustainable" by long-lasting mega-projects. However, these projects have social and environmental costs.

Every mega-project under construction produces a certain quantum of greenhouse gas that is emitted into the atmosphere. These projects are generally green open space, social movement networks, agriculture, they change land uses such as local ecologies and generate waste both during and after construction.

It is known that the costs of mega-projects are also very high. They often receive a very large share of the country's resources; however, the benefits outweigh the costs. In support of this, Flyvbjerg (2003) points out that mega projects are often expensive, but the return is less than the cost.

Although these projects are often described as proud activities in the eyes of the society, in fact, the social, economic and especially environmental costs and large-scale effects are hardly taken into account by society. Due to all these features, Zidane, Johansen, Ekambaram (2013) define these projects as "a wild animal that is difficult to domesticate" and emphasize that they cause great changes in the geography of countries and people's lives.

While they have become an icon for the country of mega projects, they draw attention to the fact that some of them also bring unforgettable disasters. It should be noted that the impact area of such projects is very wide and multidimensional; they often cause irreparable consequences in social, environmental and economic terms. These far-reaching effects are of great importance in measuring the sustainability of megaprojects in a city or region.

The Report of the World Commission on Environment and Development: Our Common Future, published in 1987 by the United Nations World Commission on Environment and Development, addresses the concept of sustainability as follows: "The concept of sustainable development does imply limits – not absolute limits but limitations imposed by the present state of technology and social organization on environmental resources and by the ability of the biosphere to absorb the effects of human activities (WCED, 1987, para 27). The report draws attention to the fact that the world's species are under threat and that the elimination of these threats is a priority task of governments, with the following statements: "The planet's species are under stres (WCED, 1987, para 52). The diversity of species is necessary for the normal functioning of ecosystems and the biosphere as a whole (WCED, 1987, para 53). A first priority is to establish the problem of disappearing species and threatened ecosystems on political agendas as a major economic and resource issue (WCED, 1987, para 54). Governments can stem the destruction of tropical forests and other reservoirs of biological diversity while developing them economically. Reforming forest revenue systems and concession terms could raise billions of dollars of additional revenues, promote more efficient, long-term forest resource use, and curtail deforestation

(WCED, 1987, para 55)". The sustainability of ecosystems on which the global economy depends must be guaranteed (WCED, 1987, para 75)".

Mega-projects play a huge role in urban and regional sustainability. Sturup and Low (2019) draws attention to the effects of mega-projects on sustainability, expressing it as follows: "What sustainability perspectives mean for the impacts of infrastructure megaprojects is twofold. First, the construction of such projects creates an impact extending out from the local space in which the project takes place to the wider region and in certain respects, to the globe. Second, infrastructure megaprojects are designed to accommodate and sustain particular kinds of human activity. That activity may have an impact on the Earth over time and space, posing the question: is the activity itself sustainable".

2. Mega Projects of Istanbul and Their Effects on the City

Istanbul continues to develop under the pressure of mega projects, especially for the last 15 years. The infrastructure of this process has been regulated by national legislation since 2004.

In addition, initiatives such as the establishment of the Ministry of Environment and Urbanization, changing the name and scope of the Ministry of Transport, with a new arrangement in the ministry structures in 2011, caused many mega projects, especially large transportation projects, to have large-scale effects on Istanbul.

Although the projects such as Eurasia Tunnel Project ($1.2 billion budget), Northern Marmara Highway (Third Bosphorus Crossing and connection roads), ($14.4 billion budget), Third Airport (with a budget of 11.2 billion dollars) and other projects which are planned in different parts of the city and are associated with these mega transportation projects are not included in the Environmental Plan of Istanbul that approved in 2009, they all are included the plan later. Among these projects, especially the Third Bosphorus Crossing Project and the Third Airport Project, suppressed the north of Istanbul, which is also under the protection of the Environmental Plan, and caused great destruction on the forested areas in this region.

If we look briefly at only two of these projects within the scope of this study, the extent of its effects on Istanbul will be clearly seen. The reason for choosing these two works is that they are part of a mega project together with the canal Istanbul Project.

Northern Marmara Highway and 3rd Bosphorus Crossing Project

Northern Marmara Highway Project, which starts from Kınalı Tolls in Silivri District of Istanbul, It passes through Kocaeli district and ends with Akyazı Trans European Highway (TEM) Tolls located in Akyazı district of Sakarya province. The sea passage of the Project is provided by the existing Yavuz Sultan Selim (3rd Bosphorus Bridge) Bridge and its connection roads, which have been in operation since August 2016. A large part of the Northern Marmara Motorway project route (approximately 35 km), It passes over the Bosphorus (Important Natural Area) stretching along the Bosphorus from the European side to the Asian side. (Important Natural Area) consists of many habitats such as dunes, rocks, maquis communities, pastures, forests and lakes on the coastline. There is also an "Important Plant Area" in the forest areas on the west and east sides of the Bosphorus. Another (Important Natural Areas) includes the West Istanbul Pastures Important Natural Area on the European side. The Important Natural Areas have a total area of 9,612 hectares between Bagcılar in the south and Pirinchi in the north. Approximately 11.4 km of the project route passes through these Important Natural Areas. In terms of habitat, the greatest impact is seen in forest areas with broad-leaved trees.

Within the 60.5 m construction corridor of the project, approximately 345 hectares of oak density, forest area and approximately 284 hectares of conifer/ The coniferous tree area was destroyed due to the project (Environmental and Social Impact Assessment (Environmental and Social Impact Assessment) for the Northern Marmara Motorway – including the 3rd Bosphorus Bridge-Project, 2013). In fact, the areas around the highway route in the 1/100,000 scale Environmental Plan of Istanbul, mainly planned as agricultural lands in rural settlements. chatalca hills and its surroundings have been determined as areas where forest and natural character will be preserved. Based on the calculations of (Environmental and Social Impact Assessment, 2013) that all private lands to be acquired within the scope of the project are agricultural lands, It is known that a total of 628.6 ha of agricultural land is permanently lost along the entire Highway. Highway passing through pasture lands, It has revealed results such as the division of pasture lands and the restriction of access between these sections (According to the calculations of Environmental and Social Impact Assessment, 2013). More than half of the pasture parcels within the Kucukkilicli and Nakkashta expropriation corridor have been lost.

Third Airport Project

In fact, Akpınar, İhsaniye, Odayeri, Baklalı, Zafer, which are located on the European side, in the north of Istanbul, in Arnavutkoy and Eyup districts. Located on the border of Karaburun neighborhoods, the Third Airport covers an area of approximately 7,650 hectares.

This area consists of 6.173 hectares of forest, 1.180 hectares of mining and other uses, 660 hectares of lakes, 236 hectares of pastures, 60 hectares of agriculture, and 2 hectares of heathland. Approximately 2,47 % (189,182 hectares) of the project area is privately owned (Third Airport EIA Report, 2013). It is seen in the comparative analysis method that the Northern Forests Defense has done on satellite images, With the Third Airport Project, excluding project areas such as bridge connection roads or other opened parts of the Northern Marmara Motorway, Approximately 13 million trees were cut (Evrensel Newspaper, 22 June 2019). However, it was calculated in the Environmental Impact Assessment Report that 2.5 million trees would be cut down, which is actually a very high number.

Terkos Lake, one of the main water resources of the city (The primary water source of the city is located 2.5 km to the northwest of the project site), The Alibeykoy dam and the chubukchi Dam, which is still in the planning phase, It is in the direct impact area of the project and will become unusable in the short term due to overpopulation and construction pressure around the project. Ceko Stream feeding the Terkos lake basin, A part of the ustunluk Stream and Yenikoy Stream has already been damaged by the project.

The area where the airport is built corresponds to 2.5 % of the forest area of the city, which is up to 240 thousand hectares. The northern forests, which are of great importance in terms of the ecology of the city, were severely damaged by the project. In addition, 17 endemic plant species in the area were directly affected by the project. The airport was built on the route through which one of Turkey's most important bird migration routes passes. Although attention was drawn to this issue in the Environmental Impact Assessment Report, the recommended bird observations were not made (Association of Chambers of Turkish Engineers and Architects Istanbul Provincial Coordination Board 3rd Airport Technical Report, 2014). Ecological-biodiversity and coastline between Terkos and Kasatura, which are among the important ecological regions listed in the Istanbul Environmental Plan, The pastures and heathlands between (Agıldere) and (Agachlı Dunes), (Gumusdere) (Kilyos) Dunes, Hadımkoy and Kemerburgaz are very close to the project area (Tolunay, 2015).

The Project (environmental impact assessment) Report also states, "There are landslides and landslides in and around the excavation dumping area located in the south-west of the project area and within the boundaries of the project area. In particular, there are slips and road deterioration due to landslides on the part of the Tayakad- İhsaniye road that coincides with the excavation storage area. In addition, there are slips on the ground in the degraded lands as a result of mining activities in the area." İt also drew attention to the landslide risk (Third Airport, Environmental Impact Assessment Report, 2013).

As can be seen, only with these two mega projects, the agricultural areas, pasture areas, water basins, forest areas and wildlife of the city have been suppressed. A large part of it has been destroyed and the future of the remaining parts is in danger. As part of these two projects, it was shared with the public by the prime minister of the time that another project, the canal Istanbul Project, would begin in 2012.

3. Possible Effects of Canal Istanbul to Istanbul and Its Region in the Context of Sustainability

3.1. General Structure of the Field

There are residential areas in the first 10–15 km of the area from south to north. The second 15–20 km. agricultural areas in the first part and then the third 15–20 km . There are forest areas in the northern part. Therefore, in the North, with the forest texture around Terkos Lake, which has the characteristics of a wetland, Buyukcekmece Lake in the south, with agricultural areas and residential areas, Kucukcekmece Lake (except for its north) is surrounded by a dense urban settlement pattern. There are many archaeological, natural and urban sites in the region affected by the project.

3.2. Canal Istanbul Planning Process

With the Council of Ministers Decision No. 12689 on 13.08.2012 unlicensed to prevent disaster risk in 3 different areas in Istanbul, The Ministry of Environment and Urbanization has been authorized in order to liquidate uninhabited and disaster-prone structures and to use them as new settlement areas. With the decision of the Council of Ministers dated 18 August 2012, the construction of the third airport, within the scope of the construction of the third bridge and the canal Istanbul projects, an area of 42 thousand and 300 hectares on the European side of the Black Sea coast has been determined as a "reserve structure area". According to the Official Gazette dated September 8, 2012, the Ministry of

Environment and Urbanization was assigned to carry out a project for the 3rd airport of 29,500 hectares, 2 project areas and 9,000 hectares. This area is the 1st degree archaeological site in and around the Kucukcekmece Basin, the natural protected area includes the Sazlıdere Dam and its basin, the military, forest and agricultural areas within the borders of Kayabashı and Sultangazi.

In The Official Gazette Dated April 30, 2014, it has been announced that the limits of authority regarding the "reserve area" have been changed. With the Council Decision No. 311 (Istanbul Metropolitan Municipality) dated 13 February 2015, the Istanbul Metropolitan Municipality Mayor was authorized for the revision of the 1/100 000 scale (Environmental Plan) and major projects were legalized with the plan. With the Omnibus Law No. 6704, which entered into force on April 14, 2016, the definition of Waterway was introduced in the Zoning Law. Canal Istanbul, the third Bridge and the third Airport, with the Omnibus Law dated August 26, 2016 and numbered 6741, to finance major infrastructure investments such as highways, Turkey Wealth Fund Management AS, which has the authority to operate without being subject to many laws, was established, The capital of the company was provided from the Privatization Fund. On 14 July 2017, Ministry of Transport and Infrastructure General Directorate of Infrastructure Investments, The tender for the survey project and consultancy service for canal Istanbul was realized, and a protocol was signed in August between the Ministry of Environment and Urbanization, the Ministry of Transport and Infrastructure and the Metropolitan Municipality.

On 15.10.2017, a lawsuit was filed by the opposition party to the waterway concept brought to the Zoning Law. The (environmental impact assessment) Report prepared on 11.12.2017 was withdrawn on 28.12.2017. On 05.12.2017, the Public Meeting was announced. On 20.02.2018, the Ministry of Environment and Urbanization (environmental impact assessment) found the file (environmental impact assessment) and started the process (environmental impact assessment). A cooperation protocol was signed between the Istanbul Metropolitan Municipality and the Ministry of Environment and Urbanization on 12.10.2018. With the Presidential Decree issued on 24.07.2018, the process was transferred to the Ministry of Transport. On 25.10.2019, the canal Istanbul (environmental impact assessment) Report was approved by the Inspection and Evaluation Board, and opened to public opinion for 10 days. Thus, the European Side of Istanbul, Reserve structure Area, 1/100,000 scale Environmental Plan Amendment was approved on 23.12.2019. When the plan is examined in detail, it differs from the 1/100 000 scaled plan, which is considered superior in terms of the planning hierarchy, with many principles and details. On January 17, 2020, the final (environmental impact assessment) Report of canal Istanbul was approved. The legality of the process is controversial in this sense, since the plans for the (environmental impact assessment) report are approved before the end of the suspension processes. In fact, on 10.03.2020, a lawsuit was filed against this decision (Union of Chambers of Turkish Engineers and Architects) and its affiliated chambers.

Therefore, when the 1/100,000 scaled and approved 15.06.2009, Istanbul Environmental Plan of Istanbul is examined, canal Istanbul planning area, within its borders, residential areas, development area, education information and technology area, military areas, urban and regional green and sports areas, university areas, agricultural areas, pasture areas, forest areas, areas whose development and density will be kept under control, coastal rehabilitation area, beach and coastal area, dam and pond areas (Fig. 1).

Fig. 1: Cannel Istanbul Project Route (Source: Environmental Impact Assessment Report, 2019)

In the northern part of the revision plan boundary, there are Nature Oriented Tourism Area, Ecological Agriculture Area and Ecological Tourism Area functions in the Istanbul Environmental Plan. Istanbul Airport, which has an area of 7740 ha, planned within the scope of the 1/100,000 scale Environmental Plan Amendment, which was approved and put into effect on 12.06.2014, is right next to the project. The planning area is an area with natural, cultural and recreational potentials in terms of natural topographic features, coastal areas and landscape values.

The European side of Istanbul (Reserve structure Area) has a 1/100.000 scaled, 1/5.000 scaled master development plan in 10506 hectares of the Environmental Plan Change planning area, and 16558 hectares of it is unplanned. The planning area includes 79 master development plans with a scale of 1/5,000 in effect, and the entire border of 18 of these plans is within the planning area.

In the planning area, 153 ha 1st, 2nd, 3rd degree protected area in Kucukcekmece Inner Outer Beach Archaeological and Natural Protected Area, Approximately 844 hectares of natural protected area and 265 hectares of Third Degree Archaeological Site in Kucukcekmece Lake and Its Environment Archaeological Site, Approximately 32 hectares of archaeological and historical sites in Resneli Farm Archaeological and Historical Site, In Filiboz Viranlıgı Archaeological Site, 56 ha first degree archaeological site, in the Spradon Archaeological Site, there are many archaeological, historical and natural.

There is Buyukcekmece Basin at the west of the planning area, and the Pirinchi Basin, which is still planning at the east, and Terkos Basin at the northwest of the planning area. A part of the northern part of the planning area is located in the Terkos Absolute, Short, Medium and Long Range Conservation Area; and some remain in the Pirinchi Basin Long Range Conservation Area. Planning area; while some of it remains in the Terkos Absolute, Short, Medium and Long Distance protection area, the distance of the canal to the Terkos goal is 1750 meters. The areas between the canal and Terkos lake are used for agriculture and forestry. Within the area, there are 1846.28 ha (approximately 10.13 %) agricultural area to be preserved (irrigated absolute, dry absolute, dry marginal agricultural lands) and 70.2 ha pastureland (approximately 0.39 %). Forest areas cover an area of 2491 ha in the planning area.

3.3. Possible Impacts of Canal Istanbul on the City and the Region

In addition, the canal Istanbul project, the Istanbul metropolitan area; It will cause far-reaching effects in the whole of Thrace and also in all Thrace and Black Sea littoral countries. These potential impacts are evaluated under several headings below:

3.3.1. In Terms of Compliance with the Upper Scale Environmental Plan

When the 1/100 thousand scale Environmental Plan and the European Side Reserve Building Area 1/100,000 scale Environmental Plan Amendment are evaluated together within the scope of general principles, the following results stand out:

The project was later processed into the upper scale plan of the city; and the plan contradicts its main decisions. In this sense, it is unlawful and void:

1/100 000 scale, plan "The sensitive ecosystems in the north; By controlling the urban development, which tends to develop towards the north, in order to protect on the east-west axis; and the provision of staggered polycentric and incremental development along the Sea of Marmara, and while speaking, Canal Istanbul puts the entire northern part of the city and sensitive ecosystems under the pressure of urban development.

1/100,000 scale plan; and plan decisions, especially in earthquake, taking into account disaster risks; and speaking of production, the planning area is a reserve area; and there are three active fault lines on the route. In this context, besides earthquake, it also includes tsunami risk.

1/100 000 scale plan; it refuses to be built within the 1,000-meter belt of drinking water basins, in absolute and short protection zones, and within the protection zones of the streams feeding the basins. However, canal Istanbul brings an intense structure and population pressure on the water basins. By opening the protection areas of the basins to construction, it invalidates the protection decisions regarding the basins. For example, Kucukcekmece Lake in the Plan; to be cleaned and rehabilitated and in the ecological corridor between the Black Sea and the Marmara Seas; While the decision to preserve the place has been taken, Cannel Istanbul Project; It destroys Kucukcekmece".

While the 1/100 000 scaled plan talks about the population and employment balance on both sides of the city and the plan foresees the 2023 population projection as 16 million, In fact, the entire population and employment balance will be upset with the Project. Residential areas around canal Istanbul; and other functions will exponentially increase the population threshold of the upper scale plan.

The 1/100 000 scaled plan (of the Trans European Motorway) adopts the principle of "purifying the north from industrial areas and preventing the pressure of urban development on the northern region, where the natural resources of the city are concentrated". Canal Istanbul, on the other hand, causes intense pressure, along with other mega projects.

1/100.000 scaled plan, the ecological corridors between Buyukcekmece-Terkos, Kucukcekmece-Terkos, Halich-Terkos and Omerli Dam-Riva Delta, natural and agricultural characteristics, wildlife; while aiming to protect and, if necessary, improve its mobility and urban air circulation function, Cannel

Istanbul; 100 forest areas in Europe that need urgent protection; It creates a strong pressure on the northern forests, which are among the forests and which are envisaged to be protected by the Environmental Plan. Approximately 20 km of the 45 km route passes through the forest area. According to this, it is predicted that the forest area, which is approximately 550 ha, calculated on the width of the Cannel, whose narrowest part is 275 meters, will be destroyed only by the effect of the cannel.

It is seen that the plan change has brought the decision of an urban development area and a university area into the archaeological site on the edge of Kucukcekmece Lake. Thus, it completely destroys a very important archaeological site within the area.

In fact, the creek along the Sazlıdere Dam, the absolute protection areas; narrowing for urban development area; protection tape along the entire stream, approximately; It is noteworthy that it has decreased by one third.

According to the Environmental Plan with a scale of 1/100,000; mines and quarries that need to be protected are becoming urban development areas. This situation will make filling in this area inevitable.

3.3.2. In Terms of Ecosystem

The Canal Project will completely disrupt the ecological balance in the region. The region vital resources will be highly affected by the project. The coastal geography of the Black Sea will deteriorate. Canal Istanbul and other mega projects, including the whole of the city and its surroundings, It is clear that it will have a cumulative effect. The main causes of these mega-projects are humidity, temperature, gas and energy flow, albedo, evaporation, It is stated that meteorological parameters such as cloudiness and wind may change (Turkesh, 2014).

It is known that there are sea, lake, river, forest, pasture, heathland, agriculture and dune ecosystems in the project area of approximately 7 thousand hectares. Besides, there are marsh habitats around Terkos Lake and rocky habitats around Sazlıdere Dam. Clearly, some of these ecosystems have been identified as Important Plant Areas. Terkos-Kastura, Agachlı and Batı İstanbul Pastures and Important Plant Areas are located in the influence area of the canal.

Importantly, natural areas have exceptionally valuable vegetation in terms of botanical science, endangered natural/semi-natural areas containing rare and endemic plant populations (Ozhatay et al., 2005). These important plant areas are endemic to a large number of It is home to rare and threatened species.

Terkos Basin, Buyukcekmece Lake, Kucukcekmece Lake, West Istanbul Pastures, Agacli Dunes, Bosphorus, Kilyos Dunes, Istanbul Islands, Omerli Basin, Pendik Valley, Shile Coasts are known as 11 important natural areas of global importance in Istanbul (Eken and et al., 2006). As can be seen, the project area will largely take place on these Important Natural Areas of Istanbul.

These ecosystems are actually the last natural habitats of Istanbul that still preserve their naturalness and offer habitats for flora and fauna. According to the (Environmental Impact Assessment) report, there are 13 endemic and 16 threatened plant species in the Canal's impact area. In addition, some of their seeds will be collected and grown elsewhere, It is explained that there is no need for such protection as some of them are also found in other habitats. This clearly shows that these endemic species will actually disappear in the region.

The world's most important gliding birds It is located on one of the migration routes (Istanbul Strait) (Arslan Gundogdu et al., 2011). Terkos Lake, Sazlıdere Dam and Kucukcekmece lake, which are located in the region covering the canal Istanbul project and in the area of influence of this region, birds, amphibians; and are extremely important ecosystems for freshwater creatures. It is known that there are 249 bird species, 29 freshwater species and 7 bi-living species in these areas (Environmental Impact Assessment Report, 2020). In the Terkos lake, a number of water birds ranging from 2,736 to 23,651 were counted during the winter months. In Kucukcekmece Lake, 25,862 waterfowl were counted in 2014, 26,601 in 2015, 29,545 in 2016, 31,912 in 2017, 22,022 in 2018 and 30,520 in 2019 (Arslan Gundogdu and Bacak, 2017, 2018, 2019). In the (Environmental Impact Assessment) report, it is stated that Kucukcekmece Lake is the richest area in terms of bird species diversity and number. It creates suitable areas around and on the water surface for both wintering species, breeding species and species that stay during migration. The project will directly affect all these living species. Loss of these areas, as a result of some critical; The breeding and wintering populations of important species will be affected. In fact, the main reason why many bird species and populations live in the lake is the brackish water, is the attribute of the lake. Kucukcekmece Lake; In the south, which interacts with the Sea of Marmara, the water may be saltier; on the other hand, in the north, it approaches is the attribute of freshwater. After the canal project, the lake water will be highly salinized and there will be a significant decrease in the aquatic life and bird species that use the lake as a habitat.

In the opinion of the General Directorate of Forestry given in the (Environmental Impact Assessment) report, it is stated that the remaining forests in the project area are 1,289,6 ha. However, in the (Environmental Impact Assessment) Report, it is stated that 421 ha of forest area will be cut for the Cannel and the number of trees to be cut is 200,878 (Environmental Impact Assessment report, 2020). The significant difference between the numbers suggests that the number of trees to be cut will be much higher and young trees are not taken into account. In the North of Istanbul, despite the information given above, 6,172 ha for the Third Airport, which is one of the other mega projects, and 2,500 ha (forest areas) for the Third Bridge connection roads were destroyed. At the same time, the fish species living in the Black Sea and Marmara will be greatly reduced.

3.3.3. In Terms of the Right to Water

The current water resources of Istanbul are barely enough for today. According to the (Istanbul Water and Sewerage Administration) Annual Report, the annual yield of the sources that provide water to Istanbul is around 1.65 billion m3.

However, climate changes, climate crises, disasters, epidemics, etc. Against possible threats, water resources will not be sufficient in the near future. It is foreseen that the population of Istanbul will increase to 26.6 million in 2050, which was approved in 2009 (in the Istanbul Environmental Plan). When the daily water consumption of Istanbul residents remains at today's levels, 1.7 billion m3 of water may be required annually in 2050 (Tolunay, 2020).

Canal Istanbul Project causes the Sazlıdere Dam, which supplies Istanbul's water for 24 days, to be completely destroyed. Also; It also narrows the water basin of Terkos Lake, which has 2 times the capacity of Sazlıdere, which is the most important water source for Istanbul. In fact, due to the narrowing of the water basin area; It is stated in the (environmental impact assessment) report that there will be a decrease of 2.7 million m3 in Terkos Lake.

Thus, a large part of Istanbul's water resources will be destroyed. The right to life and the right to water, which are fundamental rights, are taken away from the people. It is not possible to trust the Melen Dam, which is already cracked and does not hold water. In the environmental impact assessment report, the water collection basins of the dams, which are claimed to be an additional water source for Istanbul, are within the boundaries of the Terkos, Sazlıdere, Buyukcekmece and Alibeykoy basins that supply water to Istanbul. In case of storing water by building separate dams in sub-basins within a watershed, It is known that the total amount of water will not change. Therefore, whether dams are built or not, the annual water loss from the Sazlıdere Dam and Terkos Lake that will be caused by the canal will be around 52 million m3 (Canal Istanbul Environmental Impact Assessment Report, 2019).

3.3.4. In Terms of Rural Areas

Agricultural lands and pastures will be opened for development in Thrace; thus, agriculture and animal husbandry will come to an end in our most fertile lands. With the decision of the Council of Ministers numbered 2014/6028, the Ministry of Transport and Infrastructure has been given the authority to remove the qualification of such areas, which fall within the Istanbul Province European Side Project Area, which also includes the New Airport (Canal Istanbul Environmental Impact Assessment Report, 2019). Already, the Canal Istanbul project includes 440 pastures and pastures within the scope of the ownership arrangement; The nature of the immovable qualified as winter quarters has been changed.

3.3.5. In Terms of Archaeological Sites and Other Cultural Heritage

In the canal, a very large archaeological site remains on the water surface. The plan includes decisions that narrow the watershed protection zones. Likewise, it also cuts through the forest area, thus narrowing the forest area boundaries. Moreover, according to the Environmental Impact Assessment Report, many archaeological sites will be highly affected by the implementation of the plan.

3.3.6. Legal Perspective

The effects of canal Istanbul on the marine and terrestrial environment are contradictory in terms of international environmental protection agreements to which Turkey is a party. European Convention on Human Rights (especially Articles 6 and 8), Montreux Straits Convention, Bucharest Convention (Convention on the Protection of the Black Sea against Pollution), Barcelona Convention (Convention on the Protection of the Marine Environment and Coastal Zone of the Mediterranean), United Nations Convention on Biological Diversity, United Nations Framework Convention on Climate Change, Bern Convention (Convention on the Conservation of Europe's Wildlife and Habitats), Ramsar Convention (Convention on Wetlands of International Importance, Especially as Waterfowl Habitats), European Landscape Convention (Florence Convention), UNESCO Convention on the Protection of the World Cultural and Natural Heritage, International Convention for the Safety of Life at Sea.

Except for Montreux, which regulates the passage of ships, The main purpose of these conventions is that natural landscapes, conservation of terrestrial and marine ecosystems, wetlands, biodiversity, endangered or threatened living things, ecosystem services and climate. Terkos Lake Wetland, Buyukcekmece Lake Wetland and Kucukcekmece Lake Wetland are within the scope of 135 Wetlands of International Importance designated in Turkey under the RAMSAR Convention.

However, such "mega" projects that are envisaged to be carried out in Istanbul, Within the scope of the above-mentioned conventions, it is inevitable that the impacts on the ecosystems and natural processes that are intended to be protected will be "mega" on the same scale. In addition, climate change, the effects of which are gradually increasing, will give a new impetus to the negative effects on these ecosystems.

3.3.6.1. In Terms of International Legislation

Canal Istanbul project aims to protect natural landscapes, terrestrial and marine ecosystems, wetlands, biodiversity, endangered or threatened living beings; international standards for the protection of ecosystem services and climate. contradicts many documents. The project includes the European Convention on Human Rights (especially Articles 6 and 8), the Bucharest Convention (Convention on the Protection of the Black Sea against Pollution), Barcelona Convention (Convention on the Protection of the Marine Environment and Coastal Zone of the Mediterranean), United Nations Convention on Biological Diversity, United Nations Framework Convention on Climate Change, Bern Convention (Convention on Conservation of European Wildlife and Habitats), Ramsar Convention (Convention on Wetlands of International Importance, Especially as Waterfowl Habitat), European Landscape Convention (Florence Convention), UNESCO' Convention Concerning the Protection of the World Cultural and Natural Heritage, It contains contradictions to the relevant provisions of many international conventions such as the International Convention for the Safety of Life at Sea.

3.3.6.2. In Terms of the Constitution

The main basis of the project is Article 46 of the Constitution. Accordingly, canal Istanbul is justified as a major development project. When the above effects are evaluated, it is clearly understood that the project in question cannot be a development project, that is, it has no constitutional basis.

Article 17 of the Constitution states that "everyone has the right to live, protect and develop their material and spiritual existence", and in Article 43, "the public interest shall be taken into account before making use of the coasts", and in Article 44, "to protect the efficient operation of the land by the state" and It will take the necessary measures to develop and develop it, to prevent it from being lost by erosion, in article 45, "The state will facilitate the provision of operating tools and equipment and other inputs of those engaged in agriculture and animal husbandry, and plant and animal products will be evaluated", in article 56, "everyone has the right to live in a healthy and balanced environment; It is the duty of the State and citizens to improve the environment, protect environmental health and prevent environmental pollution"; Article 63 "the State's historical, cultural and natural assets and ensure that its values are preserved"; It is regulated in Article 169 that "The State will enact the necessary laws and take measures for the protection of forests and the expansion of their areas, no activities and actions that may harm the forests will be allowed", and in Article 170, "The State will protect the forest villagers". In this context, when evaluated, the canal Istanbul project contains contradictions to all these articles.

3.3.6.3. In Terms of National Legislation

In terms of this project, the environment, forest, coast, agriculture, pastures, mines, soil protection, protection of cultural and natural assets; 9 different laws on disasters and also; It contains contradictions to the Regulation on Water Pollution Control and the Strategic Environmental Impact Assessment Regulation.

3.4. Evaluation of Canal Istanbul's Impacts in Terms of Sustainability

Since mega projects are multidimensional, it is an important issue how their impact can be measured in terms of sustainability. Goldschmidt et al. (2013) underline that sustainability criteria can be qualitative or quantitative. This is an important detail; Because, an indicator that qualitatively evaluates the project as "sustainable" may actually have a structure that harms sustainability quantitatively.

According to National Research Council of the National Academies (2010), indicators selected need to be appropriate to the sustainability objectives and need to have the following characteristics: Accurately reflective of the process or function it represents, sufficiently sensitive to pick up changes over time and among different farming systems, feasible to measure in terms of time, expense, and level of skill required, understandable and relevant to end-users.

Pavlovskia (2014) notes that "Assessments of how sustainability criteria have been fulfilled, made with the help of one indicator, but applying different assessment methods and techniques, can vary substantially even when applied to the same criteria. An important question that still remains is how to make a holistic assessment of the relative sustainability of different systems given the multiple indicators that represent various sustainability goals and objectives".

According to Sturup and Low (2019), sustainability includes indicators, weights, risk assessments, etc. can be measured with; If an infrastructure megaproject is to respond to the requirement of sustainability it must be able to show how it addresses the lexical order prioritizing critical natural systems, how it reduces human social and economic inequality and how it is embedded within its technological system which in turn impinges on both the above.

So; can measure the impact of megaprojects on sustainability by asking three basic questions:

- Do mega projects prioritize the protection of critical natural systems?
- Socially; Does it reduce social and economic inequality?
- How does it take place in the technological system that will affect others?

Undoubtedly, these questions can be developed with sub-questions. The important thing is; It should be to reveal not only the spatial success of the mega project, but also the social, economic and environmental success. If a mega project; If it has achieved a success in this context, it can be said that it has a sustainable quality. Sarkhel, Rafieian and Taghvaee (2017) aimed to measure the success of mega-projects with a detailed benchmark table (Tab. 1).

Tab. 1: Factors for Megaprojects' Success Assessment in Space Reproduction

Aspects	Factors	Indexes
Economic Prosperity	Competitiveness	The percentage of active units comparing to the inactive ones.
	Private Partnership	The percentage of private investment in the whole project
	Entrepreneurship	The percentage of productive activities or trade of local productions
	Job Space	The percentage of increase of job spaces including commercial and office built area
Place Promotion	Identity Preservation	The percentage of conservation of existed buildings/previous functional activities.
	Public Space	The percentage of increase of open and green spaces.
	Desirability	The percentage of attractive land uses built including restaurants, coffee shops and etc.
Social Improvement	Participation Level	The participation level according to the participation ladder of Arnstein (1969)
	Affordability	The percentage of difference of medium price of new buildings with the old or similar ones in the surrounding area
	Social Inclusion	The percentage of residents stayed comparing to the displacement
Environmental and Infrastructure Improvement	Green Area	The percentage of protected and increased green space.
	Smart and Green Architecture	The percentage of buildings using green or smart architecture features
	Infrastructure Improvement	The percentage of increase of public infrastructure and facilities

(Source: Sarkhel, Rafieian, and Taghvaee, 2017)

The indicators listed in Tab. 1 are mostly urban; it is useful for measuring the success of mega-projects. Environmental criteria in areas where rural areas and ecologically sensitive areas are dense; Considering the conservation rates of assets such as agricultural areas, pasture areas, forest areas, water basins and wildlife, instead of criteria such as green space or smart and green architecture, which covers urban areas and their uses, will yield more rational results. Likewise, in measuring economic success, it is an important indicator how much the economic structure of a population will change in rural areas. Daly (1996) considers the protection and maintenance of economic subsystems within the carrying capacity of the ecosystem as the main objective of sustainability. The "carrying capacity of the ecosystem" mentioned here is an important point. It is not enough for a mega-project to provide economic prosperity on its own. Because there is a limit here; Welfare in the area should be limited by the carrying capacity of the ecosystem. Otherwise, the economic success of the project cannot be mentioned. These criteria will be considered in this study.

Based on our investigations on sustainability indicators, which were pointed out in previous academic studies, in this section, the sustainability indicators of the Kanal Istanbul Project, economically, spatially, socially and environmentally, will be evaluated through the environmental impact assessment report (Tab. 2).

Tab. 2: Sustainability Indicators for the Kanal Istanbul Project

Dimensions	Factors	Indexes
Economic Aspect	Competitiveness	Percentage of active units compared to inactive units.
	Private Partnership	Percentage of private investments in the entire project
	Entrepreneurship	Efficient activities; percentage or local produce trade
	Job Space	Percentage increase in business areas, including commercial space and office space
Spatial Aspect	Identity Preservation	Percentage of preservation of existing buildings; previous functional activities.
	Public Space	Percentage of open and green areas, increase
	Desirability	Percentage of attractive land uses built, including restaurants, cafes, etc.
Social Aspect	Participation Level	Level of participation according to the Arnstein in participation ladder (1969)
	Affordability	Percentage of median price difference with old or similar buildings around new buildings
	Social Inclusion	Ratio of displaced relative to displaced
Environmental Aspect	Agriculture, forest and pasture areas	Protected and declining agricultural, forest and pasture areas
	Water basins	Protected and declining watersheds
	Wild life	Protected and declining wildlife

3.4.1 Economic Dimension

According to the data specified in the environmental impact assessment report, the economic gains of the canal Istanbul project were investigated. In this context,

Competitiveness;
It is seen that the project is aimed to come to the fore with eco-tourism investments.

It has been predicted that eco-tourism will be concentrated in an area of 25,140 hectares in Arnavutkoy district. These areas are Durusu, Baklalı, Balaban, Boyalık, Bashakkoy, Celepkoy, Hisarbeyli, Orencik, Yazlık, Yassıoren Villages and Tayakadin Neighborhood, in the northern part of the European side and around Terkos Lake. This area, where eco-tourism can be intense, is located within the Terkos, Sazlıdere and Alibeykoy basins and is in the direct impact area of the Kanal Istanbul Project. The environmental impact assessment Report points out that providing an economic contribution in terms of eco-tourism depends on the protection of the natural resources of the district and ensuring its ecological sustainability. The report draws attention to the fact that any practice that will harm the eco-tourism potential can have a negative economic impact.

In this sense, it is necessary to avoid the construction that will put pressure on ecological areas. The Kanal Istanbul project has created a very intense construction pressure on sensitive ecosystems, It is clearly seen that it has dealt a strong and permanent blow to the sustainability of the ecological balance in the region. In case of the realization of the project, the region will be completely opened to construction, will be exposed to a heavy traffic load and its rural character will be completely destroyed. In this conditions; The realization of eco-tourism as a development tool is out of the question. For this reason, it is not possible for the project to compete with eco-tourism in its target.

Private Partnerships

There is no information about the partnership model of the project and its development. Only investors are mentioned.

Entrepreneurship

Bashakshehir district has an area of 104.35 hectares. Within the boundaries of the district, there are areas where the Ministry of Environment and Urbanization, the Housing Development Administration, the Ministry of Industry and Trade and the Municipality have the authority to make zoning plans (environmental impact assessment Report, Chapter 5, p. 644). 59 % of the district falls within the Reserve Area declared by the Ministry of Environment and Urbanization. It is foreseen that the district will not experience a significant economic transformation with the project, as the city is already under the influence of the urban fabric and the industry is the most important economic sector. After the Kanal Istanbul project was built, The areas entering Bashakshehir district are commercial areas, administrative centers, educational facility areas, etc. If it is evaluated as other reinforcement areas, it is thought that the urban development of the district will accelerate.

Business Area

When the effects of the project on the population and demographic structure are evaluated in terms of employment, it may lead to both positive and negative effects.

With the canal Istanbul Project, it is expected that urban development will spread towards the northern areas of Istanbul with a significant population increase and changes in demographic structure. It is inevitable that this urban sprawl will lead to a significant transformation in the settlements that have preserved their structure for many years and still maintain their rural characteristics (Bl 6, p. 237).

In the settlements living in the region and maintaining its rural structure, there is a significant population living on activities such as agriculture and animal husbandry, and if this population is exposed to external migration due to the project, an employment gap may arise. This situation may lead to sectoral employment gap as well as loss of livelihood.

Local employment in different business lines and by the Project trainings to be provided to workers will increase occupational specialization in the region; It can contribute to capacity building (technical capacity, earning capacity, wealth accumulation, purchasing power and networking), individual, household and community development.

When the economic benefits are evaluated within the scope of Gross Domestic Product, considering the MEDPRO research, it will produce an additional Gross Domestic Product of 5, 20, 126.4 billion USD annually, and it will add to the annual Gross Domestic Product (2017 Gross Domestic Product. – USD 857 billion) is calculated to contribute an average of 0.74 %. When the negative scenario is evaluated, it is calculated that it will produce an additional 73.7 billion USD, Gross domestic product in the 20-year period and contribute 0.43 % to the annual Gross Domestic Product.

If the limited agricultural lands of Istanbul are also used within the scope of the Project, it is foreseen that agricultural production in Istanbul will come to an end if rural activities are not maintained or encouraged with a resettlement nearby. In addition, with the development of the region, the rural social structure will leave its place to the urban social structure. This transformation in the social structure will greatly change the lifestyle of the population living in the area.

According to the Environmental Impact Assessment Report, considering the canal and the facilities planned together with the canal, approximately 5,000 people are expected to work during the land preparation and construction phase of the project. On the other hand, when the infrastructure displacements to be made by the administrations are taken into account, it is predicted that this figure will rise to the level of approximately 8,000–10,000 people. In the operation phase, it is foreseen that the number of personnel in the canal and other enterprises (ports, etc.) will be approximately 500–800 people. When the total number of workers to be employed in the land preparation, construction and operation phases of the Kanal Istanbul Project is evaluated, it should be evaluated that it has the potential to provide significant employment for Istanbul. Looking at the Proposed Employment Areas in the Project Impact Area, it is seen that an employment of 295 thousand people is expected. However, 230,500 of this expectation is not within the scope of the Kanal Istanbul project, but within the scope of the 3rd Airport built right next to it, and this expectation is for the year 2042. Accordingly, it is understood that an employment of approximately 65 thousand people is foreseen in the region (Number of employees in approximately 4 large shopping malls).

It is expected that the project will have negative impacts on the employment of the population living in the area of influence of the route and living on agricultural activities. It seems inevitable that employment in the agricultural sector will decrease significantly due to the fact that Istanbul has changed the nature of limited agricultural areas to a large extent.

In the environmental impact assessment report, the decrease in agriculture and livestock employment was emphasized as a long-term effect. Loss of agricultural lands, damages caused by construction machinery during the works, spillage of excavation soil, etc. It will have potential impacts on the inhabitants of the area. First and foremost, its inhabitants, whose rural economy-based lifestyles will change, will lose their basic livelihood. Project area, agriculture nearby In addition to all these, the loss of Sazlıdere dam, which is also used for agricultural irrigation in the affected settlements on the Avcılar side, will also cause adverse effects on the livelihoods of the residents.

Within the scope of the Kanal Istanbul Project, agriculture and animal husbandry is an important source of income in the neighborhoods that will be affected by the project. When we look at the number of both bovine and ovine animals per household, it is understood that there are households that make their living from animal husbandry. Livestock, which is an important source of income for some of the project-affected neighborhoods, will almost completely disappear as a result of the change in the quality of pastures and vacant private lands within the scope of the project. 100 families engaged in dairy farming in Yenikoy, 60 families engaged in fattening and dairy farming in chilingir, 40 families engaged in fattening and dairy farming in Baklalı, 50 families engaged in dairy farming in Dursunkoy, 60 families engaged in livestock breeding in Tayakad, Sazlıbosna 330 families, including 20 families engaged in fattening and dairy farming in Turkey, will lose their livelihoods. 12350 cattle, 7000 sheep and goats, 25500 poultry and more than 1000 beehives will be removed from the area.

The young population in the study area is 17.5 %, the rate of the population in active working age is 76.9 %, which is above the average of both Turkey and Istanbul. It is expected that the canal Istanbul Project will take place in the employment opportunities that will be created during the construction and operation phases. The environmental impact assessment Report predicts that the project will have a positive impact in terms of providing employment opportunities in the short and long term and reducing unemployment rates. However, considering that the construction phase will provide temporary job opportunities and only a certain part of this number can work during the operation phase, it is thought that the expected increase in employment in the field will not be remarkable. According to the environmental impact assessment report, it is anticipated that the number of personnel in the canal and other enterprises (ports, etc.) will be approximately 500–800 persons during the operation phase (Appendix 36, p. 190).

Spatial Dimension

The following effects of the property arrangement and expropriation arising from the project are revealed in general; It is expected that temporary and permanent loss of agricultural land, loss of agricultural products and trees, physical resettlement and economic relocation, loss of livestock-related structures such as barns, pens, shelters, loss of pastures and pastures, housing/structure losses, forest losses. The people who may be affected by these effects are the owner/tenant/user of land, house and other real estate and common users of areas such as pasture, grassland and forest.

Visual Quality (Rural and Urban Landscape, Design and Architectural Quality)

Along the route where the project is planned; residential areas, dam site, agricultural activities, mining activities, etc. There are natural landscape areas in the form of spots within the urban and rural landscape pattern that is shaped depending on the uses.

In an area of approximately 12 km, starting from the isthmus separating the Sea of Marmara from Kucukcekmece Lake and extending to the Sazlıdere Dam, Around Kucukcekmece Lake, depending on the lake area and protected areas, together with the natural and cultural landscape areas, the urban landscape texture formed mainly due to residential areas (Figure 5.16.1.).

Starting from the Sazlıdere Dam towards the Black Sea, it is seen that the rural landscape pattern is dominant depending on the rural settlements consisting of neighborhoods and the agricultural lands belonging to these rural settlements.

The most important natural landscape elements in the project area; Marmara Sea and Black Sea and its shores are Kucukcekmece Lake and Terkos Lake (Figure 5.16.3. and Figure 5.16.4.). In addition, the water surfaces of the Sazlıdere Dam reservoir area also positively affect the natural landscape. Most of the areas where the canal Istanbul Project is planned have a rural landscape view depending on the land use. In the north of the route, there are natural landscape areas in the form of spots between concentrated rural settlements, agricultural lands and land uses belonging to these settlements (Photo 1).

Photograph 1: View from the Canal Zone (Source: Environmental Impact Assessment Report, SECTION 5–612)

Within the scope of the project, it is planned to make zoning arrangements using (Public partnership share) or (regulation partnership share) applications in unzoned areas. The legal framework for these practices is in Section 3.1.2. explained. This situation results in that a large area from south to north along the canal route will be opened to urban development. canal Istanbul and new development areas will affect rural settlements especially north of Arnavutkoy.

Due to the canal's feature of being a waterway, it is very likely that the value of the new settlements to be formed around it will be high. This may lead to luxury construction.

Infrastructure

It is foreseen that the population increase planned with the canal Istanbul project may cause some problems in the region. problems that may arise; It is possible to deal with many aspects such as inadequate urban services (infrastructure, education, health, drinking water, etc.), transportation problems, employment gap, ecological pressure.

In the current situation, especially in the rural settlements in the northern part, infrastructure deficiencies are already experienced and the 1/100.000 scaled Environmental Plan aimed to improve the physical infrastructure services and increase the quality of life of these rural settlements. It is foreseen that infrastructure services will be developed along with the planning of these regions as urban development areas, and the project may have positive effects in this sense.

Protection of Identity

As mentioned above, the rural identity of the settlement, which has been going on since the past, will undergo a complete change. This situation has been mentioned several times in the Environmental Impact Assessment Report. The identity of the region will undergo a radical change, transforming into a rural identity, tourism, technology and commercial city identity.

Publices Space

In the project area, there will be open and green areas and other reinforcement areas stipulated by the plan standards. However, it is included in the plan decisions that the trade function will take place in the green areas and the river protection bands will be narrowed. In this respect, canal Istanbul does not have an approach that focuses on the phenomenon of public space.

Cultural Heritage and Archeology

During the impact assessment studies carried out by archaeologists, the project route and It has been determined that there are 1 archaeological site;1 historical bridge and 50 registered archaeological sites or historical sites within the impact corridor. 32 of the 50 registered areas are concrete military bunkers belonging to the Lighter Line. All 32 bunkers are located within the impact area to be directly affected by the project construction. The other 20 sites consist of important archaeological and cultural heritage assets such as archaeological sites, historical bridges, waterways and historical bends.

According to the Environmental Impact Assessment Report, many archaeological sites will be highly affected by the implementation of the plan.

With the project, it is seen that the decision of an urban development area and a university area has been brought into the archaeological site on the edge of Kucukcekmece lake. Thus, the area completely destroys a very important archaeological site within it. Two ancient cities, natural and archaeological sites will be lost in the planning area. In the Environmental Impact Assessment Report, it was determined that the project construction activities in 11 areas constitute a "Large-Scale Change".

Considering the general evaluation of the negative effects that the project may have on the determined areas, it has been determined that the project construction activities in 6 areas constitute a "Large Scale Change". The rate of change based on the destruction caused by the construction in the 2 areas on the project route and the impact corridor was determined as "Very Little", 12, and "No Change" in the area.

Charm

Within the scope of the project, besides transportation, energy and environmental applications, tourism, trade, technology, finance, etc. It is known that it is aimed to create a modern living space with functions. Therefore, the region will be under the pressure of intense construction. The population increase planned with the project is 1 million Although it is around, it is foreseen that there will be more population growth with the attraction center to be created if a large part of the reserve building area is opened for construction.

Social Aspect

Participation Level

A public participation meeting was held at the beginning of the project's Environmental Impact Assessment Report preparation process. Since this meeting was held with a sufficiently healthy organization, successful results could not be obtained.

Affordability

The two districts most affected by the canal Istanbul project and the new developments around it are Arnavutkoy and Bashakshehir.In these two districts, housing developments and real estate movements within Istanbul have varied considerably since the announcement of the canal project. In particular, it is observed that there has been a serious increase in the real estate supply after the region was declared a reserve area. In the researches, it is revealed that there has been a two-threefold increase in the monetary value and economic volume of the real estates offered in the reserve areas in recent years.

In the Environmental Impact Assessment Report, it is stated that among the possible impacts of the Project, there will be an increase in housing and land prices, and the degree of impact of this situation is defined as very high. In the interviews held in the settlements, it was stated that the lands around the Sazlıdere Dam were expropriated in 1995 and the lands were purchased by the Istanbul Water and Sewerage Administration at very low prices. While expropriation was carried out on m2/7 TL in the beginning, the prices increased as a result of the objections. Square meters of land before the projects were heard While the price was around 10–15 TL, land prices started to increase with the announcement of the Airport and Canal Istanbul projects. In the researches, according to the transferred data; After the project spread, land prices increased in quarterly increments, in the range of 50–60 TL, 80–90 TL, 120–130 TL, 160–180 TL, 200–230 TL, 260–300 TL, respectively. While the majority of the owners of these lands were previously villagers, the owner profile of the lands, some of which were purchased by the regional real estate agents, has also changed after the project.

Socialization Adaptation

According to the Environmental Impact Assessment Report, it is predicted that there will be a significant internal migration to the region with the planned new urban areas. In this sense, the canal Istanbul Project is expected to transform the population structure in the region with both internal and external migration movements and to reveal a new demographic structure. It should not be ignored that this population and demographic structure change will create a cumulative effect with the current population growth and migration movements of Istanbul (Appendix-36, p 186). With the project, it is likely that the demographic structure of the settlements on the canal route will change and population growth will occur. In particular, it is estimated that rural settlements in the north of Arnavutkoy will be more affected by the planned implementations of the project and internal/external migration movements will concentrate here.

Considering the residential areas and urban development planned around the canal, it is estimated that the settlements, which primarily preserve their rural character, will experience a great change. This will rapidly transform the rural population living in these settlements due to liquidation and/or emigration. On the other hand, it is foreseen that there will be a significant internal migration to the region with the planned new urban areas. In this sense, it is expected that the canal Istanbul Project will transform the population structure in the region with both internal and external migration movements and create a new demographic structure.

Information such as the project activities, the amount of agricultural lands that need to be expropriated due to ownership arrangement, their usage status, the type, usage status and number of buildings and structures will be made before the construction phase of the project, and will be determined during the map and expropriation processes. However, Project activities may cause some households to leave their places of residence/resettlement. This situation was evaluated as a possible social impact as it would necessitate mandatory/non-voluntary resettlement.

With the canal Istanbul Project, as explained in detail in the section above, urban development is expected to spread towards the northern areas of Istanbul, with significant population growth and changes in demographic structure. It is inevitable that this urban expansion will lead to a significant transformation in the settlements that have preserved their structure for many years and still maintain their rural characteristics. With the projects that will attract urban sprawl to the northern parts such as canal Istanbul, New Airport, and the 3rd Bridge connection roads, it is expected that the social, fabric in this region will completely change and lose its old characteristics.

According to the Environmental Impact Assessment Report, 162,964 people in Avcılar, 352,973 people in Kucukcekmece, 13,948 people in Arnavutkoy and 205,412 people in Bashakshehir will be directly affected by the project.

The route enters from a very small part of Kucukcekmece District where settlements are not very frequent, continues from the part of Altınshehir and shahintepe districts where settlements are partially dense, then near Sazlıbosna, Dursunkoy, Baklalı, Tayakadin, Terkos and Durusu districts (approximately 500–600 meters) passes. Although it is not expected to have a direct impact on settlements in Kucukcekmece, it will have a direct impact on settlements on the side of Altınshehir and shahintepe neighborhoods, where settlements are partially concentrated. In addition, the route passes through some dispersed households and summer houses in the lands between Baklalı, Tayakadin and Terkos, although they are not settlement centers.

According to the survey conducted within the scope of the environmental impact assessment report, the Participants; 55 % of more than half, their families migrated or moved here. 71 of them have been living in the region for more than 10 years.

While there will be those who welcome such a change, there will also be people who will not be able to keep up with this change and will be adversely affected. In the interviews held within the scope of the Social Impact Assessment study; Most of the people living in the area stated that they thought that if the Kanal Istanbul Project was carried out, they would not be able to stay in the region and continue to live in the same neighborhood and under the same conditions. While they are happy with the valuation of the land, the possibility of having to move is the biggest concern of these neighborhoods.

Environmental Dimension

The fact that urban development will be supported in the areas that were previously planned to be protected with the project will increase the population and construction and thus the ecological pressure. Ecological pressure caused by population growth and construction; The situation of water resources, the increase in pressure on alternative water resources, the exposure of wetlands to human intervention, especially birds and other animals will be adversely affected by urbanization.

Agriculture and Pasture Areas

The area covered by the dry agricultural fallow lands within the study area is 3,567,29 ha, and the area covered by the pasture lands is 503,89 ha. In the process of environmental impact assessment within the scope of the project; The works were carried out in a 30.019.42 ha survey area and the construction activities will be carried out in an area of 14.149.69 ha within this area, which has been processed on the 1/25.000 scale topographic map. The amount of agricultural and pasture lands that will be lost with the actual implementation of the project is approximately 4.071.18 ha, which corresponds to 59.5 % of the total area of 6.839.05 ha. In this direction, within the scope of the Kanal Istanbul Project, the pasture quality of 418 immovables (13,437.022,67 m2), out of 440 immovables with the characteristics of pastures, pastures, and winter quarters, has been removed. The works have not been finalized yet, as there are measures preventing registration and the defendant's encumbrance in the land registry of 22 pasture-qualified immovables. In case of using other pastures other than the pasture areas allocated within the scope of the canal Istanbul Project, with the Additional Article 1 added to the Pasture Law No. 4342 with the Law No. 6704; Transportation and Infrastructure; Change of qualifications with the powers given to the Ministry will be done. The agricultural areas of Arnavutkoy district, whose rural character is preserved, constitute approximately 35 % of the total area.

Forest Areas

Considering the Environmental Impact Assessment Study Area according to the canal Istanbul Project Environmental Impact Assessment Review and Evaluation Form; The area size considered as forest is 12,896.203,57 m2. 12.293.313.07 m2 of this area is within the boundaries of chatalca Forestry Management Directorate, 602.890.50 m2 of it is within the borders of Istanbul Forestry Management Directorate. The Plan Performs Scalpel Operations on Forest Areas. In the environmental impact assessment report, in the opinion of the General Directorate of Forestry, it was stated that the remaining forests in the project area were 1,289.6 ha, while in the Environmental Impact Assessment Report it was stated that 421 ha for the Canal, 200,878 ha forest area will be cut and the number of trees to be cut (Environmental Impact Assessment Report, 2020). The significant difference between the numbers suggests that the number of trees to be cut will be much higher and young trees are not taken into account. Considering the working area of the project, the size of the forest area is approximately 458.83 hectares. 287,03 hectares of the project area is within the boundaries of the "Terkos Lake Conservation Forest", which was declared as a permanent conservation forest on 22.12.1961. It is not directly stated how many trees will be cut down for the project. However, with a simple calculation, it is seen that 550 hectares of forest area will be destroyed by the product of the width and length of the canal only on the waterway of the canal.

Water Basins

It is stated that Balaban Dam (Kırklareli) and Demirkoy Dam (Kırklareli) are planned for drinking water purposes instead of Sazlıdere Dam in order to preserve the water resources potential of Istanbul European Side. In addition, Karamandere Dam (Istanbul/Terkos), Hamzalıdere Dam (Istanbul/Buyukcekmece) and Pirinchi Dam (Istanbul/Alibeykoy) by the General Directorate of State Hydraulic Works,

Hisarbeyli Dam by the General Directorate of Istanbul Water and Sewerage Administration, (Istanbul/Terkos) are dams that are in the planning stage. Accordingly, the north of the planning area is within the borders of Terkos and Pirinchi Basins. It is seen that the canal passes through the east of Terkos Lake and reaches the Marmara Sea by using the Sazlıdere Dam and Kucukcekmece lakes. The canal passing through this route includes the Terkos Lake supply basin, the Terkos-Kagithane Drinking Water Transmission Lines, the Terkos- İkitelli Transmission Line. There is a possibility that it will cut the lines, disable the Sazlıdere Dam, and reciprocal (fresh/salty) water passage to Terkos Lake from the canal. According to the drinking water requirement and population projections of DSI; current population trend and water flow trend (annual precipitation amounts and prospective precipitation and water potential calculations made with similar data), are taken into consideration; It is stated that if Sazlıdere, Terkos and Melen waters are included, the resources may not be sufficient after 2040.

Wildlife

Terkos Lake, Sazlıdere Dam and Kucukcekmece located on the canal route and its impact area are extremely important ecosystems for birds, amphibians and freshwater creatures. In these areas, there are 249 bird species, 29 freshwater species and 7 amphibian species, while in habitats such as sand dunes, stony rocks, shrubs, heathland, pasture, agriculture, forest, 37, terrestrial mammal, 239, insect species, 24 reptile (Kanal Istanbul Final Environmental Impact Assessment Report, 2020). Some of these species are protected under the BERN Convention (Bern Convention).

According to the BERN Convention (Bern Convention), it is said that it is forbidden to intentionally damage or destroy the breeding and resting places of these species and to disturb the wild fauna during breeding, development and hibernation periods. However, excavation and filling works will continue for 4 years, 365 days and 24 hours a day. Rocky areas will be detonated with dynamite. However, no measures have been proposed to prevent these activities from harming wildlife (Tolunay, 2020).

Risk and Security Dimension

Risks

In terms of risks, we will have two risky Straits instead of one. Considering that the Bosphorus is shorter and wider, the latter is much more risky.

It will increase disaster risks and create dense population accumulation in the region where the live fault line is located. It will expose the people of the region to high Tsunami risk.

There is a nuclear research center 500 meters from the shore of Kucukcekmece Lake. It is said that the domino effects of a nuclear accident can lead to a disaster when the population of Istanbul is taken into account (Appendix-26, p. 86). Theft, physical attacks, gender-based violence, human trafficking, alcohol and drug use, smuggling, etc. that may be caused by the labor flow in the canal Istanbul Project. The increase in criminal activities such as the increase in traffic and the increase in accidents and the additional burden on the transportation infrastructure include other potential negative social effects.

Disasters

Depending on the cannel route ground structure and slope sensitivity, the risk of landslides, landslides and liquefaction is high. The most important earthquake source that will strongly affect canal Istanbul is the large earthquakes expected on the North Marmara Fault, which lies on the seabed 10–12 km away from the southern part of the canal. Due to the geological-geophysical structure of the southern regions of Istanbul, earthquake waves are growing excessively. These magnification values can increase 10 times from place to place. How the channel will respond to lateral and vertical movements that may occur during earthquakes is a vital research topic. If this structure slips, breaks or twists during an earthquake, it may cause great disasters (Association of Chambers of Turkish Engineers and Architects, Kanal Istanbul Report, 2020).

Security

The cannel creates an island by tearing off a part of Thrace; A security vulnerability arises. It will be difficult to defend Thrace against a possible attack from outsid.

There are ongoing construction works near the project area. During the works carried out in the field, both local administrators, people living in the region, and representatives of some relevant institutions stated that there were problems arising from other Project activities under construction. In the interviews, it was stated that the project vehicles created a security threat for the population and animals living in the area by entering the inner streets that do not have a usage permit. The use of inner-town roads in the aforementioned project Although it has been defined, it has been stated that vehicle drivers use it without permission to shorten the road. In addition, heavy tonnage vehicles using narrow settlement roads pose a risk, especially for children. It has been stated that excessive speeding in the neighborhood also poses a safety threat for both children and animals, with or without permission.

The vehicles usually carry construction materials or excavation, and they do this work with open boxes. It has been stated that the falling of materials such as large stone boulder to the road also poses a risk (Appendix 36, p.195).

When the main land preparation and construction activities of the canal Istanbul Project started, the working area It is inevitable that similar effects will occur that will adversely affect the health and safety of the population living in the vicinity. In addition to the ongoing construction activities in the region, the start of canal Istanbul construction will increase the cumulative impact.

4. As a Result

The fact that 1/1000 plan changes were urgently included in the Environmental Plan, which is accepted as the city constitution of Istanbul, before the environmental impact assessment process was completed in the Kanal Istanbul project, points to the disruption of the legal basis of the plan. The suspension of the plan without considering the objections or even waiting for the last day of the objection period, the voices of "whatever this channel will be done" from the government, mean that an unlawful process is imposed on the people.

According to the Environmental Impact Assessment Report, it is clear that the cost of the project, whose lifespan is 100 years, far exceeds its benefits.

In terms of risks, we will have two risky Straits instead of one. Considering that the Bosphorus is shorter and wider, the latter is much more risky. The channel creates an island by tearing off a part of Thrace; Thus, a security vulnerability arises. Defending Thrace against a possible attack from outside will become stronger. Although the plan mentions a population of 500 thousand, in reality it places approximately 2–3 million people on three living fault lines and violates the constitutional responsibility of the state, its duty to take security measures against disasters. In the Black Sea and Marmara, fish species will decrease immensely, 70 living groups and 124 bird species will disappear. The project's environmental impact assessment Report states that "we allocate a certain area to the birds". However, it should not be forgotten that an address to nature cannot be shown with project reports. The Black Sea and the Sea of Marmara will smell of rotten eggs due to the hydrogen sulfide that will be released. Two ancient cities, many natural and archaeological sites will be lost. an economic disaster project that violates property rights, ignores expert participation, costs more than benefits, has a short lifespan, and takes away the basic rights of life from the people; It is clearly seen that the cannel is Istanbul. If it is started, it is inevitable that irreparable results will occur.

References

Arslangündoğdu, Z., Dalyan, C., Bacak, E., Yard, Ü., Gezgin, C. and Beşkardeş, V. 2011. Spring Migration of the White Stork, Ciconia ciconia, and the Black Stork, Ciconia nigra, over the Bosphorus. Zoology in the Middle East, 53: 7–13

Daly, H. E. 1996. Beyond Growth: The Economics of Sustainable Development. Boston, MA: Beacon Press (Eds: G. Eken, M. Bozdoğan, S. İsfendiyaroğlu, D. T. Kılıç, Y. Lise. 2006. "Important Natural Areas of Turkey". Nature Association, Mas Printing, Istanbul

Flyvbjerg, B., Bruzelius, N., & Rothengatter, W. (2003). Megaprojects and Risk: An Anatomy of Ambition. Cambridge: Cambridge University Press

Goldschmidt, K., Harrison, T., Holtry, M., & Reeh, J. 2013. Sustainable Procurement: Integrating Classroom Learning with University Sustainability Programs. Decision Sciences Journal of Innovative Education, 11(3): 279–294. [http://onlinelibrary.wiley.com/doi/10.1111/dsji.12007/pdf]. Accessed 03 June 2020

Grun, O. 2004. Taming Giant Projects: Management of Multi-Organization Enterprises. Berlin: Springer.

National Research Council of the National Academies 2010. Toward Sustainable Agricultural Systems in the 21st Century (Ed: P. T. Whitacre), Washington, D.C., [http://www.nap.edu/catalog.php?record_id=12832]. Accessed 03 June 2020, 33–34

Pavlovskaia, E. 2014. Sustainability Criteria: Their Indicators, Control, and Monitoring (With Examples from the Biofuel Sector). Environmental Sciences Europe, 26(17): 1–12

Sarkheyl, E., Rafieian, M., & Taghvaee, A. 2017. The Evaluation of Megaproject's Success in Spatial Reproduction of Urban Interests, Case Study: Great

Sturup, S., & Low, N. 2019. Sustainable Development and Mega Infrastructure: An Overview of the Issues. Journal of Mega Infrastructure & Sustainable Development, 1(1): 8–26

Tolunay, D. 2015. Evaluation of the Third Airport EIA Report in Istanbul 6th National Air Pollution and Control Symposium-2015, 7–9 October 2015, İzmir

Tolunay, D. 2020. Ecological Problems of Istanbul and Its Environment. Istanbul and Northern Forests from the Perspective of Ecosystem, Climate and Urban

Growth (Ed: Ü. Akkemik), Turkish Foresters Association Publication No: 50, p. 56–71

Zidane, Y.-T., Johansen, A., & Ekambaram, A., 2013. Megaprojects – Challenges and Lessons Learned, 26th IPMA World Congress, Crete, Greece, 2012, Procedia – Social and Behavioral Sciences, 74: 349–357

Technical Reports

Arslangündoğdu, Z., & Leg, E. 2017. Marmara Region Mid-Winter 2017 Waterfowl Counts, Istanbul University Faculty of Forestry, Istanbul

Arslangündoğdu, Z., & Leg, E. 2018. Marmara Region Mid-Winter 2018 Waterfowl Counts, Istanbul University Faculty of Forestry, Istanbul

Arslangündoğdu, Z., & Leg, E. 2019. Marmara Region Mid-Winter 2019 Waterfowl Counts, Istanbul University Faculty of Forestry, Istanbul

Environmental and Social Impact Assessment (ESIA) for the Northern Marmara Motorway -including the 3rd Bosphorus Bridge- Project, Prepared by AECOM, Turkey, 2013

Third Airport Environmental Impact Assessment Report, 2013

TMMOB Istanbul Provincial Coordination Board 3rd Airport Technical Report, 2014

Journals

"Defense of the Northern Forests: They Cut 13 Million Trees for the 3rd Airport", Evrensel Newspaper, 22 June 2019

www.ingramcontent.com/pod-product-compliance
Ingram Content Group UK Ltd.
Pitfield, Milton Keynes, MK11 3LW, UK
UKHW021922120926
8556IPUK00042BA/1120

9 783631 861127